Bridging Two Peoples

Indigenous Studies Series

The Indigenous Studies Series builds on the successes of the past and is inspired by recent critical conversations about Indigenous epistemological frameworks. Recognizing the need to encourage burgeoning scholarship, the series welcomes manuscripts drawing upon Indigenous intellectual traditions and philosophies, particularly in discussions situated within the Humanities.

For more information, please contact:
Lisa Quinn
Acquisitions Editor
Wilfrid Laurier University Press
75 University Avenue West
Waterloo, ON N2L 3C5
Canada
Phone: 519-884-0710 ext. 2843
Fax: 519-725-1399
Email: quinn@press.wlu.ca

Bridging Two Peoples

Chief Peter E. Jones, 1843–1909

Allan Sherwin

This book has been published with the help of a grant from the Canadian Federation for the Humanities and Social Sciences, through the Aid to Scholarly Publications Programme, using funds provided by the Social Sciences and Humanities Research Council of Canada. Wilfrid Laurier University Press acknowledges the support of the Canada Council for the Arts for our publishing program. We acknowledge the financial support of the Government of Canada through the Canada Book Fund for our publishing activities.

Library and Archives Canada Cataloguing in Publication

Sherwin, Allan L.
Bridging two peoples : Chief Peter E. Jones, 1843–1909 / Allan L. Sherwin.

(Indigenous studies series)
Includes bibliographical references and index.
Issued also in electronic formats.
ISBN 978-1-55458-633-2

1. Jones, Peter E., 1843–1909. 2. Indian physicians—Ontario—Biography. 3. Ojibwa Indians—Ontario—Biography. 4. Racially mixed people—Ontario—Biography. 5. Ojibwa Indians—Civil rights—Ontario—History. I. Title. II. Title: Chief Peter E. Jones, 1843–1909. III. Series: Indigenous studies series

R696.J65S54 2012 610.92 C2011-908671-9

Includes bibliographical references and index.
Electronic monograph.
Issued also in print format.
ISBN 978-1-55458-652-3 (PDF).—ISBN 978-1-55458-653-0 (EPUB)

1. Jones, Peter E., 1843–1909. 2. Indian physicians—Ontario—Biography. 3. Ojibwa Indians—Ontario—Biography. 4. Racially mixed people—Ontario—Biography. 5. Ojibwa Indians—Civil rights—Ontario—History. I. Title. II. Title: Chief Peter E. Jones, 1843–1909. III. Series: Indigenous studies series

R696.J65S54 2012 610.92 C2011-908672-7

Cover design by Blakeley Words+Pictures. Cover image: Dr. Peter Edmund Jones donned his father's headdress and buckskin suit during his 1898 visit to the Smithsonian Institution in Washington, D.C. He carried the steel peace-pipe tomahawk smoked by Iroquois and Mississauga chiefs in the 1840 reaffirmation of their treaty of friendship. Courtesy of the National Anthropological Archives, Smithsonian Institution (Negative no. 00498B). Text design by Angela Booth Malleau.

Waterloo, Ontario, Canada
www.wlupress.wlu.ca

FSC www.fsc.org RECYCLÉ Papier fait à partir de matériaux recyclés FSC® C103567

This book is printed on FSC recycled paper and is certified Ecologo. It is made from 100% post-consumer fibre, processed chlorine free, and manufactured using biogas energy.

Printed in Canada

For Fiona

Contents

List of Maps, Tables, and Illustrations

Maps

Table

Illustrations

Foreword

The lack of abundant written sources makes the writing of biographies of nineteenth-century Aboriginal leaders extremely difficult. Fortunately, in the case of Dr. Peter Edmund Jones, who was an Aboriginal politician and later Indian agent, as well as a medical doctor and publisher of an Aboriginal newspaper, an extensive paper trail exists. Dr. Allan Sherwin has carefully examined a vast array of printed and manuscript sources to produce his fascinating study.

Dr. Peter Edmund Jones, believed to be the first Status Indian to graduate from a Canadian medical school, was the third son of Peter Jones, or Kahkewaquonaby (1802–56), Mississauga chief and Methodist missionary. His mother, the English-born Eliza Field, kept her late husband's letters and historical manuscripts, a treasure trove of information about his family. Dr. Sherwin has written his book using these rich sources, as well as Eliza Field's own diaries, and added the Indian Affairs Records (RG 10) and the John A. Macdonald papers, held in Library and Archives Canada. Supplementing these accounts are the back issues of *The Indian*, Canada's first Aboriginal newspaper, which Dr. Jones published in 1886.

Not satisfied with pure manuscript work, Dr. Sherwin visited New Credit several times, where in 2002 he had the good fortune to meet the late Lloyd S. King (1915–2006), then eighty-six years old, an Elder with an incredible knowledge of the New Credit community. In the 1920s Lloyd knew William Elliott, then in his eighties, the last person living in the community, who had been born at the Old Credit Mission twenty kilometres west of Toronto. The Mississaugas resided there from 1825 to 1847, before they relocated next to the Six Nations Territory on the Grand River. William Elliott told young Lloyd about his recollections of the move from the Credit River in 1847.

Dr. Sherwin has written much more than a biography. The professor emeritus of the Faculty of Medicine at McGill University presents the story of a whole community, the Mississaugas of the New Credit First Nation, in the late nineteenth century. He describes how well they managed their affairs, such as public health and education, under the direction of Dr. Jones and his fellow chiefs and Band Council members. Through his political work Dr. Jones fought for self-government, hunting and fishing rights, and for the land claims of the Mississauga. The impressive research behind this book is one of its greatest strengths.

What makes the reading of this biography truly unique is the description of one Aboriginal community, the Mississaugas of the New Credit First Nation, from a medical perspective. Many books have been written on nineteenth-century Aboriginal Canada, but I know of no other that has been written by an individual, such as Dr. Sherwin, with half a century of medical study, teaching, and practice guiding him throughout in his research and writing.

Donald B. Smith, Ph.D.
Professor Emeritus
Canadian History
University of Calgary

Preface

That beautiful flowers such as foxglove and opium poppies contain potent drugs remains a source of amazement, even though as a physician I recognize that they have been largely replaced by synthetic chemical equivalents. In their northern climes, Canada's Aboriginal peoples discovered many medicinal plants, roots, and barks. Moreover, Aboriginal healers knew when to harvest and treat the plants and how to administer the medicinal agents that effectively relieved so many common disorders. This led me to wonder whether the first licensed Aboriginal physicians would have prescribed traditional therapies as well as European drugs.

In looking into this question, I discovered Dr. Peter Edmund Jones, the first known Status Indian to obtain a doctor of medicine degree at a Canadian medical school (Queen's University, 1866). Jones's student record consisted of an entry in a register that lists two names: "Peter E. Jones" and "Kahkewaquonaby" (The Waving Plume). During his years of medical training in then colonial Kingston, he came to realize his potential as a spokesperson for the Aboriginal peoples, many of whom had yet to learn English. Asked to provide a name for the graduation list, he selected Kahkewaquonaby, thus confirming that he regarded himself as a Status Indian whose life would be governed not by common law but by the Indian Act. Respected as a physician, a gifted orator, and writer, he would try to bridge the gap between two peoples represented by his Aboriginal father and Euro-Canadian mother. Though raised in the Euro-Canadian community of Brantford, Ontario, racial prejudice kept him outside their closely knit medical community. Who had ever heard of an Aboriginal physician? Would he perform magic cures or prescribe secret herbal potions? Dr. Jones eventually opened an office in nearby Hagersville, a village situated near the border of the Mississaugas of the New Credit reserve. As he had inherited his father's farm on the reserve, he inevitably became involved with the Aboriginal peoples, many of whom became his patients.

Band elders elected him to the posts of head chief and official band physician. He was also elected secretary-treasurer of the Grand General Indian Council of Ontario and Quebec or Grand Council, a loose union of various tribes. He published the minutes of their meetings and sent them to Ottawa in the vain hope of altering the continuously amended Indian Act. In 1886, in order to educate his people and encourage them to exercise their newly acquired voting rights, he edited and published *The Indian*, Canada's first Aboriginal newspaper. He campaigned for more municipal powers on reserves and tried to remove pejorative terms from the Indian Act. In an era when band chiefs could not yet speak English, Jones bridged the gap between Aboriginal leaders and the Department of Indian Affairs. He wrote countless letters conveying their concerns, directly to his friend and political mentor, Prime Minister Sir John A. Macdonald.

With the support of the chief and Band Council of the Mississaugas of the New Credit First Nation, I combed their archives and those of Queen's University, Indian Affairs Canada, his mother's diary, private correspondence, and many other unique sources. This century-long "paper chase" revealed how effectively this Native Indian community used the annual interest on monies derived from the sale of their former lands to promote the health, education, and social welfare of their members.

One hundred years after Dr. Jones's death, it is more important than ever that Canadians hear his story, not only in recognition of his own accomplishments but also of those made by his Aboriginal colleagues. Chiefs, band councillors, and Elders served their communities faithfully as they faced determined efforts at assimilation. They were a unique people and their actions helped strengthen that standing. These capable, informed, and caring men and women set the stage for the remarkable resurgence of Canada's Aboriginal peoples during the twentieth century and beyond.

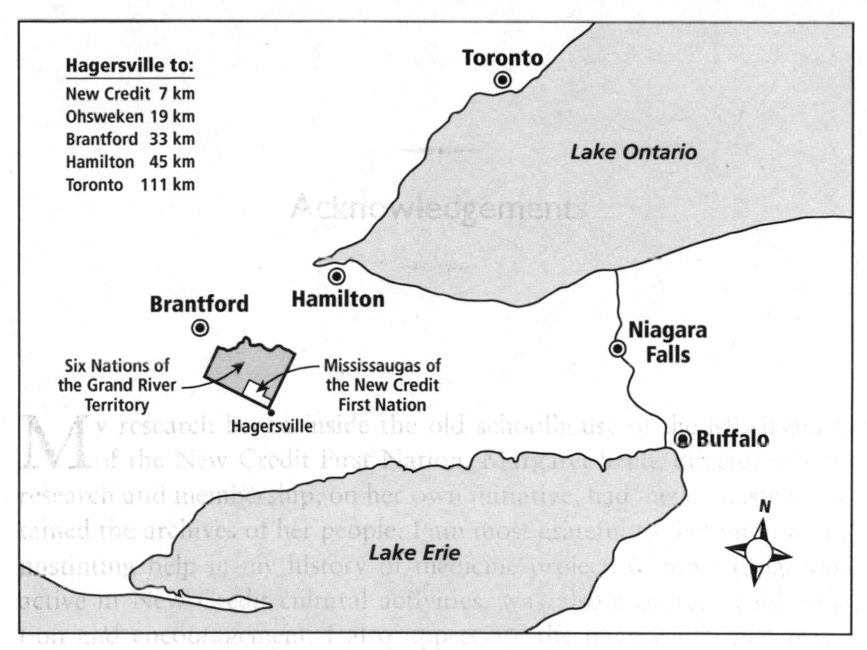

Map 1 A portion of southern Ontario occupied by the Mississaugas of the New Credit First Nation. Christine Lalonde, illustrator.

Acknowledgements

My research began inside the old schoolhouse of the Mississaugas of the New Credit First Nation. Margaret Sault, director of land research and membership, on her own initiative, had meticulously maintained the archives of her people. I am most grateful for her interest and unstinting help in my history of medicine project. Carolyn King, long active in New Credit cultural activities, was also a source of information and encouragement. I also appreciate the interest of Chief Bryan LaForme, of the Mississaugas of the New Credit First Nation. The late Lloyd S. King, a graduate of McMaster University, served as one of the first Aboriginal schoolteachers on the New Credit and Six Nations reserves. King was responsible for changing the way Aboriginal students were viewed by the provincial department of education. He was also a leader in the Aboriginal resistance movement and the respected band historian. Mr. King, who was eighty-six years old at the time of my interview, had an excellent memory and related stories told by his grandmother, Bessie King, who knew Dr. Jones. The Hagersville branch of the Haldimand County Public Library contained documentation of Dr. Jones's medical practice, and Jenifer Trigert, curator of the Haldimand County Museum and Archives, Cayuga, allowed me to search early Jones family records. The Brant County Museum and Archives' administrator, Cindy MacDonald-Krueger, and researcher Stephani Raymon-Lipinski found a silk quilt made by his mother, Eliza Jones, when Dr. Jones was a child, as well as records of Dr. Jones's brothers' later years in Brantford. Denise Kirk at Brantford Public Library provided articles from the Brantford Expositor. Tom Hill, director, and Keith Jamieson, curator, of the Woodlands Cultural Centre and Museum, Brantford, guided me through their 2001 exhibit on Dr. Jones's colleague, Dr. Oronhyatekha, entitled: Mohawk Ideals—Victorian Values. Ken Parker, of the Sweet Grass Nursery near Brantford, displayed Aboriginal plants having medicinal properties. Donald G. Jones of Dundas, Ontario, a descendant of Augustus Jones, provided me with some of his own writings, including the Jones family tree.

I thank the Wellcome Trust Library for allowing me to read first editions of early medical works as well as Dr. Jones's student textbooks. The National Library of Scotland, Edinburgh, provided similar assistance in my research on John Dunlop, the Jones's family friend and member of the Aborigines Protective Society. The Anglican Diocese of Niagara confirmed that Dr. Jones had served as a lay delegate in the 1880s. Gabbi Zalden, archivist at the Victoria University Library, Toronto, arranged for me to review Eliza Jones's diary on microfilm and boxes containing letters by his parents and eldest brother, Charles Augustus, which cast light on his childhood and the years following his graduation from Queen's University. Harold Averill, assistant university archivist, University of Toronto, generously provided much background information and records of Dr. Jones's and Dr. Oronhyatekha's student days at the Toronto School of Medicine, which later merged with the University of Toronto. Gillian F. Barlow, archivist, and Deirdre Bryden, archivist (University Records) at Queen's University, Kingston, allowed me to review the original register of students, senate minutes, and college calendars containing course descriptions, examination questions, and student lists.

Beverly Coburn and Julie Stabile, records analysts at the College of Physicians and Surgeons of Ontario, Toronto, repeatedly looked up the historical register to answer my questions. The assistance of the staff of Library and Archives Canada, Ottawa, enabled me to obtain relevant documents from the Department of Indian Affairs and the Macdonald papers. I searched the records of the Archives of British Columbia, Victoria, for information on Charlotte Dixon-Jones, while archivist Carolyn Weber helped search for Dr. Jones's Aboriginal artifacts that his stepson Elvin Dixon of Vernon, British Columbia, gave to the local museum. Christopher Lyons, of the Osler Library of the History of Medicine at McGill University, took a personal interest in my project and helped immensely. Katharine Barrette, of the government information library of McGill University, found important documents. Professor Toby Morantz kindly informed me of the rich documentation in the Robert Bell fonds of the McGill University's Archives. The Baldwin Room of the Toronto Reference Library, Toronto, supplied microfilm copies of Dr. Jones's newspaper and articles from *The Toronto Mail*. Alain Pelletier, L.L.B., assistant director, Parliamentary Affairs, Elections Canada, Ottawa, graciously assisted my review of Macdonald's 1885 Indian Franchise Act.

Special thanks are due to Sandra Guillaume, my archivist-consultant at the Ontario Archives, who took a personal interest in the project and proved to be a talented detective. Suzanne VanSickle, whose farm is adjacent to the New Credit reserve, provided photos, maps, and gracious hospitality to my wife Fiona Clark and me on our visits to the New Credit reserve near Hagersville.

Dr. Donald B. Smith, professor of history at the University of Calgary and the author of *Sacred Feathers*, the superb biography of Dr. Jones's father, enthusiastically supported and advised me throughout this endeavour. He provided unpublished notes from his earlier research and, despite his heavy academic load, allowed me to be his unofficial student. I am honoured that he agreed to write the foreword of this book. I appreciate the encouragement and advice of Dr. Jacalyn Duffin, Hannah professor of the history of medicine, Queen's University. Dr. James A. Low and Tamara Nelson guided me through the old Kingston General Hospital building, while Lorna Knight provided the 1862 drawing of the building. I am grateful for the chance to discuss the life of Dr. Jones with Malcolm King, Ph.D., who kindly read early drafts of my manuscript. Dr. King, a member of the Mississaugas of the New Credit First Nations, is professor of pulmonary medicine at the University of Alberta. In January 2009, Dr. King became the scientific director of the Canadian government's Institute of Aboriginal Peoples Health in Ottawa. Prof. Dieter Kluepfel kindly reviewed my discussion of Aboriginal herbal therapy. Christine Lalonde created the maps and drawings, and Russell Proulx digitalized the nineteenth-century photographs.

I thank Elaine Cohen, Michael Ballantyne, My-Trang Nguyen, Lesley Kelley Regnier, and Blossom Thom for editorial advice, and historians Kathryn Steinhaus and Rhonda Kronyk for reviewing the citations. Most of all, I thank my loving wife, Fiona Clark, for her encouragement and support, including searching records during field trips, keeping me on track, and providing her experienced editorial advice.

Abbreviations

ABC	Archives of British Columbia, Victoria
AO	Archives of Ontario, Toronto
BMA	Brant Museum and Archives, Brantford
CPSO	Historical register, College of Physicians and Surgeons of Ontario, Toronto
DCB	Dictionary of Canadian Biography
Debates	Official Report of Debates, Canadian House of Commons, Ottawa
DIA	Department of Indian Affairs (Annual Reports, online at http://www.collectionscanada.gc.ca/indianaffairs)
HCL	Haldimand County Library, Hagersville branch
HCMA	Haldimand County Museum and Archives, Cayuga
KGHA	Kingston General Hospital Archives, Kingston
LAC	Library and Archives Canada, Ottawa
Mfm	Microfilm
MNCA	Mississaugas of the New Credit First Nation Archives, Hagersville
MUA	McGill University Archives, Montreal
PJC, VUL	Peter Jones Collection, Victoria University Library, Toronto
QUA	Queen's University Archives, Kingston
ROMA	Royal Ontario Museum Archives, Toronto
SC	Statutes of Canada
TRL	Toronto Reference Library, Toronto
UCH	United Church Archives, Toronto
UTA	University of Toronto Archives, Toronto

Chronology of Dr. Peter Edmund Jones's Life

1843 Born 30 October to the first ordained Aboriginal minister, Rev. Peter Jones, and his English wife, Eliza Field Jones, at the Methodist mission near London, Ontario.

1851 Moved to the non-Aboriginal community of Brantford; home-schooled because of poliomyelitis.

1866 Graduates from the medical faculty of Queen's University at Kingston, the first Status Indian to obtain the M.D. degree from a Canadian medical school; receives Ontario medical licence number 678.

1869 Establishes a medical practice in Hagersville, Ontario, a village located on the edge of the Mississaugas of the New Credit reserve. Farms land on the reserve.

1873 Marries Charlotte Elvin-Dixon, an English widow with three young children.

1874 Elected head chief of his band; becomes their physician and introduces quarantine and other public health measures that helped insure the survival of the Mississaugas. Finds and begins to research an outstanding Mississaugas of the New Credit land claim.

1880 Serves as secretary-treasurer of the Grand General Indian Council of Ontario and Quebec, communicating their concerns directly to Prime Minister Sir John A. Macdonald. Actively works for the federal Conservative party.

1886 Publishes *The Indian*, the first Aboriginal newspaper in Canada in order to insure registered Indians understand and take advantage of their newly acquired federal voting rights.

1887 Responds to a request from Prime Minister Macdonald to propose modifications to the Indian Act and to consider the feasibility of a separate Act for what he called the "uncivilized" Indians living in the North West.

1888 Appointed a federal Indian agent, a post previously reserved for non-Aboriginals; no longer head chief, he remains the band's physician.

1889 Presents the Mississaugas' case before a Special Council of the Six Nations called to resolve a forty-year-old dispute between the bands over land payments.

1891 Recognized as an experienced archaeologist, he helps David Boyle, curator of the provincial museum uncover evidence of early Aboriginal settlements, and advises and collects Aboriginal artifacts for the Smithsonian Institution in Washington.

1896 The Liberal party wins the federal election. Jones, no longer Indian agent or band physician, farms on the reserve with the aid of his stepson and follows his patients in Hagersville. Maintains interests in Aboriginal affairs and helps band leaders submit their land claim.

1909 Dies in Hagersville of cancer of the tongue, and buried in family plot in Brantford.

One
Peter Edmund Jones's Origins

Prime Minister Sir John A. Macdonald rose from his seat in Canada's Parliament to read a letter from an Ojibwe chief who was also a practising physician. The letter was dated 30 May 1885.[1]

> My Dear Sir John,
> I should have written to you some time ago to thank you for making the Indian a person in the Franchise Bill. Other affairs, however, have prevented me from performing my duty. I now thank you on the part of the memory of my father and on the part of myself, as for many years we advocated and urged this step as the one most likely to elevate the aborigines to the position more approaching the whites.
>
> Kahkewaquonaby, M.D., Chief.[2]

So who was this chief who, despite nineteenth-century colonial intolerance, managed to become a physician, publisher, and political activist?

Dr. Peter Edmund Jones was the first known Status Indian to obtain an M.D. degree from a Canadian medical school. He graduated from Queen's University in Kingston, Ontario, in 1866 and received his licence to practise in November of that year.[3] Along with his general practice in Hagersville, a small town near Hamilton in southern Ontario, Jones was physician to his band, the Mississaugas of the New Credit First Nation. During his tenure as head chief, the Mississaugas became one of the first bands to have an elected Council.[4] A competent writer, Jones edited and published *The Indian*, the first Canadian Aboriginal newspaper, in order to educate his people. Male Status Indians with minimal personal property had been granted the right to vote in federal elections in 1885, and Jones wished to encourage them to register for the forthcoming election. By means of his own newspaper and letters to *The Toronto Daily*

Mail, Dr. Jones informed the general public that contrary to their government's policies, the Aboriginals were intent on maintaining their culture. In 1887, Dr. Jones even became an Indian agent, a federal civil service appointment that had hitherto almost always been restricted to non-Aboriginals.[5]

Dr. Jones was proud of his Mississauga heritage and worked tirelessly for his people's welfare. Though he lived in the adjacent community of Hagersville, Jones farmed on the New Credit reserve and tried to bridge the gap between the two cultures. He married an English-Canadian widow with three sons whom he educated in private schools as if they were his own children. Like many educated Aboriginal Protestants, Jones was a Mason, served as secretary-treasurer of the local Orange Association, and had friends and patients in the Euro-Canadian community. Because of his privileged upbringing and schooling, however, he was never fully accepted by his fellow Mississaugas, especially the more traditional members of the band.[6]

Jones served as the Mississaugas of the New Credit band's agent until 1896, the year the Conservative government lost power. He was saddened when a newly elected Liberal government repealed his cherished Indian Franchise Act, which had temporarily granted some of his people voting rights.[7] Jones continued to take an active interest in the affairs of his people until his death from cancer in 1909.[8] Today, he remains virtually unrecognized, despite his many accomplishments, foremost of which are his contributions to Aboriginal public health, journalism, and First Nations' self-governance.

Peter Edmund had opportunities not open to other Aboriginals because he came from an accomplished and well-connected family. His grandfather, Augustus Jones, was a Welsh-American surveyor who had migrated to Upper Canada after the American Revolution. Augustus was appointed deputy Crown surveyor and was the first to map Yonge Street, which followed a trade route used by the Mississaugas for thousands of years. He lived with the Mississauga chief Wahbanosay, a signatory of the 1805 Toronto Purchase, who guided him through the wilderness between 1790 and 1802 and married Wahbanosay's daughter, Tuhbenahneequay.[9] The marriage was solemnized by tribal custom and they had two sons: John, born in 1798, and Peter, born four years later. Tuhbenahneequay wished to continue living with the Mississauga band so the boys lived with their grandparents, spoke Ojibwe, and learned woodland lore.[10] After the War of 1812, a new wave of settlers occupied traditional Mississaugas' lands, and their society rapidly disintegrated in the face of infectious illness and starvation. By 1816, Tuhbenahneequay's band faced the coldest year of the century: there was frost every month, and snow fell during the summer, the result of a massive volcanic eruption in Indonesia. Crops failed, including the wild berries and plants essential to a hunter-gatherer society. With a population reduced to some two hundred people, the band faced extinction. During this crisis, Augustus brought the boys to his farm near Brantford, where they were cared for by his Mohawk second wife, Tekarihogen.[11]

Their father sent John and Peter to school in order to learn English. When they returned, he taught them basic agricultural techniques. The Mississaugas had lost their hunting and trapping grounds; agriculture was the only way they could survive. Peter, the younger brother, had just a couple of years of schooling, but he was bright, muscular, and energetic.[12] At twenty, Peter joined the Methodist church as a so-called "exhorter," translating sermons and hymns and establishing Ojibwe equivalents for Christian terms. He became a preacher in 1827 and advanced to the rank of deacon three years later. In 1833, he became the first Canadian Status Indian to be an ordained Methodist minister in British North America. Fluent in English, he served as a bridge between the government and his own people, encouraging them to embrace agriculture and move to the Methodist mission that he helped establish on the Credit River.[13]

Tribal elders realized that their ability to compete with the settlers depended on their young people acquiring at least a rudimentary Western-style education. Vocational schools were the answer, and the missionary groups responded with campaigns to raise money to build the industrial training schools that would provide a basic education so the children could at least become manual workers. Desperate to acquire skills and facing racial prejudice, Aboriginal leaders accepted this limitation as a first step. They realized that the age-old traditions of hunting, fishing, and gathering would no longer feed their people.[14] Rev. Peter Jones dreamed that educated Christian Aboriginals would eventually become the administrators and teachers in the industrial schools. Students would be able to retain their Aboriginal language and culture, but would learn to communicate in English so they could compete with Euro-Canadians. Just before he died, Peter sadly observed that non-Aboriginal teachers and caretakers, who forbade Aboriginal children from speaking their own language, staffed the industrial schools, which later became known as residential schools.

In February 1831, Peter asked the Methodist Council to allow him to preach in Great Britain in order to raise funds for the construction of an industrial school at the Muncey reserve, located near London, Ontario. After arriving in England, Jones put aside his clergyman's garb and preached in the leather leggings and headdress of an Ojibwe chief to the delight of his audiences. His lectures featured a display of pagan Aboriginal masks and symbols of deities from his own private collection to encourage the faithful to donate to the schools whose primary aim was to Christianize the Aboriginal peoples.[15] While preaching in Bristol in late May 1831, Peter was confined to bed for seven weeks with a serious illness. He confided the details of his illness to his diary, and there is little doubt that he had a severe case of pneumonia. By 24 June he was well enough to receive guests and noted in his diary: "We had several visitors at Mr. Wood's this evening, among whom was Miss E[liza] Field of London, who gave me an invitation to visit her mother."[16] Peter accepted the invitation to visit the Field family's home, where he received a warm welcome from members of the upper-middle-class family. The handsome young Aboriginal missionary's enthusiasm and future plans captivated Eliza, a twenty-eight-year-old member of an evangelical movement that sponsored social action. She and Peter spent much time together.[17]

Though they were pious and broad-minded, the Field family's expressed muted enthusiasm when Eliza announced her intention of marrying Peter and sharing his life in the Canadian colony. Fortunately, Peter obtained a strong letter of support from Rev. Egerton Ryerson, a long-time friend who had been the first missionary on his reserve. Field and his second wife, Eliza's stepmother, eventually withdrew their objections to their daughter's match, and on 5 August 1833, Eliza, chaperoned by Egerton Ryerson, set sail for New York.[18] On arrival, the couple were married at the home of a Methodist clergyman, and they departed immediately for Upper Canada on an Erie Canal boat. After reaching Toronto, they travelled five hours on horseback to the Credit reserve, where they moved into the Mission house.[19] Eliza was a devout woman, dedicated to missionary work, and she mingled freely with the women and children of the Mississauga band. Though she herself spoke Ojibwe with difficulty, Eliza taught the girls sewing and drawing. The Reverend Jones's mission was to convert all his people to Christianity, and he constantly travelled round the region, often visiting the widely scattered settlements on horseback. While away, he maintained an active correspondence with his wife, a slight woman prone to frequent illness, and gave her as much support as possible.[20]

In the coming years, after losing several children in infancy, Peter and Eliza were blessed with four healthy sons. Their first, Charles Augustus, had been born at the Old River Credit Mission on 26 April 1839, and a second son, John Frederick, followed on 29 March 1841, just before Jones was assigned to the Muncey reserve near London, Ontario. At Muncey, the main floor of the Mission house served as a school during the week and a chapel on Sunday, while the family lived on the second floor. It was here that their third son, Peter Edmund, was born on 30 October 1843. The new arrival received his father's Mississauga name Kahkewaquonaby, which means "The Waving Plume" in English.[21] The baby boy was a Status Indian since at that time, being one-quarter Status Indian was sufficient according to both Mississauga tradition and the British colonial government. He was an Anishinabe. The Mississaugas belonged to the Ojibwe nation, an Algonquian linguistic and cultural group. Individual members call themselves the Anishinabeg—"the people or good beings," the plural being Anishinabek. They spoke Anishinaabe-mowin, the Ojibwe language. Although Peter Edmund was raised and educated in English, he appears to have acquired knowledge of the Ojibwe language in adulthood.[22] All his recorded public addresses and his contributions to meetings of the Grand Council would be in English. Throughout his life, he would never relinquish his right to be a Status Indian or an Indian as defined by the Indian Act. He would be entitled to all the rights reserved for Status Indians, but would have to accept the numerous restrictions imposed by the same legislation.

In the spring of 1845, the Methodist Missionary Society, recognizing Reverend Jones's value as a charismatic preacher, sent him on a yearlong tour of the British Isles to obtain financial support for the industrial schools. It was his third trip, but this time Eliza and the three boys were able to accompany him, staying with her family in Lambeth, south London. Eliza's stepmother could not resist describing the three boys in a letter to her son Arthur, who was serving with the East India Company: "The eldest [Charles] is a fine looking boy quite European in his appearance, the second [Frederick] is rather tinged with the Indian cast and colour; and the baby [Peter Edmund] is a thorough Indian!!! His Father said he'll beat both the others."[23] While Eliza and the boys remained in London, Reverend Jones maintained contact with his family by means of regular letters. In one he writes how pleased he is that Peter Edmund is walking, and the other two suggest that the children are in good health.

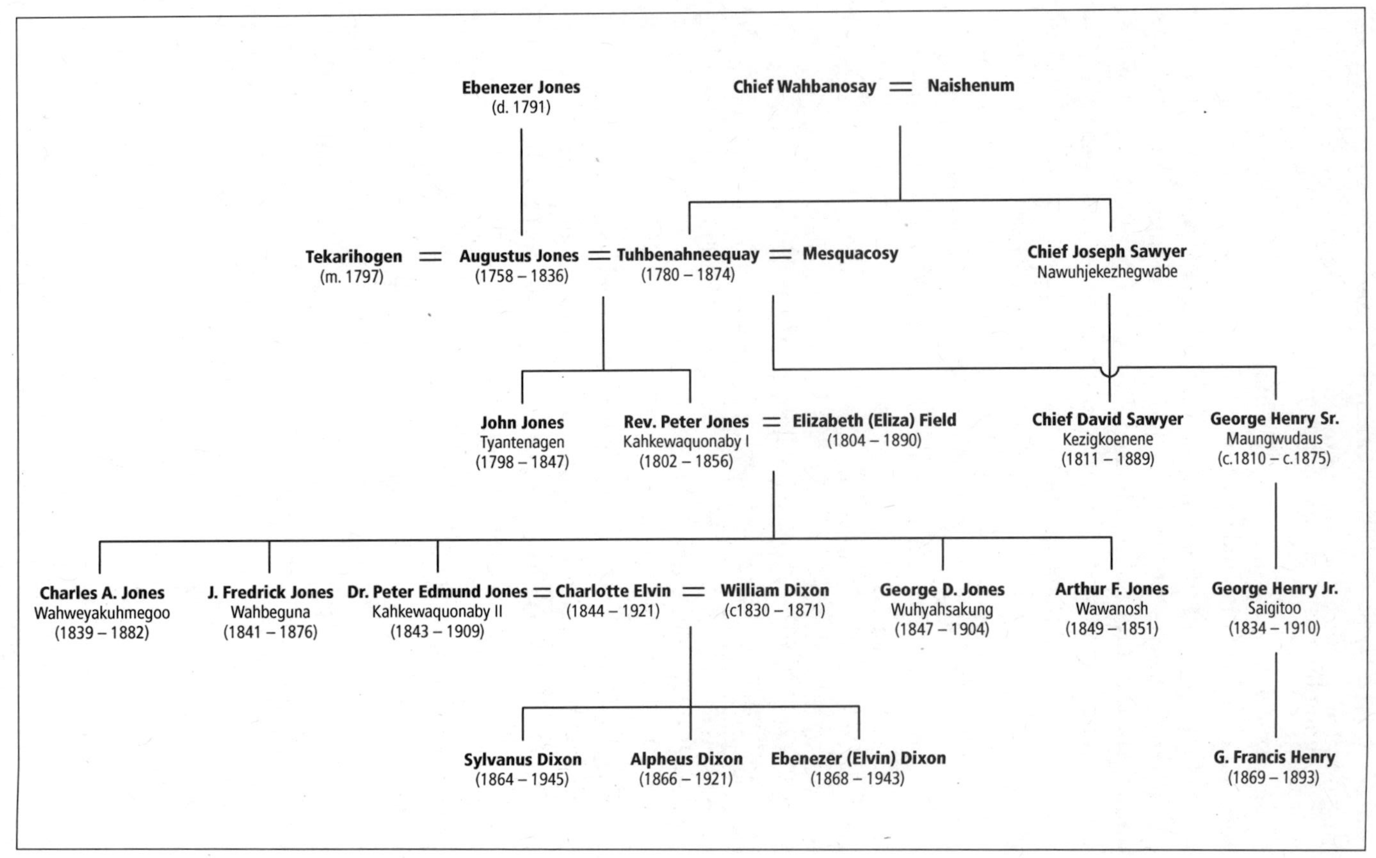

Figure 1 Jones family genealogy.

Oct. 23rd/45
How delighted I shall be to see our dear Popsey [Peter Edmund] baby trotting along like a young gosling.

Oct 29th/45
My very dear precious Newish [Eliza's Ojibwe pet name],
The account you give of the dear children is truly gratifying. Papa will not forget his sweet Popsey tomorrow the 30th [Peter Edmund's birthday]. May God bless the child and spare him to be a blessing many years to his parents.

November 1st/45, Glasgow.
Mr D [John Dunlop] has given me a silk kerchief for my sweet Popsey baby, bless his heart. How I long to see him.[24]

Not long after this letter was written, however, paralysis struck the infant, most likely due to what we now call poliomyelitis. He had already started walking; the onset of an acute illness in a child who had previously been able to walk, followed by paralysis of the limbs, supports this diagnosis as does his clinical course with eventual partial recovery.[25] Reverend Jones had ready access to medical counsel, including his friend, Dr. Thomas Hodgkin, of Guy's Hospital, who was a trustee of his Indian School Fund. A Quaker physician who is today associated with a specific disease of the lymph glands, Hodgkin was one of the founders of the British Aborigines Protective Society, a group that protested against the cruelty that the White-dominated society often displayed toward the Aboriginal peoples of the world.[26] Hodgkin was an outstanding diagnostician. He would no doubt have recognized Peter Edmund's malady from reports in the medical literature, including neuroanatomist Sir Charles Bell's lectures on the nervous system.[27]

While visiting the Island of St. Helena, Bell received a request to examine a clergyman's daughter who had suffered a paralysis of one leg during a recent epidemic of a febrile illness. This may be the earliest English reference to a polio epidemic for as Bell wrote: "it was afterwards discovered that all the children who had the fever were similarly affected with a want of growth in some part of their body or limbs."[28] Michael Underwood, physician to King George III, Queen Charlotte, and their twenty-four children, had already provided the first description of isolated cases of poliomyelitis when he noted: "Debility of the lower extremities, [which] usually attacks children previously reduced by fever ... when both [limbs] have been paralytic, nothing, has seemed to do any good but irons to the legs."[29]

Young Peter Edmund's paralysis would have reached its peak within two weeks, but any improvement would be long coming. On 4 March 1846, still visiting small communities in remote areas of the British Isles, Reverend Jones wrote Eliza, "I hope and pray that my sweet pet Popsey is still getting better. I shall be anxious to hear from you."[30] The family returned to Canada in late 1846, and over the next winter, Peter Edmund seemed to get worse rather than better. Reverend Jones wrote the visiting Indian superintendent to say that they proposed taking the boy to see the doctor as soon as the roads would permit.[31] Sometime after his sixth birthday, Peter Edmund seems to have responded to physical therapy because his father was in a more optimistic frame of mind: "Our dear boy Peter Edmund still goes on his crutches. We trust he will outgrow his disease and be able to walk in a year or so."[32]

Reverend Jones had long tried to improve the health of his people by advocating for a medical man to be stationed near each reserve. As early as 1832, he had asked Dr. John Rolph, founder of the privately owned Toronto School of Medicine, for help in preparing candidates.[33] The first of these was his Mississauga half-brother Francis Wilson Jones, but Francis would first have to acquire a general education. With Egerton Ryerson's help, he gained entry to the prestigious Upper Canada College in 1837. The principal was supportive, and the college waived the fees for their first known Aboriginal student.[34] Finally Toronto's King's College agreed to admit Wilson, and though they waived their fees, it took some time to arrange the financing. Wilson would need an additional £50 per annum to cover the living expenses of his wife and their young son in Toronto. Jones first wrote his wealthy Scottish friend, John Dunlop of Edinburgh, who agreed to send £50 a year for three years and immediately dispatched his first contribution.

Things started off well. Wilson had been attending lectures for about three weeks, he was bright and well prepared, and his professors were satisfied with his progress. Jones immediately wrote George Vardon, the deputy superintendent general of Indian Affairs, saying that he was happy to inform him that he had succeeded in getting Wilson into medical school without paying the usual fees. A Scottish banker would be sending £50 a year, but this would be inadequate to support the family in Toronto. He had consulted Mississauga Head Chief Joseph Sawyer, who agreed that part of the expenses incurred in Wilson's education ought to be paid out of the Indian School Fund: "The object in wishing to put him [Wilson] in possession of a good medical education is that he may become a useful practitioner amongst the Indian tribes...."[35] The letter went unanswered, and later a footnote was added: "No action was taken on this subject."[36] Despite this inaction, Wilson continued his medical studies. Unfortunately, he contracted smallpox during his first year on the hospital wards and died. The torch thus passed to Peter Edmund, then a mere four years old.[37]

Over the next few years, Reverend Jones's own worsening health forced him to plan his retirement and move out of the mission station. He was able to spend a great deal of time with Peter Edmund, now seven years old. The child still required crutches to get about, but loved working in the garden. His father wrote to a friend about how pleased Peter Edmund was with the way his early corn took root.[38]

The young boy's older brothers were frequently away from home. Though Charles, the oldest son, spent a short time at an Indian school, he and his brothers Fred and George later attended private boarding schools.[39] Peter Edmund's health problems, including a lifelong tendency to bronchitis, however, kept him under the parental roof as long as his father was alive.[40] By now, the Jones family had a fourth son, George Dunlop, named after Reverend Jones's Scottish financer. Sadly, a fifth child, Arthur Field Jones, named after Eliza's youngest brother, died at the age of fourteen months in 1850.[41]

In 1851, the family moved into Echo Villa, an elegant brick house in the Classical Revival style they had built on fourteen hectares of farmland a few kilometres west of the bustling town of Brantford. Funds to clear the land and build the mansion likely came from Eliza's wealthy father. Jones's friends, anxious to help, sent seeds, which enabled them to plant a typical English garden.[42] Here Reverend Jones rested, but while waiting for his strength to return, managed to build bookshelves and most certainly spent a great deal of time with his sons. Though reputed to be a disciplinarian, he tended not to interfere with their activities and allowed them more freedom than their mother with her strict Victorian rules.[43] Echo Villa, fronted by two Doric pillars, was a home fit for one of Brantford's wealthy entrepreneurs, not a retired Methodist missionary.

Young Peter Edmund, still nicknamed Popsey, had his own bedroom, complete with fireplace, on the second floor. He would hear the heated political discussions taking place below or go downstairs to meet the prominent Aboriginal and government officials who called to visit his father.[44] Both groups were anxious to hear Reverend Jones's experienced views on controversial matters as he was highly regarded by colonial bureaucrats, politicians, and the Six Nations, as well as by his own Mississaugas of the New Credit. His stepmother, after all, was the daughter of a Mohawk chief, and he had Mohawk stepbrothers, so he felt at home with members of the Six Nations. Foremost among these was Chief George H.M. Johnson, who had married an educated American Quaker woman named Emily Susanna Howells in 1853. As Strong-Boag and Gerson observed, these intermarried couples saw themselves as specially equipped to help fuse the Aboriginal and Euro-Canadian cultures.[45]

On 19 April 1854, Eliza noted in her diary: "Left my dear home in company with P.E. for England ... doctor to see P.E.'s leg."[46] The lad would be eleven years old in the fall, and as he still walked with the aid of crutches, they wished to plan his future education. Eliza, a published author, may have read how famed Scottish author, Sir Walter Scott, had suffered a similar paralytic illness (most likely poliomyelitis) at eighteen months of age, but was eventually able to lead an active life.[47] The trip would allow Eliza to introduce Peter Edmund to his grandfather, Charles Field, now in his late seventies and terminally ill. Reverend Jones, Eliza, and Peter Edmund left Brantford by train on a Saturday, but spent Sunday in Albany, where Reverend Jones had been invited to preach. His theme was taken from Acts 17:30: "And the times of this ignorance God winked at; but now commandeth all men everywhere to repent."[48] Peter Edmund listened with pride and later was overheard telling a friend: "My Papa does not read his prayers and sermons; he prays what he feels in his heart."[49]

The next morning they boarded a train for Boston, where Reverend Jones said goodbye as his wife and son boarded the large side-wheel steamship bound for Liverpool via Halifax. One can imagine the excitement: the paddle wheels were nine metres in diameter, the single black funnel was amidships, and the three masts carried auxiliary sails. The second-class fare of $60 entitled them to a carpeted cabin, about three metres square, with upper and lower berths with fine linen on one wall and a horsehair settee on the other. There was also a marble washstand, a mirror, and a glass-covered lamp. As soon as they set sail, seasickness replaced excitement as the wooden-hulled ship pitched and rolled.[50] On Tuesday, 27 April, Eliza wrote, "Being sick all day, wished to land at Halifax, P.E. sick, almost all on board sick."[51] As it was the month of May, the North Atlantic exhibited good behaviour. There were a number of children among the 120 passengers, and Peter Edmund was able to go on deck and watch them play games. The engineer proudly showed the passengers the steam engines, which burned a ton of coal every ten kilometres, but with the help of the sails propelled the ship at thirty kilometres an hour. The sailors determined the speed by tossing a log in the water and counting the length of rope released over a fixed period of time measured with an hourglass.

When stomachs settled, passengers could enjoy breakfast in their cabins, while in the late afternoon the bells summoned them to the second-class saloon located amidships. The dinner menu included barley soup, roast beef, mutton, goose, and fish, followed by desserts, including plum pudding, pies, oranges, and nuts. In addition to tea and coffee, there was a cow aboard to supply milk. By Friday, Eliza could write, "Fair wind, sails up, rather cold, felt very weak," but the next day she was able to enjoy a conversation with fellow passengers.[52] On Sunday, the pilot boarded the vessel to negotiate sandbanks in the Irish Sea and the tides of the Mersey River so the ship could dock at Liverpool.[53]

The two travellers were met by members of the Field family, who collected the boxes containing their belongings and escorted them to the family home in London. There Eliza was given the opportunity to recover from the voyage before her sister Emma called to take them all to visit her father in the countryside. They were met in the hall by her stepmother and other relatives who ushered them into Charles Field's sickroom. Eliza was immediately struck by the great change in her father's appearance since her visit the year before. In the coming months, Peter Edmund would get to know his grandfather, who was a remarkably tolerant man and had been one of the few Field family members to support his mother's marriage to an Aboriginal. The Fields' cottage in the village of Norwood Hill in Surrey was located on a hillside from which one could look down on the smoke rising from the coal fires of London some ten kilometres distant.[54]

In spite of the anxious wait at Charles Field's bedside, Peter Edmund's condition necessitated a trip back into the city. The Joneses had been advised to consult Mr. William Adams, a surgeon who was experienced in the treatment of disorders affecting the lower limbs. Adams was a former student of Dr. Hodgkin, and they had just co-authored a case report that described a patient with weakness of the limbs.[55] On 13 July, the Fields took Eliza and Peter Edmund to Adams's Harley Street consulting room. The doctor and the patient's mother had much in common; both came from upper-middle-class families and had been educated at small private schools. Adams had a soft voice and a pronounced lisp, but was never short of words.[56] The young lad was carefully examined, and Eliza was pleased by the doctor's sympathy and the many practical suggestions based on his exceptionally thorough grasp of pathological anatomy. Adams was able to assure her that the boy would eventually improve and be fit to function on his own. Eliza's diary records: "Mr. Adams says P.E. requires attention for at least six months longer, gave me instructions on how to proceed."[57]

The following day grandfather Field passed away and the family gathered for the funeral. Peter Edmund rode with his mother in a closed coach. Following the interment, there were many sympathetic visitors as the Fields were a large family and had been candle makers for two centuries.[58] In all the chaos, however, Peter Edmund was not neglected. On 12 August, Eliza wrote in her diary, "Brother Arthur kindly fetched P.E. and took him to see the Queen prorogue Parliament."[59] The state coach carrying Queen Victoria and the Prince Consort, escorted by the household cavalry, left Buckingham Palace and travelled down the Mall to the Houses of Parliament, where the Queen was to close the session.[60] The pomp of Empire impressed the young lad, and years later, when he had become a federal Indian agent, Peter Edmund wrote to an American colleague about the "prestige associated with being a British Colonial official."[61]

Once the period of official mourning had passed, Eliza and Peter Edmund returned to Canada, where they found that Reverend Jones had recovered sufficiently to take on some temporary assignments. At the request of the chiefs of the Six Nations, he had travelled to Albany to research the land surrenders of the former British colonial regime. Government officials frequently requested his opinion on matters related to Aboriginal issues.[62] Dr. Egerton Ryerson had petitioned the government to make Jones a superintendent in the Department of Indian Affairs, where he would be "a great stimulus to Indian civilization and confer a very great benefit as well as give satisfaction to the Indian tribes."[63] Though the post of visiting Indian superintendent was vacant, the department maintained its policy of restricting Aboriginal peoples to minor clerical or service employment. Peter Edmund shared his father's disappointment, little knowing that one day he would achieve his father's goal of a post in the Department of Indian Affairs, where he also would act as a bridge between the two peoples.[64]

For several years, father and son were both confined to Echo Villa. Young Peter watched, and perhaps even helped, as his father compiled his memoirs. After Reverend Jones's death, fellow missionary Enoch Wood published the *Life and Journals of Kah-ke-wa-quo-na-by (Rev. Peter Jones), Wesleyan Missionary*.[65] Eliza completed Jones's unique volume, *History of the Ojebway Indians with Especial Reference to Their Conversion to Christianity*, which was published in London in 1861 and

Figure 2 The Reverend Peter Jones as sketched by his wife Eliza when Peter Edmund was about ten years old. From Peter Jones, *Life and Journals of Kah-ke-wa-quo-na-by* (Toronto: Anson Green, 1860).

followed by a second printing a year later.[66] Eliza had entrepreneurial instincts and sent letters and descriptive pamphlets to many of her husband's friends and admirers. The readability of this work and reprints in both 1970 and 1996 reflect Eliza's proven literary skill.

Reverend Jones did more than work on his memoirs during his confinement. He was one of the regional secretaries of the British Aborigines Protective Society. His library included volumes and journals from every part of the British Empire.[67] Because he was unable to engage in strenuous activities such as hunting, Peter Edmund spent a great deal of time in the library and developed an enduring love of books. Throughout his lifetime, he continued to search for books to enrich the collection. Much of his collection now graces the archives of Victoria University and the United Church of Canada in Toronto.[68]

In the spring of 1856, Eliza, Peter Edmund and Frederick accompanied Reverend Jones on the train to St. Catharines, Ontario, so that he could try the waters of the local spa. Their friends, the Creightons, had arranged for Reverend Jones to consult prominent physicians, who, in addition to conducting a "strict" examination, asked for a sample of his urine. When the urine was heated in a spoon held over a candle, an abnormal white precipitate formed, indicating the presence of protein. Eliza recorded the sequence of events that followed: "In the evening the Doctors came and to the grief of my heart told me that by an analysis of urine they had found that my dear Peter had Bright's disease of the kidneys which if so is incurable."[69] The doctors advised them to consult Professor James Bovell, then dean of medicine at Toronto's Trinity College. Bovell was Richard Bright's student at Guy's Hospital shortly after Bright described the triad of dropsy (oedema), protein in the urine, and hardened kidneys, now called Bright's disease. Bovell later studied pathology in Scotland and worked under leading physicians in Dublin before immigrating to Canada in 1848. From 1856 to 1870, Bovell lectured on physiology and pathology at the Toronto School of Medicine.[70] He was considered a skilful diagnostician and one of the first to employ clinical microscopy.[71]

Dr. Griffin, their family doctor, accompanied the Joneses to Toronto for the visit with Dr. Bovell. The family stayed at the home of their close friends, the Egerton Ryersons, and twelve-year-old Peter Edmund likely accompanied his parents, little knowing that less than a decade later he would himself be Bovell's student.[72] Early one morning, Bovell, accompanied by Griffin, rode in a carriage to Egerton Ryerson's home, and Griffin presented Reverend Jones's case to the consultant. Following a careful examination, Bovell told the patient that in addition to his chronic heart condition, he now had congestion of the stomach and liver, his kidneys being much affected.[73] Though terminally ill, the minister insisted on returning home by train. On his return to Echo Villa, members of the Mississauga band stood vigil outside the house, chanting Ojibwe hymns translated by Reverend Jones. They also sent for a well-known Indian Medicine Man from Rice Lake at their own expense.[74] Although he was a Christian, Reverend Jones had never rejected traditional Aboriginal herbal medicines, and he must have appreciated the generosity.

On 29 June 1856, in his final hours, Reverend Jones called his sons to his bedside and presented them with keepsakes. Peter Edmund received his father's watch, his New Testament, and sixty hectares of farmland on the New Credit reserve. Most importantly, he became the heir to his father's large library and collection of Aboriginal artifacts, which he was to guard and enhance over his lifetime.[75] During the years the invalids spent together, Peter Edmund had listened to his father express his views on the important issues facing the Aboriginal community. In later life Reverend Jones had been a political leader who helped the Mississaugas develop a new legal system by modifying their traditional laws and customs so they would be more compatible with those of the colonists. The result was a remarkable example of effective Aboriginal self-government that, sadly, the government eventually quashed.[76] Peter Edmund acquired his father's legal files, which would prove to be invaluable when he became chief. Now was the time to follow in Reverend Jones's footsteps and realize his father's dream of having an Aboriginal doctor on the reserve, but first Peter Edmund must learn to walk unaided so he could study medicine.

With the help of a brace and physical exercise, Peter Edmund's mobility finally began to improve, and by age thirteen, he was able to get about easily with the aid of a cane. On 1 September 1856, Eliza received a letter from her sister in Bristol, saying, "I am glad to hear that Peter's lameness is so much better."[77] So in November little Peter Edmund was sent to the Mount Elgin Residential School near London, Ontario, built with the money his late father had raised in Great Britain. In a letter to their Scottish friend, John Dunlop, Eliza proudly wrote: "I have had many inducements to place him there ... I love the Indians, I wish my younger boys to learn the language."[78] Despite years spent in Mississauga communities, Eliza had never completely mastered their tongue. She hoped her sons would succeed where she had failed, but they lived in a home where English, embellished by an upper-class accent, was the norm. Conversing in Ojibwe, a language the Euro-Canadians hoped to eliminate, was never a viable option for the family.

Peter Edmund had finally shown considerable improvement: Now he could walk unaided, though one of his legs was shorter than the other and he still required the use of a cane.[79] He appears to have resided at the Methodist-run residential school for a relatively short time. Unable to run, play games, or labour on their farm, he could speak only English when his classmates were able to chat in Ojibwe once their teachers were out of earshot. Even though as the son of the school's founder he would receive preferential treatment, the discipline was harsh and the food horrid. The unhappy boy was no doubt pleased to return to Echo Villa.

Figure 3 Eliza Field-Jones (Carey), age seventy-two years in 1876. (*Source:* Courtesy of Victoria University Library, Toronto)

When he returned home, he found that his mother had hastily remarried. Her new husband was John Carey, who had called on Eliza following the death of his wife. The Joneses were old friends of the Careys. Though he was a farmer, John had also taught at the Indian school connected to Reverend Jones's Muncey Mission near London, Ontario, but Carey was neither as refined nor as considerate as her beloved first husband. Eliza soon recognized her mistake. The four boys were revolted at the thought of such a boorish man occupying their revered father's room. Jennifer Lund's detailed analysis of Eliza's diaries revealed that as a woman, she was denied any form of credit, and Carey refused her repeated requests for financial assistance.[80]

By January 1860 Peter Edmund's health had recovered sufficiently to commute to the Brantford Grammar School, which had moved to

Figure 4 Peter Edmund Jones's childhood home, Echo Villa, in Brantford. (*Source:* Courtesy of Louise Thorp, Vancouver, British Columbia)

the upper part of the North Ward School on Albion Street after amalgamation with the Public School Board. A review of Peter Edmund's attendance record through to December of that year reveals numerous prolonged absences, especially during the winter months. He suffered frequent bouts of bronchitis, and going to school entailed travelling several kilometres by sleigh or buggy. Nevertheless he passed the final examinations and was qualified to begin what would be a multifaceted career.[81]

Two
Medical Education

His year at an approved preparatory school enabled Peter Edmund Jones to gain entrance into the privately run Toronto School of Medicine in 1862.[1] The University of Toronto had been forced to privatize its medical and legal training programs in 1853 because the government believed that the province should not have to support the education of those who wished to enter what they called the "lucrative professions."[2] The University of Toronto's dean of medicine, however, remained responsible for setting the examinations and granting degrees, and the university's medical library was open to the students. The largest commercial school was the Toronto School of Medicine, located near the university, with a faculty providing both basic science and practical instruction. Dr. John Rolph established the school in 1843. Although he later became embroiled in politics and was no longer in charge when Peter Edmund applied for admission, he provided the boy with a recommendation that would have carried considerable weight because he knew Reverend Jones from working with him on a number of past occasions.[3]

In Peter Edmund's time these private schools provided reasonably good training. Because the medical profession was not well policed, many final-year students merely fulfilled the course requirements and opened a practice without a degree. A year before Peter Edmund graduated, provincial authorities finally obtained laws to control untrained medical practitioners. The General Council for Medical Education was authorized to regulate medical training, including examinations, licensing, and the right to discipline physicians, but in 1869 the newly formed College of Physicians and Surgeons of Ontario took charge.[4] Importantly, in 1887 the University of Toronto regained the right to offer medical training and adopted an improved curriculum. Within two decades it was considered one of the top medical schools in North America.[5] The Toronto School of Medicine welcomed Peter Edmund. He had the necessary premedical training and could pay the fees. He was given a unique opportunity. Generations of Aboriginal lads had attended schools dedicated to assimilating them into the majority population, but only as semi-skilled workers. Bright boys could aspire to becoming a teacher, interpreter, or missionary, but never a physician. Slight of build and modest in height, Peter walked with a limp aided by a cane. He had Native features and could have had problems being accepted by his peers because prejudice ran high among the local population. Well-spoken and raised in Brantford, however, he was at ease with his classmates. Peter Edmund was able to make friends because of his familiarity with the Euro-Canadian community, his scholastic abilities, and his skill at the then very popular game of chess. Unable to take part in sports, he busied himself by becoming a member of various organizations.[6]

Peter Edmund was not the only Aboriginal attending classes at the Toronto School of Medicine. The other was Oronhyatekha, who in later life seldom used his Christian name, Peter Martin. As far as we know, these two young men were the first Canadian Status Indians to study medicine. They had attained the necessary level of education to apply to medical school, and both had strong links with influential people, which probably helped them gain entry. Unlike Peter Edmund, who had family connections, Oronhyatekha came from a simple background and had to work hard to gain recognition. Also in contrast to Peter Edmund, he was a particularly striking figure: the powerful Mohawk had shiny hair and prominent eyes that topped his two-metre frame. He spoke with a deep resonating voice, was always in fine spirits, and excelled at virtually every sport.[7] His confident manner was the result of having overcome unbelievable odds. Oronhyatekha was born on the Six Nations Territory in 1841 and was attending school when a visiting phrenologist, impressed by his large head, recommended him for further education at a Wesleyan academy in Massachusetts. He did manual work, taught school, and acted in Indian shows to finance his education. Joining the militia he became a medal-winning sharpshooter. When he finally gained admission to the Toronto School of Medicine in 1863, he must have been surprised to meet Peter Edmund. Both young men buckled down to work, dressed like the other students in stylish suits under black academic gowns.[8]

The University of Toronto followed the English system in which students first obtained a Bachelor of Medicine degree, which entitled them to sit the licensing examination and to practise. An M.D. degree required the submission of a thesis a year or so later. However, Peter Edmund spent only two years in the Toronto program while Oronhyatekha, who married soon after beginning his medical studies, remained in Toronto and obtained his M.D. degree from the University of Toronto. He received his licence to practise in 1867.[9]

Peter Edmund elected to transfer to Queen's University in Kingston in order to complete the last two years of his program. Queen's had an Edinburgh-style four-year program, which enabled him to obtain his M.D. degree in the spring of 1866 and his provincial licence to practise in the autumn of that year.[10] The motivation for this move is unclear, but Eliza's finances had become tenuous especially after she separated from her second husband. It would certainly be less expensive for her son to live in a smaller town such as Kingston and attend Queen's University. It is unclear how Peter Edmund financed his medical education. His mother still lived in Echo Villa, but her estate suffered from poor investments. The family's Scottish friend, John Dunlop, was still an active member of the British Aborigines Protective Society and had been kept informed of Peter Edmund's progress. Since he had helped pay the medical school fees of Peter's deceased uncle, it is possible that he would have been willing to assist Peter Edmund in following the same path.[11] Eliza's family in England was another source of funds. They loved and supported their eldest sister and had been kind to Peter Edmund when he was in London for his grandfather's funeral. Dr. Thomas Hodgkin also offered advice on how to proceed with Peter Edmund's medical training, but as the Quaker physician seldom collected his fees, he was not in a position to offer financial support.[12]

Peter Edmund arrived in Kingston in the fall of 1864, a few weeks after his twenty-first birthday. The population then was approximately twelve thousand, including the three thousand men of the British colonial garrison with their families and the inmates of the provincial penitentiary.[13] Immigrants arriving by boat in Quebec City would catch a train bound for Upper Canada or board a smaller vessel to Ottawa, then transfer to a small steamer that passed through the multiple locks of the Rideau Canal to Kingston and the Midlands Region. These poor, malnourished people were ready victims of infectious disease, especially cholera, typhus, and even smallpox, while many indigent patients required hospitalization. Peter presented himself at Queen's College, where the registrar neatly inscribed his name in the broad pale-grey pages of the student register: "Student No. 596: Peter Edmund Jones, Kahkewaquonaby (The Waving Plume); preparatory school, Brantford Grammar; age 21 years; religion, Wesleyan Methodist; home address, Brantford and, father's occupation,

Missionary."[14] It was noted that Peter had completed two years at the University of Toronto. He was to attend the college's daily chapel service, board with Mr. Hunter on Bagot Street, and attend Sunday services at the Sydenham Street Wesleyan Methodist Church. The university's Board of Trustees assured parents that they would supervise student morality, making arrangements for undergraduates to attend divine worship in a church of the family's denomination. Scottish Presbyterians were the source of all theology students and also constituted a large part of Jones's medical class, the remainder being Anglicans, Methodists, Baptists, or Roman Catholics.[15] Peter Edmund was assigned to the church where his future professor of midwifery, Dr. Michael Lavell, was in charge of the Sunday school. The two men had much in common: an 1863 Queen's graduate and also a son of a Methodist preacher, Lavell had once worked alongside Peter's father at the *Christian Guardian*.[16]

At the time it was founded in 1842, Queen's University boasted two professors and ten students lodged in rented premises. The institution had strong Scottish traditions and was initially dedicated to training Presbyterian ministers, but Kingston itself was unusual as it had attracted a small but impressive group of experienced physicians trained in Britain and the United States. Among them were Dr. John Robertson Dickson, a surgeon, and Dr. Horatio Yates, a physician with an interest in basic science and therapeutics. Both men had obtained their M.D. degrees in 1842 and were ambitious, hard-working, and interested in upgrading medical education and hospital practice.[17] Dickson happened to have the member of the legislature for Kingston, John A. Macdonald, as a patient, and the two men became close friends. On 7 February 1854, John A. Macdonald, M.P. hosted a meeting at his new home on Brock Street to discuss the possibility of establishing a medical faculty at Queen's University.[18] Dickson had provided him with a list of invitees, including Dr. Yates, Dr. James Sampson, and Dr. John Stewart, as well as a number of potential medical teachers. The desire of nine final-year students to transfer from Toronto to Kingston if a medical school could be organized provided a strong sense of urgency. The future faculty rushed to meet this need. Dr. Sampson chaired a committee of physicians that prepared a syllabus with a list of potential lecturers. In April, the Medical Board of Upper Canada met in Kingston, where they examined and certified those found qualified to teach. They also inspected the Kingston General Hospital, which had benefited from the administrative talents of Dr. Horatio Yates.[19] To further improve matters, Yates had persuaded Dickson to join him in running for town council, a prerequisite for appointment to the hospital's Board of Governors. Both men, now in their early thirties, were elected to the council in January 1854, and Yates was elected chairman of the Board of Health. Acting on faith, the trustees courageously agreed to establish a medical faculty. To avoid delay, the school was started as a private venture in rented premises, beginning on 5 November 1854 with twenty-three students: nine in their final year, thirteen entering second year, and one freshman. The college co-operated, and the final-year students who had transferred from Toronto graduated in the spring of 1855.[20]

This success encouraged the Queen's trustees to establish a Faculty of Medicine located on the college campus in June 1855. The six staff members were given the rank of lecturer rather than professor, but the medical faculty did get a government grant of £1,000. That the dean of a faculty should receive a government grant angered the Board of Trustees, who believed that only they should receive such grants.[21] The new medical students and faculty swamped the college's four professors who were busy preparing thirty-six theology students to become Presbyterian ministers. As a result, the faculties of arts and theology protested the right of the medical faculty to receive such a grant.

Once registered, Peter Edmund was confronted with the task of submitting the title of a thesis to be presented two years later at the time of his final examinations. A list of well-documented topics in the medical literature of the time was provided, so picking a common disease or surgical procedure was the easy way out. His record reveals that, without hesitation, he submitted the title "The Indian Medicine-Man." He would have been familiar with the topic because of his father's convictions and the time his mother spent poring over her late husband's notes, which included details of what he had learned from Aboriginal healers. Peter Edmund understood how much Reverend Jones respected many of the traditional medical practices of his people.[22] Indeed, Reverend Jones had believed in the superiority of Aboriginal medicinal agents and made a point of recording the means of preparation and usage of these herbs during his travels. He even administered them to his wife, who appears to have suffered from migraine and had frequent bouts of the flu.[23] This acceptance of the benefits derived from blending of traditional Aboriginal knowledge and European technology must have stuck in the young boy's memory.[24] In his thesis, Peter Edmund would avoid citing the contemporary medical literature, which was plainly dismissive of the Aboriginal peoples and their "pagan" medical practices.

Peter Edmund faced a heavy schedule as each professor gave a daily lecture, and there were laboratory demonstrations several afternoons a week. Though the students wished to see patients, observe operations and obstetrical deliveries, they would first have to attend didactic lectures in chemistry and natural history, the name then used to describe all the other basic sciences. Just before Peter Edmund transferred to Queen's, the university's popular chemistry and natural history professor, Dr. George Lawson, left for Dalhousie University in Halifax.[25] While at Queen's he had founded the Canadian Botany Society and established a museum, which eventually became the Department of Biology. The medical students appreciated both botany, involving the study of medicinal plants, and zoology, in which students dissected vertebrate animals. Darwin's theory of the evolution of species by natural selection also intrigued them. Botany and natural history were the most fun, however, because students collected their own specimens and put them under one of the new English microscopes purchased by Dr. Lawson.[26]

Chemistry, especially the way it was then taught, was unpopular with medical students. It took real talent to make inorganic chemistry relevant to clinical practice, even though compounds containing mercury and iodine were the drugs of that era. Without consulting the medical faculty, which had insisted that an M.D. be appointed, the Board of Trustees made Mr. Robert Bell, a recent McGill graduate in engineering and geology, interim professor of chemistry and natural history.[27] His salary of $500 used up one-half of the medical faculty's highly coveted government grant. Equally galling was that Bell received permission to collect fees from students, heretofore an exclusive privilege of the medical faculty. The fees were to remunerate local physicians who took time out to teach students at the bedside. The indignant faculty refused to invite Bell to its meetings and encouraged the students to make his life intolerable. Many of the students were older than Bell. Peter Edmund was just two years younger, and he would find Bell's classes disrupted by objects, including snowballs, flying through the air. Students repeatedly sabotaged Bell's chemical apparatus and stole his chemicals. The last straw was the so-called shoulder incident.[28] Every time Bell turned to face the blackboard, a ringleader shouted "shoulder," a signal for the students to noisily slap their chests. Bell eventually identified the ringleader and entered a complaint, but the medical faculty took it as proof that this non-doctor was unable to control his students. The university Senate was more realistic, however. It suspended the student and forced him to write a letter of apology.[29]

Though Bell now held a permanent university position, the medical faculty still felt that he was simply unable to teach, though he was a capable researcher. They continued to make his life difficult, and Bell eventually decided to return to his first love, the exploration of Canada's North. In 1869 he was appointed an officer of the Geological Survey of Canada, based in Montreal at the time. While there he used the periods between expeditions to obtain an M.D. degree from McGill University and to practise medicine for a time in Montreal. This allowed him to serve as both medical officer and chief geologist on all future expeditions.[30] Bell was profoundly interested in Canada's Aboriginal populations and spent more than thirty years among them. Throughout his career he collected Aboriginal legends, and though he wrote countless geological papers, Bell left but one medical report. Curiously, he gave it the title *The Medicine-Man*, perhaps recalling that two decades earlier he sat on the committee that voted to accept Peter Edmund Jones's thesis, "The Indian Medicine-Man."[31]

Anatomy was without doubt the major preclinical subject. Although students found the details somewhat tedious, in those days it distinguished the future doctors from the other students. By Peter Edmund's time, the medical school's facilities included an anatomy building, where he would have registered for courses and spent time visiting the anatomical museum. The course itself would have consisted of lectures, demonstration of specimens, and the dissection of a cadaver. The dissecting laboratory was a frightening experience from the first whiff of formaldehyde at the door to the sight of the cadavers in various stages of dissection. The anatomy professor arrived early to prepare his presentation, and the students worked in groups: one reading the dissection manual while another exposed the structure to be identified. Supervised by Dr. Michael Sullivan, the dissecting room was open every weekday and Saturday mornings for individual study. Usually the students worked in groups as it was hard to identify individual muscles and nerves in the emaciated cadavers. They may not have realized it, but the students were learning several thousand new words that would be with them until the end of their careers. With time, they overcame their fear of working in the dissecting room.[32] The museum enabled the students to observe expert dissections of key regions that had been prepared by the professor or his assistant. They would also be able to memorize the anatomical relationships of various bones, muscles, tendons, and organs, which would someday guide their own surgeries. Jones's training differed from that of Aboriginal healers who believed in the integrity of the body and considered post-mortem examinations to be a violation of that integrity. Though they did not dissect the human body, traditional healers knew the function of the various organs from their experience with wild animals. They understood the importance of the heart, lungs, and brain and knew these organs were essential to life. They also had detailed knowledge of the skeleton and impressed early explorers with their skill in treating fractures and dislocations of the limbs. Following the death of their ancestors, they carefully reassembled the bones and honoured their memory with an appropriate burial.[33]

Queen's University anatomist and medical historian Anthony A. Travill records that the university trustees were distressed by the boisterous behaviour of the medical students. They were more difficult to discipline than those in the faculties of arts or theology. As the university arranged for the students to be accepted as boarders in local homes, busybody gossips informed all and sundry that they occasionally stayed in bed on Sunday mornings and sometimes skipped their church services. The members of the board held firmly to Queen's founding tenets of Presbyterianism, and they worried that the medical students were being influenced by Charles Darwin's recent writings on the theory of evolution.[34] More likely, however, the theologians and businessmen on the board simply failed to realize that the medical students were merely responding to the stress associated with being exposed to the fears and realities of post-Civil War surgery. Because it was the first major conflict to utilize the newly developed high-velocity rifles, the American war had changed conceptions of surgery. The new rifles inflicted terrible wounds that soon led to gangrene and, before the age of antibiotics, amputation of the affected limbs was the only way to prevent death from septicemia. Abdominal surgery, however, was not routinely practised when Jones was a student; these operations would have to await Louis Pasteur's discoveries of the role played by bacteria in wound infection.[35]

After much hard work, twelve medical students finished their courses and sat the primary examination in 1865. Three students obtained over ninety-five percent and thus were excused from sitting the oral examination. A further six passed the oral exam. Three more, including Peter Edmund Jones, were considered insufficiently prepared. They were given the opportunity to retake the examination and then passed.[36] The whole class celebrated the successful completion of their basic science training. Now they were going to enter their version of the Promised Land, the Kingston General Hospital. They eagerly awaited their chance to follow the attending surgeon on a "walk-about" on the hospital wards. No doubt they could watch him perform operations and, if they were lucky, watch while their instructor delivered a baby.

Situated on its own 2.5 hectare grounds and overlooking magnificent Lake Ontario, the Kingston General Hospital was a brisk walk from Peter Edmund's boarding house. The hospital was built in 1835 by stonemasons who had settled in Kingston after completing Colonel By's Rideau Canal, which connected Kingston to Ottawa. Its classic design suited a hospital because large windows and balconies on each of the three floors provided cross ventilation. The front and rear facades were identical, with the front door facing the lake across a field kept trim by farm animals.[37] The only snag in this idyllic scene was that the government had not provided funds to operate the hospital. For a time, therefore, it served as a military barracks, and from 1841 to 1844, the building housed the Parliament of Upper and Lower Canada. Temporary alterations were made to accommodate the legislature, and the walls echoed the voice of Louis-Hippolyte LaFontaine, who defied the English-only provision of the Act of Union of Upper and Lower Canada by delivering his inaugural opening address in French. The gradual acceptance of both languages in the first Parliament of the United Province of Canada was a crucial step in Canada's evolution as a nation.[38] Because of Kingston's proximity to New York State, the capitol eventually moved to Montreal, and the building returned to the community. Despite limited funds, they finally had it refitted and opened as a hospital in 1845. Finally, the community established a charitable institution with a lay board to relieve the sick and destitute, the immigrants, and the mariners plying Lake Ontario. Male and female wards were set up, and in the early days one woman, aided by her daughter, prepared all the meals. According to Dr. James A. Low, the hospital museum curator, patients were expected to help keep the building clean.[39] There were no nurses, but relatives were allowed to visit. Physicians made rounds and surgeons performed operations in a room on the top floor. These patients were all indigents, so the medical men's only compensation was heartfelt gratitude. Although ether anaesthesia had been discovered in 1846, followed by chloroform a year later, some conservative surgeons still used whiskey and laudanum, a tincture prepared from raw opium. In this pre-antiseptic era, the infection rate was astronomical, but over the next few years, both medical techniques and hospital facilities improved, encouraged by the development of the medical school.[40]

The Queen's medical faculty maintained a close relationship with the hospital, which by 1864 could accommodate 150 patients, the same number as McGill's Montreal General Hospital.[41] Peter Edmund's decision to transfer to Queen's University may even have been influenced by the hospital's construction of the Watkins Wing in 1862, which provided fifty more beds. The new wing was certainly in operation when Peter Edmund arrived. Male and female smallpox wards were located in the basement.[42] *The Kingston Daily News* reported: "Four wards on the main floor were intended for the admission of a respectable class of patient who may be able to pay a certain amount for the medical attendance and nursing."[43] The gallery of the operating theatre on the top floor could accommodate the whole class. In those days, patients were presented in the amphitheatre, and medical students never ventured onto the wards by themselves to examine patients. Intimate exposure to patients would have to await graduation. An attending staff member served as daily visiting surgeon and supervised the senior students whose curriculum included twelve months of hospital practice.

Dr. Horatio Yates, as president of the medical board, introduced many improvements, including the appointment of a house surgeon selected from the recent graduates, a forerunner of a resident physician. Now that the patients were closely supervised, the quality of care improved. The year Peter transferred from the Toronto School of Medicine to Queen's University Yates became dean, replacing Dickson, who had resigned following a dispute with the trustees of the college. After receiving his M.D. degree from the University of Pennsylvania, Yates had benefited from a

Figure 5 The Kingston General Hospital as it appeared in an 1862 drawing. (*Source:* Courtesy of Kingston General Hospital Archives)

year of post-graduate training in England. At Queen's Yates became professor of the institutes of medicine, an important subject that embraced physiology, general pathology, and therapeutics.[44] Lectures were held five days a week from eleven until noon and were illustrated by drawings, specimens from the museum, and the use of the microscope, a new tool in clinical practice. The fee for the basic six-month series of lectures was $12, the equivalent of several hundred dollars today. Yates gave lectures on clinical medicine twice weekly while his colleague, Dr. John Dickson, performed operations in the theatre on the top floor of the Watkins Wing. The students had to purchase tickets in order to attend these extra teaching sessions. These were signed by the professor and at the end of the course the tickets would be presented to the examining board as proof of attendance. Peter Edmund had to purchase tickets from his professors to attend their lectures and clinical demonstrations or accompany them on their hospital visits. As many students were often short of funds, they could pay on account, though some of the early graduates remembered Professor Fife Fowler reminding students in his thick Scottish brogue to "Pay y'ere fees."[45]

Kingston has long been the location of a major penitentiary, and some of the professors were charged with caring for the inmates. Students sometimes accompanied the visiting doctor, but strictly as observers.[46] The college calendar for 1865–66 proudly notes that Professor Dickson had been appointed surgeon of the provincial penitentiary, which provided an additional teaching facility.[47] Another department was devoted to women's and children's diseases, and the students were required to have observed at least six cases of midwifery. The course on forensic and state medicine was also to prove useful to Jones. As one of the first physicians to establish a practice in Hagersville, Jones would later act as local coroner, investigating crimes that frequently involved poisoning or abortion.[48]

Students learned how to examine patients and perform laboratory tests such as urine analysis and therapeutic procedures such as cupping, bleeding, and the application of mustard plasters. One essential faculty requirement was that "the student must have prepared medicines for two periods of six months or one period of twelve months in the offices of a duly qualified practitioner."[49] In some instances this involved synthesizing the drug from the raw ingredients. In the final *Materia Medica* [pharmacology] examination, students were questioned on the properties of inorganic chemicals such as bichloride of mercury, which druggists called calomel. They also had to describe how to prepare these medications employing toxic substances, including metallic mercury and sulphuric acid. For example, in 1866, question four on the final examination read: "How are Calomel and Corrosive Sublimate made? State minutely how they differ as to their effects on the system."[50] Correct use of herbs and other plant products was important and comprised half of the medicinal agents on the final examination, but agents were mainly restricted to those natural products widely used in Great Britain. Physical treatments such as bleeding, either by means of cutting veins with a scalpel or by placing hot glass cups on the chest and back immediately after lacerating the skin with a sharp instrument (a procedure called cupping) were still widely employed in Canada during the 1860s. Watson's well-known 1858 textbook of physic [internal medicine] claimed that bleeding was the best remedy for inflammation because it decreased the flow of blood to the inflamed organs.[51]

During his last six months at Queen's, Jones was fortunate to have been taught by Dr. Yates, who was in charge of the wards until 31 December 1865, followed by Peter Edmund's Sunday school teacher, Dr. Michael Lavell. There were no specialists in Jones's time. Yates preferred his role as an experienced physician, but would perform surgery if there was nobody else available. For his part, Dr. Lavell had built a fine reputation in obstetrics, gynecology, and diseases of women and children.[52] A recently appointed instructor, Dr. Donald Maclean, a clinical lecturer in surgery, had fought on the Union side in the American Civil War and in the process had performed numerous amputations and other operations on the battlefield and in the large military hospitals. Peter Edmund no doubt would have appreciated how quickly Dr. Maclean could amputate a limb. As the era of Lord Lister's antisepsis only began in 1867, in Jones's student days amputations were frequently marred by secondary infections and the terrible complication of gangrene.[53] The hypodermic syringe had recently been introduced to deliver morphine subcutaneously, but it still was not possible to quickly alleviate pain by administering the drug intravenously.

A combination of basic science and clinical experience is important in evaluating medical training. In Peter Edmund's day, there were no clinical trials. Doctors merely recounted how they diagnosed an "interesting case," and rare diseases received unwarranted attention. In spite of this shortcoming of the time, Peter found conscientious and well-prepared teachers at both basic and clinical levels. Though Kingston was a small town, one-half of the hospital's patients came from the surrounding area, so the hospital continuously had a heavy patient load. There were 567 admissions in 1865: 301 surgical, 236 medical, and thirty lying-in cases.

The hospital boasted that it had the lowest death rate in Ontario. These cases gave Peter Edmund a wide-ranging exposure to both disease and trauma.[54]

In addition, Peter spent time with a local practitioner, observing office patients or more likely accompanying him when he treated his patients at home. In that era, middle- and upper-class patients did not receive treatment in hospital; it was safer to be treated at home because hospitals were a source of infection, particularly obstetrical cases, which would usually be managed at home by a midwife with a physician being called in to handle complications. Since the doctor's unwashed hands and clothes carried germs from operating theatres or even from the morgue, there was less risk of infection if the delivery was performed by a midwife. Fortunately, Kingston was spared from the scourge of major epidemics while Peter Edmund was a student, but the army and naval garrisons were a unique source of patients: veterans of campaigns in the Middle East and India who had unusual ophthalmologic diseases. These would have been especially interesting because the cornea, lens, and retina could now be visualized by means of the newly invented ophthalmoscope.[55]

Peter Edmund would even receive an introduction to the emerging discipline of psychological medicine during his visits to the Rockwood Lunatic Asylum, the second mental hospital in Ontario.[56] The facility provided a kind environment under medical superintendent John P. Litchfield. Psychiatric patients were no longer chained and incarcerated in the penitentiary. In that era the sole therapy was rest in a quiet hospital atmosphere, a wholesome diet, and some exercise. The aim was to do away with physical restraints, but this was not always possible. Drug therapy in 1866 included sedatives. One favourite, a bottle of the best Scotch ale or Dublin stout, was said to be demonstrably more effective than a straitjacket when repeated as needed![57]

Peter Edmund's textbooks from this period reflect the state of medical education in the mid-nineteenth century, particularly its emphasis on the theoretical. His school books from the mid-1860s are equal in size to, or in some cases somewhat larger than, those used by present-day medical students. They contain a number of simple illustrations and many fine woodcuts, but the textbooks often merely recount the daily experiences of highly respected medical practitioners—a series of individual case reports describing afflictions of various organs and regions of the body or of behavioural disturbances such as epileptic seizures.[58] The first scientifically organized medical textbook was not written by Sir William Osler until 1892. Six years younger than Jones, Osler was raised in Dundas, Ontario, forty kilometres from Brantford. He combined his skills as a pathologist, laboratory researcher, and bedside physician to arrive at evidence-based conclusions.[59]

Medical progress was slower than today when continuing medical education is essential. Victorian-era physicians and surgeons tended to practise the way they'd been taught. Rural physicians were tied to their practice, competition being intense in many areas. Consequently, they relied on consultation with more experienced doctors to keep up to date.[60] In spite of this slow movement of knowledge, medical care was evolving. One of the major innovations was the improvement in diagnostic instruments whose development had benefited from both surgical and post-mortem examinations. Laennec's stethoscope, often a shortened model, was employed to examine the heart and lungs.[61] One end could even be used as a rudimentary tool to elicit deep tendon reflexes. The dedicated reflex hammer, however, would not become part of a doctor's armamentarium until Erb and Westphal first reported the diagnostic utility of the knee-jerk reflex in the 1870s.[62] The doctor could guess whether the patient was febrile by feeling the forehead, and clinical thermometers became available only a year after Peter Edmund's graduation.[63] With regard to the use of medication at that time, opium or tincture of opium (laudanum) or morphine were potent analgesics. General anaesthesia could be induced by means of ether or chloroform inhalation. Chloral hydrate, still a useful hypnotic, was discovered in 1868, while potassium bromide was not only a sedative but also proved to be the first effective anti-epileptic drug. Physicians were reluctant to abandon their old remedies even though some, such as tarter emetic and the mercury-containing drug calomel, were toxic. They prescribed potent laxatives such as jalap and calomel and also administered emetics such as ipecac to induce vomiting.[64] Then, as now, the key to successful therapy was to administer just the right dose of medication for a sufficient period in order to obtain the desired effect without inducing toxic side-effects. Herbal products posed a problem in that they contained varying amounts of their active ingredients depending on when the plants were harvested and how they were stored. The wise physician selected his pharmacist with care and became a regular customer. Medicines, such as the cardiac stimulant digitalis, obtained from the leaves of the foxglove plant, could be safely prescribed to patients with heart failure. Medicines have been an expensive commodity throughout history.

Surgical management of trauma, toothache, and abscesses fared somewhat better than medical treatment, despite the high infection rate, but diagnosis was still hit or miss. Even acute appendicitis, which then and now affects approximately ten percent of the population, was unknown until the 1880s.[65] Jones graduated the year before Joseph Lister's landmark paper, "On the Antiseptic Principle in the Practice of Surgery." Lister recommended soaking all sutures and dressings in carbolic acid, a chemical selected because it had been used to disinfect sewage at Carlisle in northwest England.[66] Louis Pasteur's and Robert Koch's observations of the role of microbes in infection were being disseminated together with hygienic measures such as hand-washing and the sterilization of instruments by boiling (termed "asepsis"), which eventually proved to be more effective than antisepsis.[67] Hygiene was yet to become a full-fledged university course, although Toronto's Trinity College led the way in 1870 with a course called "Sanitary Science."[68]

Medical theses were the nineteenth-century equivalent of an undergraduate term paper as there were no facilities for active basic or clinical research. The only requirement was that they be composed and handwritten by the student. The theses titles published in the university calendar offer an insight into what the students considered important. Jones's classmates chose topics such as "On Mumps," "On Signs of Pregnancy," and "On Digestion."[69] The case histories of one or more patients with a review of the relevant literature from textbooks and journals would suffice. Peter Edmund's title was dramatically different from those selected by his classmates, but the faculty board accepted it nevertheless.[70] In order to pass, Peter Edmund's own thesis would have placed some distance between himself and the non-Christian rituals associated with traditional Aboriginal medicine. When it came to Aboriginal herbal therapy, however, he would be treading on safer ground because North American physicians had accepted many proven Aboriginal remedies. Over the centuries, they had learned when to harvest, store, extract, and prescribe these medicinal agents. The *United States Pharmacopoeia*, first published in 1820, was parsimonious in selecting drugs considered effective at the time. Most of the drugs accepted by earlier texts were eliminated.[71] The editors note, however, that a considerable number of indigenous vegetables and herbs employed by Aboriginal healers had medicinal properties. "In several instances Aboriginal plants have been substituted, for European ones of the same genus where their qualities were esteemed to be the same."[72] This was allegedly done because in the days of sea travel, it was not possible to obtain fresh plants from Europe or Asia (and dried vegetable matter often lacked the medicinal properties). But Peter Edmund's textbooks insisted on citing the experience of American and European professors and ignored the contributions of Aboriginal healers, which by means of their oral tradition had been handed down over the millennia.[73] For example, of the 296 substances of vegetable, mineral, or animal origin listed in the volume, 130—nearly all of vegetable origin—were products previously employed in traditional Aboriginal healing.[74] The Aboriginal peoples received no credit for discovering the medicinal properties of these plants. As Vogel, who compiled a massive compendium of American Indian medicine, once remarked: "This is one more example of how the conquered people contributed to the conquerors far more than they received."[75] In fact, some Ojibwe healers tended to prescribe medication prepared from a single plant in contrast to the complex mixtures employed by some of the other North American tribes, and whenever a medicinal herb exhibits therapeutic effect when given by itself, it meets the scientific standard accepted by physicians.[76] In his book, *History of the Ojebway Indians,* Peter Edmund's father included a list of effective Aboriginal medicinal products.[77] Fifteen of these drugs (all approved at one time or another by an official body) are listed along with the Latin terminology and references from Peter Edmund's own textbooks in Table 1.

At the end of March 1866, the Senate of Queen's University accepted the recommendation of the Faculty of Medicine and voted to confer the degree of Doctor of Medicine on Peter Edmund Jones and six of his classmates. Peter Edmund did not know that his guardian angel, Dr. Hodgkin, was on his deathbed, his mission to help little P.E. become a doctor completed.[78] In the Senate minutes, Peter Edmund Jones is identified by his English given names and surname, but in the official printed calendar of Queen's University, he followed his former classmate Oronhyatekha's example and used his Ojibwe name, Kahkewaquonaby. This provides an important clue to his mindset: like all his brothers, Peter Edmund rejected the government's call to give up his Indian status and be enfranchised, even after the government sweetened the offer with twenty hectares of land and a cash payment from his band's trust fund.[79] Jones remained true to and proud of his Aboriginal heritage and made every effort to show that those he frequently referred to as "educated Indians" could compete with Euro-Canadians. He would later claim in a letter to the editor of *The Toronto Mail* that "with education and the passage of time the Indian could achieve a level approaching that of the white man."[80]

Once he had been granted his degree in the spring of 1866, Dr. Jones would have to sit the examinations of the newly formed General Council for Medical Education. Fortunately, Peter Edmund was reassured to learn that his former professor of surgery, John Dickson, was their first president.[81] On 14 November 1866, Peter Edmund Jones, M.D., became the first-known Status Indian student of a Canadian medical school to pass the licensing examination and received medical licence number 678. His colleague, Oronhyatekha, who qualified for a Bachelor of Medicine degree in 1866, delayed sitting the exam until 22 May 1867 when he was granted licence number 709.[82]

Table 1 Indigenous Herbal Medicines Appropriated by the Europeans*

Herb (Scientific Name)	Preparation	Therapeutic Use
Sassafras[a] (*Sassafras officinalis*)	Decoction[b] of bark Volatile oil	Abdominal cramps Used externally as a rub
Seneca snakeroot[c] (*Polygalia senega*)	Decoction of bark	An expectorant[d] and cough remedy
Poke-root[e] (*Phytolacca decandra*)	Powdered root Decoction	Fomentation[f] Liniment[g] for itchy skin
Gold thread[h] (*Coptis trifolia*)	Infusion[i] of dried rhizome	Inflamed eyes and mucous membranes
Lobelia[j] (*Lobelia inflate*)	Infusion of dried leaves and tops	Expelling intestinal worms
Wintergreen[k] (*Gaultheria procumbens*)	Infusion of leaves	Headache, fever, and rheumatism; contains methyl salicylic acid, which irritates the stomach, but is as effective as acetylsalicylic acid, marketed in 1898 as Aspirin®
Red willow[l] (*Salix lucida*)	Infusion of roots	Same as above
Wild cherry[m] (*Prunus serotina*)	Infusion of bark	Coughs and colds; is also a flavouring; berries are used as a tonic
Slippery elm[n] (*Ulmus fulva*)	Pounded inner bark	Wound dressing, sore throat medicine, tooth ache remedy; emergency food as mucilage later shown to be as nutritious as oatmeal.
Canada balsam[o] (*Abies balsamea*)	Resin is collected from trunk and branches	Wound dressing, soothes sore nipples and abrasions, decongestant, stops runny noses, and relieves headache
Sumach[p] (*Rhus glabra*)	Infusion of bark	Astringent,[q] haemostatic; leaves are used as fomentations and the fruit as throat cleanser

continued

Table 1, conclusion Indigenous Herbal Medicines Appropriated by the Europeans*

Herb (Scientific Name)	Preparation	Therapeutic Use
White oak[r] (*Quercus alba*)	Decoction of inner bark	Decoction is antiseptic-astringent as wash for eyes; used internally for dysentery, as fomentation for wounds, enema[s] for hemorrhoids
Flowering dogwood[t] (*Cornus florida*)	Infusion of bark	Intermittent fever and malaria (Northern Indians did not have access to Peruvian bark, which contains quinine)
Creosote bush[u] (*Larrea tridentate*)	Boil branches to extract gum (Sonora gum)	Infusion of leaves diminishes bronchial secretions and cough; for toothache, a hot branch is inserted in cavity or extract is applied locally
Witch hazel[v] (*Hamamelis virginiana*)	Infusion of bark and leaves	Astringent; inflamed eyes, bruises, aching muscles, hemorrhoids; twigs are added to hot water in steam baths

* All listed in various editions of *The United States Pharmacopoeia* (USP)[w] and the *Dispensatory of the United States of* America,[x] published in Dr. Jones's lifetime.

a Virgil J. Vogel, *American Indian Medicine* (Norman: University of Oklahoma Press, 1970), 361–65.

b A liquid obtained by boiling medicinal vegetable substances in water.

c Ibid., 372–73.

d A medication that expels fluid or semi-fluid, matter from the lungs or air passages.

e Ibid., 350–1.

f The substance applied to a part to convey heat and moisture to relieve pain or inflammation.

g A liquid intended for application to the skin by gentle friction.

h Ibid., 311.

i The process of extracting the active principles of a substance by means of water without boiling.

j Ibid., 330–32.

k Ibid., 395.

l Ibid., 393.

m Ibid., 388–90.

n Ibid., 302–4.

o Ibid., 278–79.

p Ibid., 376–78.

q A medication that produces contraction of tissues or that arrests hemorrhages, diarrhea, etc.

r Ibid., 342–43.

s The rectal instillation of a liquid for therapeutic or nutritive purposes.

t Ibid., 299–301.

u Ibid., 296–97.

v Ibid., 395–96.

w *The Pharmacopoeia of the United States of America* (Boston: Printed by Wells and Lilly, for Charles Ewer, 1820), 272. Microfilm 413, Osler Library, McGill University. Creosote was listed in the 1842 edition; witch hazel was listed in the 1882 edition.

x George B.B. Wood and Franklin Bache, *The Dispensatory of the United States of America*, 11th ed. (Philadelphia: J.P. Lippincott & Co., 1885), 1583. This edition lists all herbals cited in Table 1, but with the exception of witch hazel. This Eurocentric compendium neglects to credit Aboriginal herbalists.

Three
Country Doctor

New doctors were encouraged to work as an assistant to a registered practitioner following graduation, an early equivalent of a year spent as an intern or resident. In those days, as now, it was necessary to be fully responsible for patients before setting up one's own practice. The medical school was well aware of the need to have hands-on experience, and the twelve months the students spent observing a local doctor while he examined patients in his office was deemed insufficient.[1] To fulfill this requirement, Peter Edmund returned to Brantford in the spring of 1866. He apprenticed with family doctor and friend, Dr. Egerton Griffin, an established practitioner who also served as public health officer and coroner of Brant County. Eliza's diary contains numerous references to their friendship with the Griffins right up until the 1880s.[2]

By the time Peter Edmund returned, his older brothers had both left home: Charles had joined the Union army and was now stationed in Alabama, one of the recently defeated Confederate states, while Frederick was working as a newspaperman in California. Eliza sadly confided in her diary:

> It should seem strange that my two eldest sons should leave the maternal roof to seek their fortunes in foreign lands so soon after my second marriage, but alas when, too late, I found to my grief, that their domestic happiness was blasted by the entire contrast they experienced in the conduct of a stepfather in the room of the loved one they had lost.[3]

Eliza's marriage to John Carey had been short-lived. Neither Peter Edmund nor his youngest brother, George Dunlop Jones, appears to have lived with their stepfather for any period of time, although the exact date at which Carey left Echo Villa is not known. Eliza came from the British upper-middle class. She was educated and quite able to live on her own, as suggested by her sons. Reverend Jones's career involved prolonged periods away from home, and Eliza had played the major role in raising the boys and managing their affairs. She also continued to visit her family in England at remarkably frequent intervals despite the inconveniences and hazards of a prolonged sea voyage. Soon after Peter Edmund returned to Brantford, Echo Villa was sold, and Dr. Jones helped her find a small home, the purchase price of which was $700, far more than she could afford. Charles, Peter, and George helped their mother move into 101 Brant Avenue in Brantford, which she nostalgically named Lambeth Cottage after her English birthplace. Because she had remarried so soon after Reverend Jones died, she had been entitled only to a clergyman's widow's pension for the first six months and would be both lonesome and short of funds for the rest of her life. Her son, "The doctor," would have many opportunities to repay his mother for her attentive medical care and home schooling.[4]

Had things gone smoothly, Peter Edmund should have been able to continue living with his mother and serve as Dr. Griffin's assistant for an extended period in order to gain valuable experience. The apprenticeship was unpaid, however, and Dr. Jones found it impossible to attract his own paying patients in Brantford.[5] This colonial town was not yet ready to accept an Aboriginal medical practitioner. Realizing that he faced overwhelming racial prejudice, Jones wrote the Department of Indian Affairs asking if he could succeed the late Dr. Alfred Digby as one of the physicians attending to the Six Nations.[6] When this effort also failed, he decided to move to Niagara, Ontario. Now called Niagara-on-the-Lake, the town is located at the entrance of the Niagara River into Lake Ontario, facing Fort Niagara on the American side. The population of three thousand was half that of Brantford, but there was a locomotive and car factory in addition to the Niagara Dock Company, which built steamboats. The town had a courthouse, a jail, three churches, twenty shops, and ten hotels and taverns. Steamers provided daily service to Toronto.[7] In Niagara Jones seems to have had better luck attracting patients. However, in a letter dated 19 April 1867, his brother Charles revealed that Peter had developed restless feet when he asked: "When does the Dr. leave for New York? I trust you will write me on his arrival sending me his address."[8]

Biographical sketches published during his lifetime and several obituaries after his death indicate that Peter Edmund worked for a time in a New York City hospital. It is difficult to imagine how he managed to survive because hospital physicians were not paid salaries and were lucky enough to obtain room and board. The hospitals in the United States, however, were seriously short of physicians as all available men were in either the Union or Confederate armies. In the emergency, even nurses and students, including Canada's first female physician, Emily Jennings Stowe, who was attending a women's school of medicine, looked after the patients in New York's Bellevue Hospital.[9] Another of Charles's letters tells of Peter Edmund's return to Canada and hints at what may have happened in New York City when he wrote:

> Mobile, Ala., Sept 14th, 1868.
> The reappearance of *Pills* [Peter Edmund] on Canadian soil somewhat surprised me though I must confess that I did not expect him to stay in New York long, as I believe him to be destitute of that capital which is so essential for a professional man's success in that town. I daresay it's all for the best and now if he will only content himself at Hagersville and follow out the programme hinted at by him and you. I daresay he will never regret the want of those means which might have kept him from his country and so much happiness (in future).[10]

Jones appears to have started his Hagersville practice in 1868 or 1869.[11] The small village was located on the edge of the Mississaugas of the New Credit reserve in southwest Ontario. It was about to have a railway station, and Hagersville's location on the plank road between Hamilton and Port Dover on Lake Erie amid the region's rich farmland offered potential for growth.[12] Unfortunately, there were a number of local physicians so competition for practice in the town was keen.

Struggling to make a living, Jones tried to obtain a loan to help him open a drugstore, although a chemist was already in business in the village. Eliza even wrote a family friend, the Scottish philanthropist John Dunlop, in 1869: "Trying to obtain a loan for Peter to open a drug store, but to no avail."[13] That Peter Edmund wished to open a drugstore was not unusual. Many physicians were directly or indirectly involved in commerce in the nineteenth century. Their patients often encouraged them to invest in their businesses, lumber mills, and real estate ventures.[14] In addition, the training in *materia medica* at Queen's would have prepared Peter Edmund to prepare prescription drugs such as mercurial ointment and tincture of opium. Physicians purchased drugs in bulk from pharmacies, compounded the final prescription, and administered the medication to their patients when making house calls. They were also permitted to operate drugstores in small communities. In view of Dr. Jones's Ojibwe background, his patients would likely feel he had an advantage in the preparation of herbal products such as senna, aloe, and Peruvian bark, all medications accepted by the *United States Pharmacopoeia*, in contrast to herbal remedies sold by unqualified practitioners.

Dr. Jones eventually did go into the drug business in his Hagersville Medical Hall, likely selling medicinal plants that Aboriginal herbalists (primarily middle-aged women) harvested in the wild. Herbalists knew when the active medicinal agents reached peak concentrations either in roots, leaves, or bark, and how best to store them to maintain their potency. The Roseau River Anishinabek peoples supplied tons of Seneca snakeroot to dealers at an average price of 17 cents a pound. No longer considered a sure cure for rattlesnake bites, it had earned a place in the pharmacopoeia as an expectorant useful in the treatment of coughs and colds.[15] Jones's partner and salesman was his cousin Frank G.H. Wilson, son of the Francis Wilson (Whabunoo), who died before receiving his medical degree from the University of Toronto. Frank, like his late father, was well educated and taught school for several years, but when the herbal medicine business lagged, he left the reserve to travel the world as an advance sales agent for the Royal Italian Circus and Menagerie. He kept in contact with his mother Phoebe, who had been widowed a second time and lived on the New Credit reserve. The Band Council, always concerned with the welfare of their members, gave her a pension of $25 per annum.[16] Dr. Jones later reported Wilson's international adventures in a newspaper column titled "A Mississauga in Japan: An example of what education and an energetic character can do for the Red Men of America."[17]

The doctor was kept busy with his professional activities, but at the same time his elder brother Charles hinted at Peter Edmund's romantic life in a letter he sent to Eliza during a visit to Washington, DC:

> Washington, DC, 29 April 1869,
> I am pleased to hear of dear Peter's success also that Dodo [youngest brother, George Dunlop] is doing so well. It must indeed be a source of pleasure to you to have such good tidings of your boys. I suppose it will not be long 'till [*sic*] the Doctor settles down as a staid married man. So should it be.... It seems as if I was destined to become a confirmed old bachelor.[18]

On 3 April 1870, Charles wrote an intriguing note to his mother from the editorial room of the *State Capital Reporter* in Sacramento. "I am sorry that the Doctor's love affair has fallen through. Ask P. Edmund when you see him to write."[19] Who was the lady in question? Where did she live? Why did she reject him? Eliza's diary, usually a reliable source of information, does not offer any other details, but the need to share his life was clearly beginning to make itself felt. At the time, Dr. Jones was boarding with a family in Hagersville.[20]

Eventually, a well-educated woman, a recent widow raising three children alone, entered the picture. Charlotte Elvin Dixon was six months younger than Peter Edmund. She was born in Burlington, Yorkshire, England, and immigrated to Canada with her parents at the age of four.[21] The Elvins settled on a farm in Ontario, but the terrain proved unsuitable for growing wheat, so they moved to Badaxe, Michigan. Charlotte later returned to Ontario, where she married William Dixon. Dixon was a yeoman, but because he had his land in freehold, he was considered a member of the minor gentry and called "Sir" by the tenant farmers. Tragically, he died intestate on or about 25 December 1871. Although he left an estate worth $1,100, it remained so mired in legal issues that Charlotte lost the farm. Charlotte appears to have had no means of supporting her three sons: Sylvanus, age seven; Alpheus (Alph), age five; and little Ebenezer (Elvin), just three years old.[22]

The young widow was a member of the Anglican Church, and Charlotte and Peter Edmund seemed to have much in common. Peter Edmund was an Anglican by this time and genuinely fond of her sons. He was ready to finance their education, although, as he recalled in a letter to the prime minister, he had expected to be repaid within a few years from the proceeds of the sale of his wife's farm.[23] The plan was that he would be repaid after Charlotte sold her first husband's farm, but women had few rights in those days. Despite protracted legal actions undertaken in the hope of securing her estate, they were never successful. For her part, Charlotte, to her dying day, would be proud of her relationship with Eliza Jones.[24] She could expect, however, to face the same racial prejudice that Eliza endured when first married. Educated Aboriginal peoples did occasionally marry middle-class Anglo-Canadian women in the nineteenth century. Women from families that had been associated either with the Christian Evangelical or anti-slavery movements were likely to be more accepting of an interracial marriage.[25] Peter Edmund's mother Eliza was one of those women, and years earlier she had supported Emily Howell in her decision to marry Six Nations chief and interpreter George H.M. Johnson. The famed Mohawk poet Pauline Emily Johnson was one of the children in their happy family.[26] Eliza and Charlotte seem to have enjoyed a good relationship, perhaps because it was Eliza who had encouraged her bachelor son to marry the young widow. As Eliza's vision failed in later life, Charlotte journeyed to Brantford to be at her side, and the older woman's diary refers to her frequently.[27]

On 27 February 1873, the day Peter Edmund married Charlotte, Eliza wrote the following note in the family bible: "On the 27th ult., by the Rev. J.G. Salter, M.A., Peter Edmund Jones, M.D., third son of the late Rev. Peter Jones, to Mrs. Charlotte Dixon, all of Hagersville." The marriage was solemnized at St. Jude's Anglican Church in Brantford.[28] Charlotte's younger sister, Drusella, and her husband, Dr. Robert McDonald probably attended. Guests on the groom's side would have included Eliza and his youngest brother George, now a painter employed by the Brantford Carriage Company. Brother Charles, who had finally returned to Brantford in 1870, would have been there with his new wife, Hannah Ellis, and widowed brother, Frederick, whose young wife had died in childbirth seven months earlier.[29]

The newly married couple returned to Hagersville, where they occupied a frame house on the south side of Main Street at the corner of David Street.[30] Charlotte's second marriage produced no children. This surprised band members since they seemed a healthy couple, and she had already borne three children. Dr. Jones left a clue to his own hopes for a family. At a meeting of the Grand General Indian Council, held one year after his marriage, he spoke against the Indian Act, which now specified that Indians with less than one-fourth Indian blood would in future no longer be considered Status Indians. Jones spoke out against this rule, saying: "Although he was married to a white lady, it was his wish to train his children to be Indian children."[31] His children would be only one-eighth Indian and would be unable to inherit his farm or receive the interest payments and other benefits accruing from membership in the Mississauga band. Perhaps the Jones's lack of children together ultimately came about because Charlotte may have felt threatened by the prejudice engendered by mixed-race children as well as the need to pay for the education of her own three boys. The small Mississauga band needed as many children as possible because the mortality rate was high during the early years of life.

As the wife of a Status Indian, Charlotte was accepted as a band member, receiving her share of interest monies as long as she lived on the reserve. Peter Edmund applied to have Charlotte's sons receive annuity payments, but his head chief refused because they had no Indian blood.[32] Although he always referred to the boys as his sons, Jones was never able

Figure 6 Dr. Peter Edmund Jones and Charlotte Dixon-Jones when married in 1873. (*Source:* Courtesy of Louise Thorp, Vancouver, and Donald B. Smith, Calgary)

to legally adopt them because he was considered an Indian under the Indian Act, and an Indian could not have his case heard by an Ontario court. The three boys did not attend the school on the reserve but went to private schools. The two youngest attended colleges in Toronto, entirely at Dr. Jones's expense.[33]

Hagersville had grown into a market town where local employment came from the quarry supplying the crushed stone used to macadamize the plank road between Hamilton and Port Dover. The work was done by local farmers who were excused from paying taxes and benefited from the fact that the toll road was free of charge on Sundays. Gypsum mines and a variety of other businesses operated in the adjacent town of Caledonia, while Hagersville benefited from the town's location on three major rail lines.[34] One would imagine that a young doctor, accompanied by an attractive and socially active wife, would slowly build up a thriving practice. Though there were other practitioners in Hagersville, some families would have had to find a new physician whenever their own doctor moved away. In the days before telephone service, farmers from the surrounding area visiting on market day would leave a note requesting a doctor visit them on his rounds. Peter Edmund would have seen more opportunity here than he had had in Brantford, although his family worried over his lack of patients. Charles wrote in a letter to his mother, found in Toronto's Victoria University Archives: "Pills is well but has no practice; he devotes a great part of his time to shooting and stuffing birds, etc. Whether this occupation pays is very problematical. It is a great pity for him and family he never received any encouragement to come to Brantford—Charlotte is well. One of the boys, the eldest, has the mumps."[35] Perhaps Charles believed that because Peter Edmund had been raised in Brantford and his mother was a respected local artist and teacher, success would come easier there. Certainly, wherever they lived, nineteenth-century Aboriginal physicians faced a conundrum: their Euro-Canadian patients believed either that they were racially inferior and therefore incapable of becoming physicians, or were mere Medicine Men treating incurable diseases by means of incantations and secret potions.

Despite initial hardship, Jones managed to establish a paying Euro-Canadian practice over time. A family doctor seldom leaves detailed records of his house calls, and at the time Hagersville was too small to support a hospital. It is clear, however, that for more than two decades fees derived from clinical practice paid for his house and supported his family. Jones would have had no Aboriginal patients. They could not afford to pay his fees and were required to consult the medical officer appointed by the Band Council and approved by the Department of Indian Affairs.

Jones called the office located in his frame house Hagersville Medical Hall. It was only a short distance from the reserve, but apart from a few Mississauga women who were employed as domestic servants, there was little contact between the townsfolk and the Mississaugas. Dr. Jones was caught midway between villagers who regarded him as an Aboriginal and some of the principal men of the Mississaugas of the New Credit reserve who did not. He was an educated man who had never lived at New Credit and had only distant relatives on the reserve. The problem of gaining the trust of the Aboriginal community was hardly unique; even long-time residents of a reserve who left to study, travel, or work away from home for a significant period of time had to prove themselves when they returned. The Elders feared that their contact with the non-Aboriginal community altered their perception of traditional cultural values and mores.

Although Dr. Jones built up a medical practice among the Euro-Canadians people of Hagersville and those who farmed in the vicinity, he grew increasingly concerned with band politics. In his application for a post in the federal Department of Indian Affairs, Jones stated that his involvement with the band started as early as 1869.[36] He faced a number of obstacles: he had been raised in Brantford, he had never lived at New Credit, and he had no close relatives on the reserve other than his aged grandmother Tubenahnequay.[37] Jones owned two separate plots of farm land on the reserve, which engendered jealousy, and he always lived in the adjacent town of Hagersville, where he developed many friendships and was active as the secretary of the local Orange Association, in the Masonic Lodges of Hagersville and Hamilton, and in the local Chess Club.[38] His working language was English, and he was not at all fluent in Ojibwe. Jones's decision to play an active role in band politics placed him in direct opposition to members of certain leading families who had long fought to maintain the Mississaugas' language and traditional lifestyle. They had opposed the pro-government stance of his late father, Reverend Jones, with its emphasis on agriculture and strict discipline in the school. The traditionalists also included two relatives of Dr. Jones: his uncle, former Chief David Sawyer, and his cousin, George Henry Jr., who advertised himself as a Mississauga Medicine Man.[39] Peter Edmund and George would always be political competitors, Jones favouring the frequently amended Indian Advancement Act and George as a band councillor who wished to preserve the Mississaugas' traditional lifestyle.

In spite of these limitations, Jones had skills and connections that would help him negotiate band politics. He was no doubt well suited to conducting negotiations with the bureaucrats of the Department of Indian Affairs because he had acquired a firm grasp of the legislation affecting Aboriginal peoples. He was also active in the governing Conservative party and wrote frequent letters to the official party organ, *The Toronto Mail*. This was important because as a Native Indian community, the New Credit band was controlled by the deputy superintendent general of Indian Affairs in Ottawa. All communications had to be handwritten and sent by post. Indian agents, invariably Euro-Canadians, exercised "imperial powers" over their charges. Only the local band agent could

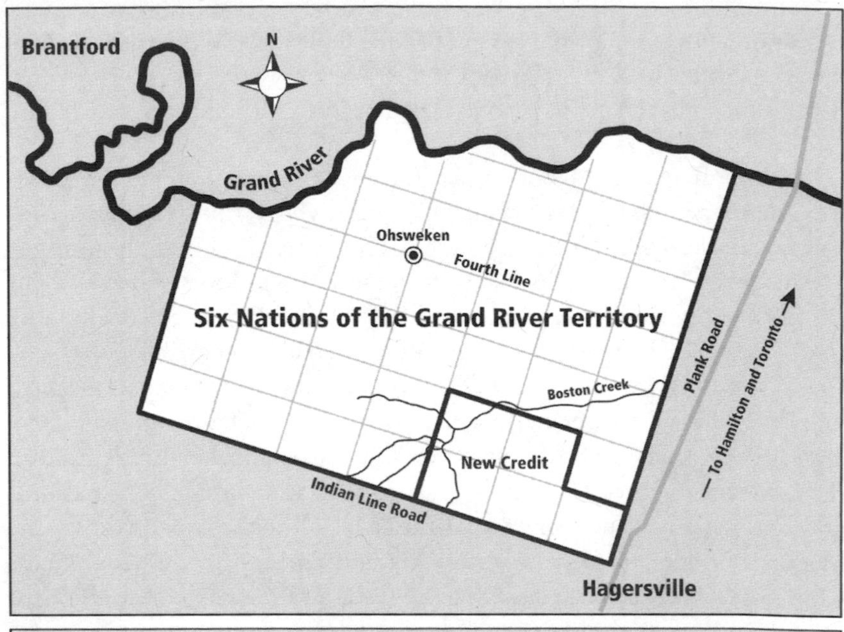

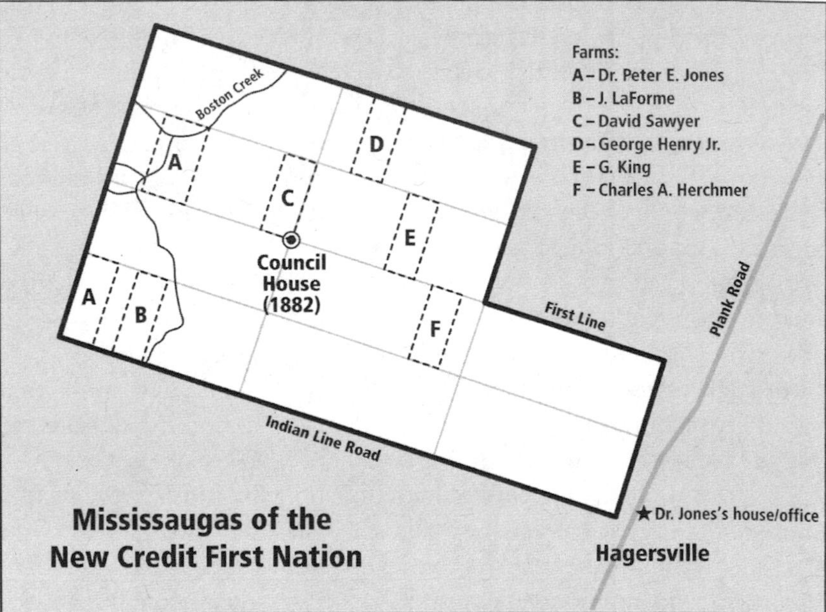

Map 2 The Six Nations and Mississaugas of the New Credit reserves as they appeared in the late nineteenth century. Modified from *The Illustrated Historical Atlas of the County of Haldimand, Ontario* (Toronto: H.R. Page, 1879) by Christine Lalonde.

purchase livestock, seed, and implements or authorize the sale of produce. In those years when crops were insufficient to carry the livestock through the winter, the agents purchased additional supplies of fodder. The chiefs were even dependent on the goodwill of the agent to forward special requests to Ottawa.[40]

Dr. Jones received a warm reception when he visited the small log cabins scattered about the New Credit reserve. His late father had been a band hero, and many of the women remembered how his mother had taught them sewing. They were his people, and he and his brothers Charles and George were still members of the small Mississauga band even though they chose to live off reserve. After years spent in communities where people looked him up and down and wondered what he was doing in their midst, Jones felt at home. Mothers asked him questions, and soon whole families began to entrust him with their health problems and ask him for medicines, which were always in short supply. The new arrival's activities soon annoyed the Indian agent, who insisted that his charges consult Dr. Thomas Pyne, the doctor paid by his department. Pyne, now in his sixties, had practised in the United States before moving to Hagersville. As well as his part-time position on the reserve, he was the coroner and had been elected to represent his colleagues on the Medical Council of Ontario.[41] Things came to a head in the spring of 1872 when the Band Council opted to replace Dr. Pyne, despite his good record, because "one of their number, Dr. Jones was attending some of the members, and having confidence in him, they too desired his appointment."[42] Pyne was dismayed, but wrote back saying, "Jones was one of themselves and he would not stand in his way."[43] The respected physician decided to move to Toronto and become the registrar of the newly formed College of Physicians and Surgeons of Ontario.

The Brantford agency's superintendent, Lt. Colonel Gilkison, did not take the matter lightly and informed Ottawa that "Dr. Jones had undermined Dr. Pyne by the very act of attending the Indians, exacting from them fees, when he knew that Pyne was their band medical attendant."[44] Jones would have to cool his heels for a few years before he could even hope to become the Mississaugas medical attendant. [45] Adjacent to Hagersville, the band community continued to rely on the town's physicians, one of whom would serve as their medical officer on a part-time basis. In the years that followed Dr. Pyne's departure, however, the band had trouble retaining the services of a physician for any length of time. One of the reasons doctors were reluctant to accept the position was the reserve's distance from Hagersville, which was quite cut off from the other areas covered by a Hagersville doctor's customary rounds. The country doctor travelled by horseback or, if passable roads existed, took a buggy in warm weather and a sled in winter. The roads were either poor or nonexistent, with primitive bridges over Boston Creek, which winds through the reserve.

In the autumn Peter Edmund's medical competitor and relative, George Henry Jr., inadvertently provided him with a new opportunity when he informed the agent that the band wished to change from traditional hereditary chiefs and choose their next chief by election. When band members were asked if they agreed, a majority of those present responded positively by rising.[46] Indian Affairs was pleased to agree as the Mississaugas of the New Credit were the first band to take this big step. Jones now had a chance to lead his band, provided he could convince the Elders to lend their support. This would not be easy as not only was he young and inexperienced, but, like his late father, he believed in accommodating the provisions of the existing federal Indian legislation rather than outright opposing it. Head Chief George King's term expired in 1873 and, in gentlemanly fashion, he agreed to run in an election. Peter Edmund campaigned for the job, but was easily defeated by the experienced incumbent.[47]

Bachelorhood over, Jones was faced with mortgage payments and the household expenses of a wife, three stepchildren, and a mother without a pension. The growth of his practice was blocked by stiff competition of newly arrived physicians, including his brother-in-law, the affable Dr. Robert McDonald. Hagersville had fewer potential clients than most towns, as it was surrounded by the Indian reserve on the north and Lake Erie on the south. So when it was rumoured that Dr. Robert H. Dee, the medical attendant to the Six Nations, was about to resign, Jones rushed to consult the missionaries attached to the Six Nations. They pledged their support and advised him to write the superintendent general of Indian Affairs, Sir Alexander Campbell. In his letter, Jones made a point of mentioning that he was a graduate of Queen's, for by chance, Campbell was from Kingston and was dean of the Faculty of Law when Peter was admitted to the university. Jones offered to provide a petition signed not only by a large and influential group of his "White acquaintances," but by the leading "Chiefs and Warriors" of the Six Nations. Jones concluded by stating that if Dee resigned, he had "not the slightest doubt that all other things being equal, you would feel a pleasure in conferring the position on a duly qualified Indian."[48]

In fact, Dr. Dee had merely sent a polite letter to Indian Affairs requesting a substantial raise in pay and a much needed increase in the amount budgeted for medications.[49] Dee had served the Six Nations for twenty years, first from his home on the Grand River, but in 1866 he agreed to give up his "White" practice and move on to the reserve. He reminded Indian Affairs that in addition to a stipend of $1,200 per annum, plus $300 for medications, they had promised to erect a brick or stone house on a two- or four-hectare lot. The home was yet to be built and he had to be satisfied with a $75 grant for rent and had spent a considerable amount to make his rented house livable. Recently the owner had reoccupied his house, so Dee's family was forced to relocate to a small and uncomfortable log building, which again required further repair.

Dr. Dee, who was responsible for the health of the 2,200 people living in the "central beat" running north and south through the reserve, presented a detailed record of his labours during the year 1871. He had examined and prescribed medicines to 2,460 patients in his clinic and made 492 home visits, about the same total number of patient visits as a busy Euro-Canadian physician in a nearby town.[50] In doing so he travelled 5,000 kilometres over roads that were often barely passable, so bad that both the horses and buggies were quickly worn out. Often he would have to tie the horse to a tree and be compelled to walk long distances in order to reach the patient's home. If he delivered a baby or performed an operation, it might be too dark to return home and he would bunk in with the family. Over the years Dr. Dee had established good relations with members of the Six Nations, including the eight hundred or so who followed a non-Christian lifestyle, taking part in ceremonies conducted by their Shamans, who would prescribe traditional herbal remedies. A sensitive man, the doctor supported their views. In fact, he considered that Aboriginal herbal medications were often as good as and, in some cases, more efficacious than those employed by mainstream physicians who prescribed arsenic and mercury. In the past nine months he had noticed a significant increase in his office practice, in part because more traditionalist families were arriving at his door. Surgical techniques had improved following the American Civil War and some of the operations were quite effective. Surgeons could now alleviate pain by means of the anaesthetic gases, ether or chloroform. Morphine, the active ingredient of opium, could be administered by mouth or, if necessary, by means of the newly invented hypodermic syringe with its hollow needle. Malaria and other intermittent fevers were a major cause of illness on the reserve during the summer months, carried by the mosquitoes that bred in local swamps and streams. Dr. Dee could prevent the high and often fatal intermittent fevers characteristic of this parasitic infection by administering quinine. His allowance for medications was feeling the strain of the need for these expensive drugs, aggravated by the recent surge in the number of patients, thirty percent of whom were children.

An 1852 graduate of the University of Buffalo, Dr. Dee was one of the first physicians licensed by the College of Physicians and Surgeons of Ontario. Despite his seniority, his base pay of $1,200 per annum was lower than that of many employees in the home office of the Department of Indian Affairs. Mid-level office workers, lacking post-secondary education, received at least $200 a year more, plus a pension on retirement. Indian agent J.T. Gilkison, who at the time earned $1,584 per annum, did not think the doctor's patient load was excessive.[51] His negative opinion of Dee's request might have been the source of the rumour that the band physician would likely resign. The Department of Indian Affairs finally asked the Six Nations council to deal with the matter. The chiefs always selected and hired their physicians and, importantly, were responsible for their salaries, which were deducted from their own bank account, held in trust by the government in Ottawa. The Six Nations hereditary council, satisfied with the doctor's performance, made a modest adjustment in his salary and the matter was settled. Eventually the Band Council built a substantial brick building in their "capital," Ohsweken, to house their doctor's residence and office. The Six Nations were among the first Aboriginal communities to have their own medical clinic. Dr. Dee laboured for thirty-six years and remains a role model for non-Aboriginal physicians who take up the challenge of providing much needed services to Aboriginal peoples.[52]

When he recovered from his disappointment at not obtaining a full-time job, Peter Edmund was a changed man. Realizing that he would never be able to support his family on fees derived from the Euro-Canadian community of Hagersville, he began to use his Ojibwe name, Kahkewaquonaby, more often and visited his grandmother, who still resided on the New Credit reserve, where he could practise his Ojibwe. The following spring long-time Chief King passed away and in the election that followed, Jones was elected head chief by a margin of one vote. His mother was visiting England at the time and had to wait to hear the good news, but on 4 June 1874, she received letters from Charles and George bearing the happy report that "Peter made Chief."[53] Her beloved husband's fondest dream had been to have one of his four sons inherit his title of chief, and as head chief, Dr. Jones was entitled to a stipend of $200 per annum.[54]

The Joneses seem to have had favourable relations with both the Iroquois of the Six Nations and the Mississaugas of the New Credit. Dr. Jones was given the opportunity to step further into the limelight when the Six Nations invited him to give one of the speeches of welcome when the governor-general and the Countess of Dufferin visited the Six Nations Territory in August of that year. The chairman reminded the audience that in 1812 General Sir Isaac Brock had made an urgent visit to the Six Nations in order to invite the "Feathered" United Empire Loyalists to go to war against the American invaders. His wish had been granted and their warriors once more took up their weapons to defend the Crown.[55] This time it was a social visit, however, and civic dignitaries, Six Nations chiefs, and two former Mississauga chiefs filled the platform.[56]

In October 1875, Dr. Graham, the band's physician at that time, asked to be relieved of his duties. An election was called, and members of the Band Council gathered to cast their vote. Dr. Jones was the only nominee. After waiting a full hour to ensure that there were no other nominations, the council unanimously elected Dr. Jones as his successor.[57] Like everything on an Aboriginal reserve, the appointment had to be approved by Ottawa, and Jones appears to have been the second Status Indian to become a band physician. Two years earlier Sir John A. Macdonald had appointed Jones's colleague, Dr. Oronhyatekha, to the post of medical consultant to the Mohawks of the Bay of Quinte.[58]

The Mississauga Band Council approved a stipend of $250 per annum, which came from the band's own interest monies, as did the salaries of schoolteachers and widows' pensions. The government and the Band Council administered these monies, originally derived from land sales; therefore, the Mississaugas of the New Credit were not receiving federal handouts but were paying their own way. These accounts were submitted to the Dominion Parliament for review annually. Since Dr. Pyne had received only $200 per annum, the Department of Indian Affairs thought Dr. Jones should be satisfied with the same amount. On 12 April, however, the Band Council unanimously recommended an increase, and Department of Indian Affairs Superintendent Gilkison reported: "His predecessor always considered that the salary of $200 per annum was insufficient and that, considering the extent of the reserve and the frequent calls for expensive medicines and the number of people in the band, a salary of $250 would not be exorbitant."[59] The deputy superintendent general of Indian Affairs, Lawrence Vankoughnet, relented on 22 June 1876.

The total population of the New Credit band was 204 when Jones became band physician and would rise to 242 during his tenure.[60] The birth rate was modest, infant mortality was high, and infectious diseases, such as diphtheria and scarlet fever, took a toll. The death rate from consumption (tuberculosis) was very high, even among adolescents, because families were confined to single-room cabins, which encouraged the spread of infection. Variants of acute infectious diseases, mainly scarlet fever, whooping cough, and diphtheria, were observed. Jones made certain that the council purchased smallpox vaccine and that all band members were vaccinated.[61] To his credit, there were no cases of this dangerous illness during his tenure. Eye disorders were also a frequent cause of disability caused by smoke emanating from stoves that were less efficiently vented than traditional fireplaces. Fortunately, bathing the eyes with traditional Aboriginal herbal infusions was usually efficacious.[62]

Environmental hazards began to complicate life on the reserve now that the inhabitants lived in cabins. There was a lack of open space about the dwellings so that children from different families came into close contact and, if ill, could spread one of the infectious diseases. The Mississaugas had been encouraged to adopt European-style housekeeping when the cabins replaced their more widely scattered wigwams, but they resented the change and had difficulty abandoning their traditional way of living. Winter garbage had to be collected and burned when the snow melted, and they no longer had a ready source of clean water. A new problem arose when some of the more prosperous Mississauga farmers were able to purchase steam-operated machinery with exposed belts and pulleys. The incidence of trauma soared because children, fascinated by the machinery, would play in front of the moving pieces and could be severely injured.[63]

The importance of isolation as a means of controlling infectious disease was already well recognized when Dr. Jones had been a student in Kingston. He observed the tragic effects of malnutrition, overcrowding, and epidemic diseases such as cholera among the immigrants streaming into Kingston, and he would face a similar situation when he took up his post as band physician. With the Band Council's support, he enforced quarantine regulations, thereby reducing childhood morbidity and mortality from acute infectious disease. Unfortunately, there was little he could do to halt the deadly menace of tuberculosis. Quarantine practices were not new to the Ojibwe. In the past, the chiefs had been able to isolate the sick by sending them far into the forest until they recovered. This was no longer feasible, of course, once Aboriginals lived on reserves and a single extended family shared a one-room hut. Tuberculosis was so prevalent that there would be a carrier in virtually every family.

Few escaped the ravages of the disease. Another threat came from the piles of refuse that accumulated over the winter, and the Department of Indian Affairs Reports made note of this problem.[64] Before the discovery of micro-organisms, accumulation of wastes associated with a miasma (noxious vapour) was held to be responsible for what we now know are infectious diseases. Although the theory proved erroneous, the clearing of the English slums had successfully prevented disease by removing sources of bacterial, viral, and parasitic infection. Draining the swamps created by dams on the Grand River at Caledonia similarly helped reduce the incidence of malaria on the Six Nations and New Credit reserves in the days long before it was realized that the Anopheles mosquito carried malaria parasites.[65]

Dr. Jones occupied the post of head chief from 1874 to 1877 and again from 1880 until 1886. Under his leadership, the Mississaugas of the New Credit adopted a code of rules and regulations for the governance of their community. By 1883 officials were elected, and they established a municipal-style government on their reserve. Prime Minister Sir John A. Macdonald, who also served as his own superintendent general of Indian Affairs, was thrilled by this development. In his 1883 Annual Report to the governor-general, the Marquess of Lansdowne, he noted:

> The small Chippewa [Mississauga-Ojibwe] Band are a progressive people, their advancement being very marked. They have recently adopted a code of Municipal Laws, so far as the existing general law of the land admitted of their doing so, for the better government of their people, which is remarkable for the ability displayed by their Council in framing of its provisions, and will no doubt be productive of much benefit to the community.[66]

Two years later, the prime minister, echoed his earlier compliments, recognizing the contribution of his loyal Tory supporter:

> The efficient head chief of this band, whose Indian name is Kahkewaquonaby, but who is better known under his English patronymic of Dr. Jones, has been largely instrumental in bringing about the satisfactory condition in which matters are at present on this reserve. For although he has his professional practice to attend to (Dr. Jones holds a diploma from Queen's College, Kingston), he takes a deep and active interest in the welfare of his people.[67]

Opposition to these "colonial" measures came from the traditionalist faction, led by former Chief David Sawyer and George Henry Jr. They preferred to allow everyone to speak before arriving at a decision by consensus. Though time-consuming, this approach encouraged compromise and provided some solace to the opposition. Election by a one-vote majority, as happened when Dr. Jones was first appointed head chief, had left many band members dissatisfied. As a part-time farmer, Dr. Jones had to supervise the men working his sixty hectares on the reserve and attend to the upkeep of the barn and equipment. Here too he had to withstand criticism from fierce political opponents who felt he had no business belonging to the band because his father and Uncle John had supposedly renounced their band memberships when they accepted a land grant of forty hectares in 1805. Though the Band Council had approved the deal in 1835, their critics, including the Sawyer family, believed that without exception all land belonged to the community.[68]

Members of the original group who inhabited the first Mississauga reserve on the River Credit also felt that they should not have to share the band's annual interest payment with those who joined after the move to New Credit in 1847. They therefore lodged a protest with the Department of Indian Affairs in Ottawa.[69] The department appointed one of their seasoned officials, Mr. A. Dingman, as a special commissioner and instructed him to verify the New Credit band membership list. He held hearings in Council House in the spring of 1888 and kept meticulous records with the help of Dr. Jones, who found himself in a delicate situation. Jones had to act as the agent and secretary of a hearing in which he was one of the people targeted by the complainants. Jones prepared detailed tables, one of which shows that most of the families could trace their band membership back some twenty-five years (the minimal residence being eleven years). The commissioner conducted the hearing in a manner that respected the Ojibwe's cultural values, and the minutes show that the band Elders documented their cases and responded eloquently to cross-examination.[70]

Dr. Jones was obliged to defend his family's right to remain members of the band and stay on the payment roll. In a manner befitting a barrister, he presented deeds, census records, Band Council minute books, and pay lists, proving that his father and members of their families had been continuously on the membership list since 1828. The heads of other families also pleaded their cases eloquently, making use of both written and oral evidence.[71] On 15 May 1888, Dingman called for a vote to decide whether the disputed families should be removed from the band's membership list. They would forfeit their annual interest payments and lose their right to live on the reserve. Those who remained would divvy up the interest monies formerly paid the expelled families. Both men and women voted, the latter being subdivided into wives, widows, and spinsters. The show of hands revealed that siblings often voted against each other, while wives were forced to support their husbands, but no matter how the vote was tabulated, in each instance a slight majority of band members voted to exclude many of their fellow families. The commissioner declared that he would leave it up to Ottawa to decide whether to consider the female vote. He knew full well that women—deemed "non legal persons"—were still denied the franchise at all levels of government. The federal department refused to change the pay list because many of the contested members had been admitted in good faith by previous Band Councils.[72] The band could not have survived with such a drastically reduced membership. This incident reveals the divisive nature of arrangements dependent on subdividing a fixed income within a community.

Jones also had an earlier history of conflict with traditionalists, including one of his cousins, that would plague him for much of his adult life. Serving as physician to a tightly knit group of people, especially when many are interrelated, is a daunting occupation, but Dr. Jones was shocked in 1879 when his cousin, George Henry Jr., supported by a few of other members of the New Credit Band Council, attempted to have him fired from the post of band physician.[73] At a council meeting they were critical of the care their families had received and wished to hire one of the Euro-Canadian doctors from Hagersville. Following a heated debate, the chiefs and the rest of the Band Council declared that they were perfectly satisfied with Dr. Jones. In an effort to lay the matter at rest, Jones drafted a petition that was distributed to all the households on the reserve. Always aware of the niceties of medical practice, the doctor did not disturb one of the families because that very morning they had just lost a daughter, another young victim of tuberculosis. In the end, all but four band members signed in favour of his continuing to be the band's physician. Jones wrote the Department of Indian Affairs, saying: "I considered it quite flattering that after nearly four years of practice that there were so few complaints."[74]

George Henry Jr. and his clique were not to be defeated so easily. They reorganized and a couple of years later levelled a more serious charge when he accused Dr. Jones of both inattention and incompetence.[75] The complaint had nothing to do with professional incompetence or malpractice, but annoyance that he had not always been easily available to see patients or make house calls. Jones explained that he had been ill for six weeks and had contacted another doctor to replace him. Repeated entries in his mother's diaries indicate that Peter Edmund, a polio victim, suffered from repeated respiratory infections in adult life. On 20 April 1882, he went before the council, stating that he had no desire to continue as their medical attendant without the support of at least two-thirds of the band. His only object in coming to Hagersville, he told them, had been to serve his brethren. Thereupon, he withdrew, and the Band Council voted on a motion put forward by John LaForme, seconded by William Elliott, that his services be retained. The vote was thirteen in favour, nine against. Dr. Jones then returned to the meeting room and informed the assembly that he had received a memorandum of support signed by thirty-two members, who, together with their families, constituted the large majority of the band. He would not, therefore, resign.[76]

The matter didn't end there. Jones's cousin, George Henry Jr., had apparently been the complaint's instigator, and he wrote to Mr. Vankoughnet, the deputy superintendent general of the Department of Indian Affairs, to say that he had brought charges last spring, substantiated by a majority of the band, alleging that the doctor had used his position as head chief, which traditionally implied that he was first among equals, to shield himself from exposure. He did not repeat his long-standing accusation that Jones was not entitled to be a band member because he was only one-quarter Aboriginal. In reply, Vankoughnet pointed out that the band had become dissatisfied with five or six doctors in succession. The problem, as the past Band Council minutes documented, was that these town doctors "had their general White practice which they could not neglect" and came to the reserve only when summoned.[77] Vankoughnet remembered that when he first joined the Indian Department in 1873 they had to deal with an identical charge levelled at young Dr. Oronhyatekha, who had just been appointed medical consultant to the Tyendenaga Mohawk reserve near Belleville.[78]

A word should be said about the warring cousins. Their fathers, Reverend Peter Jones and George Henry Sr., were both sons of Tuhbenahneequay or Sarah Henry. Peter Jones's father was Augustus Jones, while George Henry Sr.'s father was Mesquacosy, Sarah's second husband. According to the Credit River Reserve Register, Reverend Peter Jones and George Henry Sr. were half-brothers, but the two men grew up to espouse directly opposing views.[79] Whereas Reverend Jones dressed in Protestant garb and lectured on the civilizing power of Christianity, George Henry Sr. assumed the role of traditional Medicine Man and, using his Aboriginal name, Maungwudaus, organized a travelling Indian show. Following each performance he presented himself as an experienced Aboriginal Medicine Man and sold packages containing a variety of herbal cures.[80] His son, George Henry Jr., had travelled to Europe in order to take part in his father's performances and acquired his father's herbal recipes in due course. In 1889 the *Oakville Star* published an account of the visit by George Henry Jr., referring to him as Saigitoo, the Medicine Man from the Mississaugas of New Credit and the son of the well-known Aboriginal doctor, Maungwudaus. Saigitoo had just visited Urquhart's Medical Hall in Oakville with a full supply of medicines concocted from his father's recipes.[81] Both Medicine Men claimed to "cure diseases every time while they were still curable."[82] The list of treatable problems included an inability to hold water, scalding of urine, change of life, skin rashes, fainting spells, loss of voice, dropsy, stomach worms, and other nameless diseases. His medicines were "roots, herbs, barks, pleasant to the taste, devoid of nauseating properties and suitable for little children as well as adults."[83] By their choice of professions, Dr. Peter Edmund Jones, a licensed physician, and his cousin George Henry Jr., a Medicine Man, were destined to carry on the same conflict that had kept their fathers at odds.

In the final third of the nineteenth century, Dr. Jones and Medicine-Man George Henry Jr. farmed nearby acreage on the New Credit reserve. The two cousins, both former band councillors, were temporarily brought together by a family tragedy. George's twenty-four-year-old son Francis left home on 3 November 1893 to seek work, but never returned. The winter months passed without word of his whereabouts, so George consulted a lawyer in Hagersville whose research turned up a grisly possibility. On 4 November a man had been run over and killed on the Michigan Central's tracks near the nearby town of Cayuga. The body was terribly mutilated, but foul play was suspected. The coroner conducted an inquest. On 14 May 1894, Dr. Jones, the helpful lawyer, and the distraught father watched while the grave in the local Potter's field was exhumed, and Francis's clothing was identified. A scrap of paper found in a trouser pocket bore the name of a man known to be involved in criminal activities, supporting their belief the youth might have been murdered.[84] Jones supported the grieving parents and immediately set to work arranging a proper burial on the reserve. He bluntly informed Ottawa: "Henry, like most Indians is a poor man," and asked that his legal expenses should be paid by the government. He also requested that the burial costs of $7.50 be paid by the Band Council. Deputy Superintendent Hayter Reed approved these expenditures.[85]

Four

Pride in His Heritage

The Mississaugas of the New Credit reserve gradually became a successful farming community, complete with roads, fences, and bridges. In 1881, Chief Jones, supported by his council, decided that they were ready to have their own Council House.[1] Built at a cost of $550, the brick building had a high ceiling with a balcony encircling a large chandelier. The walls were graced by portraits of Queen Victoria, Prime Minister Sir John A. Macdonald, and six prominent chiefs, including the current head chief, Dr. Jones.[2] Built a mere thirty-five years after the band was evicted from the River Credit reserve, the building declared that the Mississaugas were here to stay. Head Chief Jones lost no time in organizing a mammoth reception. To his delight, the Grand Council accepted an invitation to hold their September meeting in the new facility. Many Aboriginal peoples consider the opportunity to be a generous host to be a great honour, so the formal opening of the building was scheduled for the end of the Grand Council meeting.[3]

Press for the event came from Dr. Jones's reputation as an avid chess player. He was considered a "chess master" and won first prize in a chess competition sponsored by the *Detroit Free Press*.[4] The paper's Indian Affairs reporter, J. Grensell, whose nom de plume was Yusif, was so impressed by Dr. Jones that he arranged to come to Hagersville and cover the Council House inauguration. Dated 15 September 1882, Yusif's report provides an independent account of the event. He noted that there were some three thousand people, "red-men" and "pale-faces," assembled with four brass bands. Playing "Pull for the Shore" and resplendent in red-trimmed uniforms with Prussian helmets and red and white plumes, the musicians marched smartly up to the Council House. Chief Jones, attired in broadcloth "as if for a wedding reception," invited all to take seats in the bower.[5] The clergy, head chiefs, and visiting members of Parliament sat arranged in order of rank on the platform. The

Figure 7 The New Credit First Nation's Council House as it appeared in 1882. Christine Lalonde, illustrator.

superintendent of the Brantford Indian agency, J.T. Gilkison, presided and the ceremonies began with a prayer and a selection of hymns sung by a choir accompanied by a young Aboriginal girl on a portable church organ.[6]

Dr. Jones spoke in English, followed by different chiefs who made several other speeches in their Native tongues. Especially noteworthy was a speech in the Mohawk language by Chief John Smoke Johnson, a warrior over ninety years of age who had fought under Tecumseh in 1812. About Johnson's neck hung the large silver medal he had received from King George III.[7] Chief Sampson Green, the president of the Grand Council, complimented Dr. Jones in his address to the audience. He admired the substantial Council House the band had built, and he declared that "the beautiful trees he had planted would be a monument to the doctor's energy and good advice long after he had passed away."[8]

Later the audience called for a war dance, and with some reluctance a man stepped forward, removed his coat, and tied a red sash about his waist. When no one else volunteered to join in, Dr. Jones put aside his cane and came to the man's assistance. The drum struck up, and the two men began to foot it in time to the beat's increasing cadence. Trying to keep up, Jones raised several war whoops, which were received with laughter but at least encouraged another dancer to come to his relief. Just as the dance grew fast and furious and the dancers' arms swayed rapidly, the drummer delivered the drum with an unlucky stroke, splitting the drum head from hoop to hoop.[9] No music, no dance, so dinner was called. The guests sat down to a fine repast of poultry, meats, vegetables, fruits, and pastry organized and prepared by the women of the band, which was described as being "more than ordinarily rich and savoury."[10] After dinner there were bass solos by Chief Herchmer featuring a repertory of amusing English songs. The *Detroit Free Press* correspondent concluded by reporting:

> The afternoon closed with the formal adoption and naming of the wife of Chief Dr. Jones, a white lady. She came forward dressed in a short gown of dark green cloth, trimmed with blue silk and artistically ornamented with beadwork. She wore earrings, bracelets, broach and necklaces of silver filigree and various ornaments of pearl. A circlet of golden beads was round her head; her hair hung loosely down. A very pretty picture she made as she stood before the audience, just the least bit flustered at being the cynosure of so many eyes. Rev. Mr. Chase spoke briefly in Indian and again in English, gave her his hand and led her forward, addressing her by the name of Wabunooqua—the "Lady of the Morning." And all the people thrice repeated the word Wabunooqua and gave three cheers. And so when evening had come on a great display of fireworks and a set concert by the Ojibway band finished the dedication ceremonies.[11]

Dr. Peter Edmund Jones always presented himself as a Status Indian who farmed land on his band's reserve, never as a Métis or non-Aboriginal. Despite his upbringing in Brantford and his years at university, he made no effort to become enfranchised in order to acquire the legal rights of a Euro-Canadian. His writings suggest that he was pleased that his skin colour resembled his father and that everyone considered him an Aboriginal. The so-called "Red Men versus White Men" controversy began with a racist letter from R.W. Phipps, printed in the 30 November 1875 issue of *The Toronto Mail* newspaper, a forerunner of today's

Globe and Mail.[12] Under the subtitle "Reasons against Prohibition," Phipps argued that North American Indians enjoyed a state of perfect prohibition because they did not make fermented beverages, but attempting to support his argument that prohibition was not necessarily a good thing, he went on to claim that the Indians were lazy, their sins of morality were unquestionable, and their treachery and inhumanity proverbial. Dr. Oronhyatekha wasted no time in dispatching a strong retort. A few days later a second letter, signed B.A. of Peterboro, made scurrilous reference to members of the Mississauga tribe.[13] Dr. Jones decided to join the fray:

> I am one of the Mississaugas, a branch of the Ojibways, and head chief of that part of them called the New Credit band and I will commence by stating that there is not in Canada a tribe of Indians more clean, industrious, and sharp in business, than are my people. Although a band of only a little over two hundred souls, we have two schools in active operation, taught by well-educated members of the tribe. Our women are treated as much like ladies as the wives of the white farmers about here.... Indirectly I suppose I must thank the white man for being able to write a letter, though my father was much better educated than I am. But "B.A." must also thank the Romans and 1,800 years of improvement, while we poor Indians have only had some forty or fifty years since paganism. Let "B.A." give us a few more years and then perhaps we will be able to camp out under snow-white canvas, hunt all day with kid gloves on, and bring home ground birds and red squirrels à la manner of B.A.[14]

A few days after the above letter appeared, Dr. Oronhyatekha also wrote a reply to B.A.:

> But when I see my people wantonly assailed, in a leading public journal, by a gentleman who ought to have known better, as "immoral, treacherous, and inhuman," I am prepared to show that, in all that is truly noble and good, the Indian has always been, is now even in his degenerate days, and ever will be, better than any white man on the face of the earth. And I see no reason why B.A. should thereby allow his angry passions to arise, for I can assure him he has my cordial sympathy for having been so unfortunate as not to have been born an Indian.[15]

The letters clearly demonstrate the pride both physicians exhibited in their Aboriginal status, even though it impeded their smooth entry into their chosen profession. Oronhyatekha was an early proponent of the teaching of Mohawk in schools located on reserves, and about the same time as this controversy's editorials, he published two articles on the Mohawk language in the Toronto-based *Canadian Journal*.[16] Both physicians were excellent writers and knew how to use the media to defend Aboriginal rights and reputations.

Political struggles co-existed with family difficulties as Peter Edmund outlived all three of his brothers. Though the Jones family was distinctly proud of their best-educated member—Eliza referred to her son as "The Doctor"—it was Charles Augustus who had become family head following the death of Reverend Jones. Like Peter Edmund, Charles was first educated at home before attending the Indian day school on the reserve for a short time. Eliza soon noted in her diary: "But being greatly in advance of the scholars there, we removed him to a private school."[17] He then went to Victoria College, in Cobourg, Ontario, intending to study law, but his plans were dashed when Eliza was unable to pay the fees. Ill advised, she had lost most of her savings in the investment market.[18]

Charles joined the newly formed Canadian Volunteers and was sent to Sarnia to guard the Canadian border against the Fenian incursions during the brief but violent agitations for Irish independence.[19] In 1865 he decided to seek his fortune in the United States. The Union army still needed soldiers for its army of occupation, and Charles unwittingly signed up for a three-year term. He was assigned to a hospital in Georgia; not only were the soldiers severely wounded, many had recently contracted yellow fever. Eliza desperately wanted him to come home. She wrote to the president of the United States and the secretary of the army asking to be pardoned as it was the anguish of a mother, but the army held firm to his contract. In November 1867 Charles wrote, "I hardly dare hope for release, unless I release myself."[20] Eliza's letter to Charles's company commander, begging for a more honourable type of work did, however, strike a favourable chord, and he was appointed the military hospital's librarian. Peter Edmund was relieved that his brother no longer had to work in the infectious disease wards. Always helpful, he mailed his brother the weekly *Toronto Leader*, which Charles proudly placed in the reading room. Charles now enjoyed carrying out his duties and wrote his mother that he was now determined to remain in the army and hoped she would approve. The Jones family was staunchly Conservative and supported Macdonald in his 1867 election campaign. The voters were being asked to approve a Confederation of the colonies of Nova Scotia, New Brunswick, Upper Canada (Ontario), and Lower Canada (Quebec).[21] Learning of the prime minister's success, Charles wrote his mother that he was pleased that the elections in my "beloved country" had gone as they have, and that "Canada would become one great country."[22]

Honourably discharged from military service, Charles took the train to San Francisco, where he joined his younger brother Frederick.[23] The most independent of the Jones boys, Fred had left home in 1862 and made his way first to British Columbia, then to California, where he found employment as a newspaper reporter.[24] Charles, well read because of his classical education and service as a librarian, also found work as a journalist. On 17 February 1870, he wrote his mother from Sacramento that *The Chronicle* and the other papers "gladly take anything I write."[25] The two brothers roomed together and were able to enjoy life, though they had little money. Charles's talents earned him a job with *The Sacramento Reporter*, and he was soon made a department head. The work was stressful, and in May 1870 the brothers decided to return to Brantford. Charles's editor was sad to see him leave and wrote a fine testimonial. Armed with this letter of reference, he was invited to join the reporting staff of the local paper, *The Expositor*.[26] With Eliza's home as his base, he courted Hannah Elda Ellis, daughter of an old United Empire Loyalist family, and they were married later that year. Tangible evidence of his acceptance by the non-Aboriginal community came with his appointment as an officer in the Canadian Revenue Department.[27] Charles was a talented writer like his mother Eliza. One may ask how a member of a local Aboriginal band could obtain a job in the federal civil service in the nineteenth century, but the family had long had the respect of Brantford citizens. Eliza herself taught drawing and was active in church circles. County Judge Stephen James Jones was a United Empire Loyalist descendant of Augustus Jones's older brother Stephen Jones Sr. He had prepared the petition Eliza sent to the secretary of the army to aid her futile effort to secure Charles's release.[28] Though sensitive and retiring, Charles had a strong attachment to his friends and family. Charles and his family's involvement with Macdonald and his Conservative party had antedated Confederation and the prime minister, who had a fabulous memory for faces and names, kept tabs on his supporters, who were usually entitled to at least one favour. In nineteenth-century Canada, jobs were scarce, and the sons of prominent families, who were neither professionals nor tradesmen, eagerly sought out such appointments. The editors of *The Expositor*, an influential newspaper, were happy with their new colleague and appreciated what they later referred to as Charles's "sterling qualities."[29]

When Frederick Jones returned to Brantford, he became an ornamental painter and married Mary Fuller, a local non-Aboriginal woman. Eliza was delighted when Mary became the first of her daughter-in-laws to become pregnant, but later she was heartbroken after mother and baby died during childbirth in August 1872. Still mourning his tragic loss, Frederick moved to Chicago early in 1873 to pursue his trade in what was a rough-and-ready city, still growing rapidly as a railway hub supplying the western states. Post–Civil War Chicago was also a favoured destination for recently freed slaves and other immigrants determined to find jobs and better lives for their families. Competition was high and racial prejudice fierce; because Frederick had the features of an Aboriginal, he suffered from both.[30]

In July 1875, Frederick married a widow of Irish descent who had a young daughter, but in the late autumn tragedy struck again when he developed "galloping consumption," a rapidly progressive form of tuberculosis. He wrote his mother that he was being treated with a mustard plaster poultice on his throat.[31] Unable to provide for his family, he brought them home to Brantford by train, arriving in March 1876. Eliza received them at her home on Brant Avenue and called her long-time family friend, Dr. Egerton Griffin. Sadly there was nothing Griffin could do, and Frederick lived only another two weeks. The family was heartbroken: only thirty-five, he was the first brother to pass away. Charles had to provide the civil information required for the death certificate, giving his occupation as Inland Revenue officer, Brantford, Ontario. Griffin's diagnosis was pulmonary tuberculosis; duration of illness: about four months.[32] The family had not known death since Reverend Jones died twenty years earlier. Charles found refuge in poetry and composed a long poem entitled "In Memory of Brother Fred." The lines reflected the happiness experienced by Charles and Frederick when they shared a flat in Sacramento and afterward when Frederick faced poverty and prejudice alone in Chicago:

> Far from the old home, far from the brothers,
> Far from the mother, whose love passeth others;
> Fighting the cold world, sharing its cares,
> Tasting its hardships, sharing its snares
> Longing for peace and rest
> Striving to do the best
> Yet oft cast down.[33]

The still grieving Charles was recognized later that year when he was appointed official secretary of the Brant memorial committee. The hereditary chiefs of the Six Nations had voted to erect a memorial to their legendary war chief, Joseph Brant, in Brantford's Victoria Park. Brant was one of Britain's heroes in the American Revolution as he supported the Crown. His memorial would be one of the first pieces of statuary of its kind in North America, and its patrons included leading men and government officials. Charles's committee included Judge Stephen James Jones, Six Nations Chief George H.M. Johnson, Brantford Mayor James W. Digby, M.D., and Head Chief Peter E. Jones, M.D. Eliza even prepared a fine biography of Brant, which was offered as a bonus to prospective donors.[34] Charles would prove to be a superb intermediary between the Aboriginal peoples and the British-Canadian sponsors of the memorial, which included the Dominion and British governments, the United Empire Loyalists, and patriotic Canadians. After years of planning, Joseph Brant's monument was finally unveiled on 13 October 1886, but Charles was not present at the Brant celebration. He had died on 19 June 1882 at the age of forty-three after an illness of several months' duration.[35] Chief Dr. Jones spoke on behalf of the Mississaugas of the New Credit, however. Their proud band added zest to the ceremony.[36]

Charles, the son born after four miscarriages, had always been Eliza's pride and joy. He was the only one of her five children whose milestones were tabulated in her diary. The loss of both Frederick and Charles at so young an age was particularly hard for Eliza, but despite failing vision, she busied herself teaching drawing. Her "drawing master" had been Monsieur Bocquet, a French artist who had exhibited landscapes and portraits at the Royal Academy between 1817 and 1849. Eliza, whose miniature watercolour portraits won prizes at an 1854 exhibition, is recognized as one of the early painters and engravers in Canada.[37]

Eliza always remained close to Peter Edmund, who provided financial support, which she earned by writing his letters and possibly the minutes of the Grand Council's meetings. Entries in her meticulously kept accounts noted: "2 November received from PEJ, $50; 21 November from Dr. Jones, $20."[38] On Christmas Day 1882 she boarded a train to Caledonia. Peter Edmund then drove her to his home for a festive dinner with old friends.[39] Eliza also developed a closer relationship with her youngest son George, though she had often expressed dismay at his past wayward behaviour, especially his use of alcoholic beverages. George lived close by and held a steady job as a painter at the Brantford Carriage Works. Most importantly, his wife Minnie eventually provided Eliza with three grandchildren, two boys and a girl. Minnie brought them to see Eliza frequently. Raised in Brantford, the boys would someday request that the Department of Indian Affairs allow them to give up their membership in the New Credit band. They were the first members of Dr. Jones's family to become enfranchised, and shortly after they moved to the United States.[40]

In her mid-seventies, Eliza's vision began to fail. Whether she had developed cataracts or retinal disease is not recorded. Peter Edmund took his mother to Toronto, where she was examined by Dr. George A.S. Ryerson, professor of eye, ear, and throat surgery at the Trinity College Medical School. A nephew of her late friend, Reverend Egerton Ryerson, George had trained in Europe and is remembered in Canadian medicine for his innovations in ophthalmology.[41] Although after her visit she confided to her diary that "thank God the news was favourable," this did not turn out to be the case.[42] By the end of 1882, at seventy-eight years of age, a progressive loss of vision curtailed activities essential to her well-being, and she feared she would soon be unable to see her grandchildren. Eliza's eyes had served her well, though. She spent a lifetime able to select just the right colours for a portrait or a quilt. A quilt she crafted in the 1840s is preserved in the Brant County Museum in her beloved Brantford, fashioned of hundreds of small hexagon-shaped silk blocks in a myriad of colours and bordered with triangular pieces. Eliza had bequeathed the silk quilt to her son Charles's widow Hannah, who had a difficult time following his death, and before leaving Brantford, Hannah generously gave her prized possession to the Brant County Museum.[43] Despite this prestigious past, Eliza was totally blind by the time she died at the age of eighty-six in 1890. The *Christian Guardian*'s obituary commented: "A little time before her decease she was taken very ill and to all appearance, for death. However, she was very much disappointed that the Lord did not take her home.... She longed to go home with her precious loved ones ... my eyes shall be opened ... no more darkness."[44] The editor added: "We trust she is ever with the Lord."[45] Dr. Egerton Griffin sadly signed the death certificate; the diagnosis was "Old Age." A friend who had attended to all the Joneses for more than half a century, the doctor seems not to have realized that he too had grown old.[46] Tragedy came again within a few years. Family and friends were shocked when George suddenly collapsed in July 1893 and died three weeks later at the age of forty-six. In his Annual Report, Indian agent Dr. Jones was forced to include a painful statistic: "Only one adult member of the band died, my brother George D. Jones."[47]

Jones's strong interest in his people's history might have provided some solace as he fought grief and political opponents. Peter Edmund had long been fascinated by the fact that Aboriginal peoples had resided on the banks of the Grand River for thousands of years, and he ultimately made an important contribution to knowledge of early Aboriginal culture through his lifelong passion for collecting prehistoric Aboriginal artifacts. Not only did he collect Aboriginal relics, but Jones also conducted his own archaeological digs, finding broken pottery, flints, and ossuaries that confirmed the presence of prehistoric Aboriginal nations who had lived on his farmland centuries before the European conquest. He wanted to show that the Aboriginal peoples of North America were thriving prior to the arrival of Columbus.[48]

In his quest to find physical evidence that prehistoric peoples had occupied the same territory as the present-day Six Nations and New Credit reserves, Jones found a willing ally in David Boyle, curator-archaeologist of the Canadian Institute Museum. Boyle studied human prehistory by excavating promising sites and analyzing pottery, flints, and burial sites. Dr. Jones and Boyle were the same age and became lifelong friends.[49] In the summer of 1890, Boyle visited the Six Nations reserve, and the two men explored Baptiste's farm, close to Jones's own property on the New Credit reserve near Hagersville. They found an encampment where a line of ash beds indicated that Aboriginal peoples had occupied the area in ancient times. In his 1891 archaeological report, Boyle observed that the whole of the Grand River Valley was rich in evidence of Aboriginal settlement more than 5,000 years earlier, long before the Six Nations settled near Brantford. Several amateur archaeologists had already found pottery and ossuaries at the site of an early village on the Six Nations reserve.[50]

Jones was able to lead the archaeological team to a site on Boston Creek, where he was convinced that the clay forming its right bank had been worked by peoples of yore for pottery-making. The creek ran through his farm, and examinations proved Jones correct. Boyle's report was accompanied by a drawing entitled "Tuscarora Village—site and Clay-bed," which indicated Jones's discovery. Many other areas were examined, and Boyle deemed it worth reporting that the "Indians" he had hired showed no superstitious fears in connection with their work, even when handling the bones of departed warriors. Today the excavation of these sacred sites is forbidden, and museums have returned skeletal remains to First Nations authorities for traditional burial.[51]

Aboriginal peoples had certainly been a continuing presence in Jones's region from very early times. For example, the ancestors of the

Figure 8: Chief Peter E. Jones at thirty-nine years of age, pictured in a portrait commissioned for the 1882 inauguration of his Council House. (*Source:* Courtesy of the Mississaugas of the New Credit First Nation, Hagersville)

Hurons, Neutrals, and Iroquois likely spoke Iroquoian, and it appears that a series of hunter-gatherer peoples had evolved an agricultural way of life. As archaeologist Bruce Trigger observed, the spread of ideas from one group to another could not by itself explain internal changes. These early societies had to evolve to a point where they could make use of these ideas and be capable of integrating them into their way of life. The gradual changeover to horticulture involved major changes in their traditional habits, an alteration that he believed need not be explained by migration.[52] Studies of pottery, burial mounds, and crops such as corn indicate dynamic and creative changes as new inhabitants occupied the area. Some of these groups spoke totally unrelated languages and do not appear to have descended from a common ancestral culture. The

Anishinabek, an Algonquian linguistic group that included members of the Ojibwe, Mississauga, Chippewa, and other tribes, migrated to southern Ontario at the end of the seventeenth century following a series of battles with the Iroquois. By 1720 they were well established and maintained their hunter-gatherer way of life; though they had gardens, they were not accomplished agriculturalists like their predecessors.[53]

Besides the specimens Boyle retrieved on his own, the Canadian Institute received many unique donations from Jones and his collector friend, James Wood. Boyle was thrilled to obtain a beautiful ceremonial weapon of Huronian slate and an ingenious arrangement of conical bones on a string used by the Ojibwe people as a gambling game. Jones's personal collection—the largest in the province—combined his late father's efforts with his own. It was insured for $1,000 until many items were acquired by the Smithsonian Institution in Washington, DC, in 1898.[54]

In the ceaseless battle to establish their traditional occupation and use of their territories, Canadian bands sought the aid of sympathetic intellectuals in order to document and promote their claims. Though the British had given the Six Nations their land in appreciation for their help during the Revolutionary War, settlers frequently harassed them and their Mississauga neighbours, who later occupied the southwest corner of the Grand River Territory. In the late nineteenth century, Chief George H.M. Johnson, the official translator of the Six Nations, formed a committee of chiefs to co-operate with linguist Horatio Hale to study the mnemonic belts of wampum, beads that remind a storyteller of what comes next in a tale. These wampum belts document the Iroquois people's oral history. Deciphering the ritual text of the condolence ceremony at which deceased chiefs were mourned and their successors installed still ranks as a major discovery. After publishing *The Iroquois Book of Rites*, Hale had the rare opportunity of witnessing a Condoling Council, following which he described the procedure's sequence in a paper published by the Royal Society of Canada.[55]

While studying various Aboriginal dialects, Hale realized that language could supplement archaeology as a reliable tool for uncovering history, and his work demonstrated that these languages, far from being primitive tongues, enabled the speaker to classify information in a sophisticated manner. The Smithsonian Institution in Washington later enlisted Dr. Jones's assistance in identifying the meaning of place names in the Ojibwe language. One such was the Toronto Islands, which Jones translated as *Mi-ni-sing*, "On the Island." The translation may well have supported the Mississaugas of the New Credit First Nation's claim that the Toronto Islands were part of their traditional territory.[56] James Pilling, editor of the Smithsonian Institution's *Bibliography of the Algonquian Languages*, also recognized the linguistic contributions of Dr. Jones, which included the name of the Etobicoke River, *E-o-bi-coke* or "The place of the alders."[57]

Five

Active Critic of the Indian Act

For many years Dr. Jones was actively involved in the Grand General Indian Council of Ontario and Quebec or Grand Council. While serving as head chief he led the elected delegation to the council, and the community paid the expenses. Every band had the right to send one delegate for each hundred or fraction of one hundred members.[1] The council relied on oral presentations, such as traditional storytelling, which celebrated identity and affirmed strength and spirituality, and delegates carefully used persuasion in their debates rather than the confrontational techniques enjoyed by British parliamentarians. Norman Shields expertly reviews these deliberations of the Grand Council in his M.A. thesis, "Anishinabek Political Alliance in the Post-Confederation Period."[2]

North American Aboriginals had organized such meetings for centuries in order to settle disputes, organize war parties, and foster trade with their neighbours. Each tribe had trade routes to ensure a supply of such essentials as flints, foodstuffs, shells, copper, and medicinal herbs. Some Grand Councils evolved into long-standing alliances: The Three Fires united three Anishinabek tribes living around the Great Lakes: the Ojibwe, Odawa, and Potawatomi. The Iroquois formed the Confederacy of the Five Nations, which became the Six Nations in 1722 when the Tuscaroras joined their league. The Six Nations designated themselves Haudenosaunee, which translates loosely as "people of the longhouse."[3] By means of these unions the Anishinabek and the Six Nations acquired state-like powers, useful when negotiating with the British and later American governments.

In the latter part of the nineteenth century, laws passed by the colonial government became the focal point of Grand Council deliberations. The first Acts dealing with the Aboriginal peoples were actually designed to protect their lands from encroachment by both settlers and squatters who stole tribal lands and resources. The British Parliament responded to this problem because the London-based Aborigines' Protection Society members, like Dr. Thomas Hodgkin, wrote letters to the newspapers and lobbied members of Parliament demanding that the Empire protect Aboriginal peoples' lands. Responses were limited, however, because the Aboriginal peoples still occupied land, and conventional wisdom of the time dictated that they must be assimilated into the new Euro-Canadian society.

The first legislation, the Gradual Civilization Act, was enacted in 1857, a full decade before Confederation, by the Parliament of Upper and Lower Canada. It was prepared by a young attorney general from Upper Canada named John A. Macdonald. In its summary of the legislation, *The Toronto Globe* of 15 May 1857 reported that William Benjamin Robinson, who had negotiated the 1850 treaties on the north shores of Lakes Huron and Superior, criticized the government: "Why should this bill be pressed through, without getting on it the opinion of the Indians themselves or their chiefs. At their council meetings the Indian chiefs deliberated quite as sensibly as honourable members did in this house, and sometimes even more so."[4] As Sidney L. Harring reveals in *White Man's Law*, the Act created a system of legal dualism that became the basis of all subsequent legislation concerning Aboriginal peoples both in law and in policy. Status Indians were placed in a distinct legal category under the paternalistic protection of the government. This unique form of social control enabled the authorities to train them for the responsibilities of citizenship, at which point males could apply to abandon their Indian status. They would then acquire the same rights as non-Aboriginal citizens. Because citizenship also included the right to vote, the process whereby registered Indians surrendered their treaty rights erroneously came to be called "enfranchisement." While individual Canadian Status Indians, unlike their American counterparts, could acquire legal rights, their communities were denied any form of legal status as a group except for minor municipal powers.[5]

The principles laid down in 1857 would be refined and adjusted in subsequent decades. For example, the enfranchised man (women were not eligible) would have to leave his reserve, accompanied by his wife and children. Once struck from the band membership list, he would lose all rights to own land on the reserve, to receive interest payments, to serve on the Band Council, or to otherwise enjoy the support that came from band life on the reserve. The gift of a personal deed to twenty hectares of land and the applicant's share of the band's funds held in trust by the government seemed to sweeten the buy-out deal, but the twenty hectares of land came from the reserve, reducing it in size. The deal, therefore, removed both land and funds from the band.[6]

Reverend H.P. Chase, of the Alderville reserve, later described attending an 1858 Grand Council at which the Gradual Civilization Act was discussed. Council members were unanimously convinced that "when the Indians came under the control of the Canadian government, efforts would be made to encroach upon them and drive them away."[7] The delegates rejected the 1857 Act and were not interested in the so-called enfranchisement provision, but the die had been cast. From this point on, Aboriginal leaders at successive Grand General Indian Councils would choose to organize and oppose the frequently amended Indian Act, which was largely but not entirely created by Euro-Canadians. They would debate the issues raised by this complex legislation, protest the seizure of their lands and the restrictions imposed on their members in a civilized manner without resorting to protest, confrontation, and armed conflict. They continually reaffirmed their loyalty to their "great mother," Queen Victoria, and her representative, the governor-general. Was this a carefully engineered ploy to keep these eloquent and effective politicians busy? In *A Fair Country: Telling Truths about Canada*, John Ralston Saul bemoans the wasted talents of gifted Aboriginal leaders, forced to devote their most productive years to trying to settle incredibly complex land claims.[8]

After Confederation in 1867, Macdonald became prime minister as well as minister of justice. His government merely refined and cosmetically renamed his old provincial legislation a year later. Then, in 1869, Canada's Parliament legislated more stringent restrictions on Aboriginal rights when it passed an Act for the Gradual Enfranchisement of Indians.[9] Wasting no time, a wide representation of bands from Ontario and Quebec took trains to Brantford in 1870 in order to attend an urgent General Council.[10] The chance to discuss the threats to all tribes posed by the 1869 Act attracted Mohawks from Oka, Kahnawake, St. Regis, and the Lake of Two Mountains, as well as Abenaki from St. Francis in Quebec. Ontario delegates included Mohawks from the Bay of Quinte, the Six Nations, and the Oneida of the Thames. Ojibwe bands, now part of the Anishinabek First Nations, included Mississaugas and Chippewas living on the shores of the Great Lakes.[11] All these bands had been deprived of land, lumber, and mineral rights—not to mention fishing and hunting grounds—by settlers, many of whom were squatters.

In all, a total of ninety-one delegates from twenty-one bands listened as the Onondaga Fire Keeper opened the 1870 Grand Council by thanking the Great Spirit for preservation. He then kindled the council fire, symbolically uncovering the slumbering embers of former councils. The names of the delegates were recorded, followed by ceremonial shaking of hands, but conflicts arose both in style and substance between the Haudenosaunee (Six Nations) hosts and their Anishinabek visitors. Before tackling the 1869 Act, Chairman Chief W.J. Simcoe Kerr encouraged the delegates to carefully review each section of the Act in the hope that their report would encourage the government to consult them in future. As Shields notes, the co-operative posture of the Grand Council toward the Canadian government would be maintained: it seldom communicated with the Department of Indian Affairs in anger. This polite approach, however, had more to do with the traditional Anishinabek and Haudenosaunee codes of behaviour than a desire to be obsequious.[12] The council reviewed each new Act in detail and usually provided sound reasons, and at times an alternative, when rejecting contentious items. In spite of this behavioural pattern, the 1870 council voted to reject ten of the first eleven sections of the Act. Chief George H.M. Johnson, of the Six Nations, seconded by Chief George King, of the Mississaugas of the New Credit, moved that only Section 3 banning intoxicating liquors remain. It was carried unanimously with the recommendation that fines be doubled.[13]

Unanimity came to an abrupt halt when Section 12 came up for review. Band Councils were to be able to frame their own regulations on subjects such as public health, maintenance of roads and bridges, and the building and maintenance of schoolhouses. The Six Nations did not like this legislation because they wanted to continue to be ruled by their hereditary chiefs. A few of the Anishinabek delegates, on the other hand, favoured adopting some of these rules. The final section dealt with enfranchisement, setting out the criteria whereby Status Indians could no longer be deemed Indians within the meaning of the laws relating to Indians. While the majority of the Anishinabek had no quarrel with the concept of enfranchisement, especially of educated young men, the Six Nations opposed the measure, and it was left in abeyance.[14]

Dr. Jones only represented his band at council for the first time in 1874 when they met on the Sarnia reserve. In fact, he was not the only Aboriginal medical doctor in attendance; Dr. Oronhyatekha and a final-year McGill University medical student, George Bomberry of the Six Nations, also played an active role in the proceedings.[15] Their presence was living proof that the government's attempt to dismantle the reserves by offering citizenship to educated Aboriginal peoples would be doomed to failure. The doctors wished to play an active role on their own reserves and represent the interests of all Aboriginal peoples, particularly in matters of health, education, and self-respect. The delegates enthusiastically welcomed the doctors, and both Jones and Oronhyatekha were nominated for the post of Grand Council president. They reportedly made eloquent and powerful speeches; Oronhyatekha did well enough to force a runoff vote, but in the end the election was won by Chief Reverend Henry P. Chase.[16] Dr. Jones was later elected to the post of second vice president. At the end of the meeting the council voted to approve Jones's proposition that Status Indians and their families who had acquired the legal rights of citizens would retain their rights to participate in the interest money and councils of their band. The government would later adopt Dr. Jones's enfranchisement scheme with some added provisions. Norman Shields notes that this was one of the times the government showed a willingness to implement a recommendation of the Grand Council, a considerable accomplishment for Jones.[17]

In 1876, a short-lived Liberal government that supported Macdonald's Indian policies consolidated all his laws and coined the now familiar eponym, the Indian Act.[18] Conservatives and Liberals thus worked together to abolish the traditional tribal government and assimilate band members into the majority Euro-Canadian population. Once the legislation was enacted, federal agents would be instructed to encourage and, if necessary, bribe band members to accept the government's offer of full political rights after they had voluntarily relinquished their Indian status.[19] In *The Ojibwa of Southern Ontario*, historian Peter S. Schmalz describes how the government bullied Aboriginal leaders into accepting the new Act. He notes that Chief John Henry, of the Chippewas of the Thames, and Chief William Wawanosh, of Sarnia, were called to Ottawa in February 1876 to evaluate the proposed Indian Act. They were joined by Reverend Allen Salt, a missionary with a biblical flowing beard, said to be half-"Indian." Salt also practised herbal medicine.[20] The three men were handed the complex legal document and told to read it over. Help was available in the form of the government officials, who stood over them and eagerly pointed out the benefits of enfranchisement. At the end of the meeting, the three Aboriginal leaders signified their approval.[21] The government's propaganda proved to be so effective that they presented an enthusiastic report when they attended the Grand Council meeting in July 1876. Moreover, a motion proposed by Chief John Henry to accept the 1876 Indian Act was passed by a margin of sixty-six to one.[22] Following the meeting, Council President Henry P. Chase took the initiative to write then Superintendent General David Laird, informing him that they approved of the Act and the offer of enfranchisement. Chase may have wished to enhance his own private relationship with Ottawa as he had been asked to go to England in order to help solicit funds for the establishment of the University of Western Ontario. Laird swiftly replied, declaring how gratified he was by the council's decision.[23]

In 1878, the Grand Council was once again held at Sarnia, and Head Chief David Sawyer, Chief Charles Herchmer, and Councillor George Henry Jr. represented the Mississaugas of the New Credit. The Six Nations sent a large delegation, which included Dr. George Bomberry, now one of their attending physicians. The delegates who had so readily approved of the 1876 Act when it was briefly presented were now aware of its oppressive nature and realized they had been fooled. Chief Wawanosh was criticized for signing a document at the government's request, though he too had been given scant opportunity to review it in detail. He had no excuse and could only say "that as a member of the delegation he had done his best," a reasonable answer considering how the Aboriginals had been tricked by the government officials.[24] Many sections of the Act were rejected, including those dealing with Aboriginal professionals, who stood to lose all their rights as Status Indians. Section 63, however, which dealt with the organization of Band Councils and the replacement of hereditary chiefs by elected officials, drew an angry response from the tradition-minded Six Nations. They insisted that it be removed from the Act, while the Anishinabek delegates, including those from New Credit, refused. Outnumbered, the Six Nations requested permission to leave the council. This was denied. They departed anyway, though as a conciliatory gesture they invited the other delegates to a meeting at the Grand River in two years' time. The delegates strongly opposed this motion, but Chief David Sawyer, whose New Credit band was on the Grand River Territory of the Six Nations, asked for permission to intervene. He then begged delegates to accept the Six Nations' generous invitation in order to have "the sympathy and good-will of his friends the Mohawks and so all 'Indians' would be on good terms."[25] David Sawyer was Dr. Jones's uncle, thirty years his senior. He had been a government translator, an assistant Methodist preacher, and an Aboriginal leader at Owen Sound for fifteen years, but had just recently returned to his home in New Credit. Sawyer's efforts on behalf of his people are enumerated in an 1867 volume by missionary Conrad Van Dusen, entitled *The Indian Chief*.[26] A visiting English clergyman once described him as "a tall fine man with a sensible-looking face."[27] Many of the delegates respected Chief Sawyer for work he had performed in their territories, and the 1878 Grand Council delayed voting on whether to accept the Six Nations' invitation. In the end, however, Sawyer was to be disappointed; the Grand River site received only five votes and these were from the New Credit delegates. This stood in comparison to thirty-five cast for the winner, Saugeen Village, near London, Ontario.[28] Because they lived in close proximity to each other on the Grand River territory, the Mississaugas of the New Credit and the Six Nations had gradually established a working relationship despite differences in language and culture, but the Anishinabek nations living in western and northern Ontario continued to distrust the Iroquois, their traditional enemies during the fur trade wars of past centuries.[29] Their links were with the local Métis and Euro-Canadians with whom they were involved in joint ventures in fishing, trapping, and lumbering.

The Six Nations rejoined the Grand Council in 1880, the same year that the government revised and consolidated the Indian Act.[30] Once again the delegates would have to examine this complex legal document and discuss how it would affect their communities. In what appears to have been a fruitful compromise, Chief Jones and the Mississaugas of the New Credit Band Council were invited to host this important meeting. The Six Nations delegates took part in the meetings, and all attendees joined in celebrating the opening of the new Council House. Before they left for home, all the delegates were invited to the Six Nations Council House in Ohsweken, where speaking, music, singing, and feasting were the order of the day, and a most enjoyable afternoon was spent.[31] The Grand Council was a great success! Now seventy-one, Chief David Sawyer was pleased at the outcome, even though he realized that differences remained between the Anishinabek and Iroquoian peoples.

Mindful of the traditions and languages of his people, Jones opened all sessions of the Grand Council held on his New Credit reserve with prayer, song, and due reference to the role of the Great Creator, but added British parliamentary rules. Unfortunately, Prime Minister Macdonald was unable to accept Head Chief Jones's invitation to meet the delegates.[32] He would have been impressed to see the 118 delegates from twenty-one Ontario bands, accompanied by educated men who could translate English into the Ojibwe or Mohawk languages. The council sessions included detailed discussions of the latest Indian Act. There was concern over the fact that there had been greater satisfaction and confidence in the government's role when the affairs of the Aboriginal peoples had been under British government control. Since the management of their communities had been transferred to the Canadian government in 1860, however, confidence had evaporated. Dr. Jones argued that in the case of minor grievances, it was more convenient to approach Ottawa than Westminster, and despite the transfer of management, there was nothing to prevent an appeal to Queen Victoria.[33] Jones had been elected secretary-treasurer of the council, and he dutifully recorded the views of the delegates, identifying with much respect those who took part in the deliberations, along with the reserves they represented. The words were rhythmic and conveyed the thinking behind each resolution the council passed. Even so, the reports had little effect. As the council had no legal standing, the government took no interest in their views. Each time Jones mailed a report to the Department of Indian Affairs, a bureaucrat would quickly dispatch the identical reply: "Their proposed changes to the Indian Act would receive close consideration."[34] Superintendent Alex Logan's remark about the council held at Parry Island in the late 1870s provides an insight into the Department of Indian Affairs' attitude: "I do not know if their meetings are any good, but it seems to please some of them."[35] The Ottawa bureaucrats faithfully followed policies bearing the imprint of successive Canadian prime ministers, but lower level officials who lived near reserves and interacted with Aboriginals and their leaders were often more in tune with reality.

Dr. Jones had twice asked Prime Minister Macdonald to make a brief appearance at a Grand Council meeting without success.[36] Nevertheless council efforts to gain government recognition continued. Deputy Superintendent Hayter Reed accepted an invitation to attend the Grand Council, but as a patronage appointee of the Conservatives, once the 1896 general election was called, he was away campaigning for his party. Disappointed, the council would have to settle for the inspector of Indian agencies, James A. Macrea. A veteran with fourteen years of service in Indian Affairs, Macrea's observations were penned the day he returned home from the fourteenth Grand Council. Given the smug attitude of his Ottawa colleagues, it is surprising to find that Macrea's bravely written nine-page report concluded that the Grand General Indian Council was a competent body that should be respected:

> Proper rules of debate were adhered to and the utmost decorum prevailed. Speeches were not only intelligent and occasionally eloquent but were well marked by moderation. Speakers made it evident that they had given attention to what they spoke of and that much good sense and truth lay in their remarks. The utmost courtesy was

> invariably displayed between those holding opposite views and rulings from the chair were unquestionably accepted.... The Grand Council might well become the theatre for larger discussion of more grave matters to afford opportunity for all the more advanced bands to speak directly to the Government.[37]

Macrea was not fired for his views, but his report was ignored as the government wished to assimilate the Aboriginals rather than listen to their opinions. Later the department rejected his expense account: Neither the 50 cents for repairs to his valise nor the cost of renting a replacement valise at 25 cents a day was reimbursed.[38]

This meeting and others illustrate why the Grand General Indian Councils of Ontario and Quebec are considered forerunners of twentieth-century Aboriginal organizations such as the Assembly of First Nations and the Union of Ontario Indians.[39] If the Department of Indian Affairs had bothered to read Dr. Jones's minutes and negotiated with his patriotic organization, it would have been good "preventive medicine" because, as Antonio Lamer, the chief justice of the Supreme Court of Canada, remarked in his 1997 landmark decision on Aboriginal treaty negotiations: "Let us face it, we are all here to stay."[40]

The Grand Council also had sophistication beyond the Canadian government's in some areas. For example, Jones and his committee provided the Grand Council with a written constitution.[41] At the 1882 Grand Council, there had been a dispute concerning the qualifications of the president, and Chief Sampson Green strongly advised the council to frame a constitution.[42] Jones drew up and published a constitution for the Grand Council, which bridged traditional ways, including songs and oral history, with British parliamentary rules and written history. A review of early councils, however, indicates that Jones largely updated and codified long-standing Aboriginal rules of behaviour.[43] Speakers were usually asked to abbreviate their remarks and votes were taken, though both Anishinabek and Iroquois delegates were committed to consensus decision-making, especially on controversial issues. One such instance is when the question of enfranchisement was not put to a vote in the 1870 council.

Jones's constitution was adopted at the 1884 Grand Council meeting, held at Cape Croker, a beautiful peninsula extending into Georgian Bay.[44] At the same council, the delegates from the Garden River and Sault Ste-Marie bands expressed hope that their colleagues at the Grand Council would petition the Department of Indian Affairs on their behalf.

They were disappointed that the delegates spent all their time dissecting individual sections of the Indian Act. By the second day, Chief Augustine Shingwauk, finding no opening to present his grievances, called a separate council of the Sault Ste-Marie and Garden River bands.[45] The delegates from the northwest reserves ultimately expressed their frustration at the workings of the Grand Council and decided to return home. When the president of the council heard Shingwauk was about to leave, he promised to insure that these bands would be able to express themselves. The next morning he arranged to amend the council's agenda, and the chief was allowed to present what would turn out to be an important issue. Traders and miners had come into his neighbourhood, not only for lumber and whitefish, but seeking all manner of minerals. Geologists dug pits while surveyors laid out roads, all with total disregard for Aboriginal lands. Shingwauk had offered to co-operate with road building and other matters, but in nearly every case the contractors and miners had not fulfilled their promises.[46] The Grand Council, through the offices of their secretary, Dr. Jones, agreed to write the Department of Indian Affairs in Ottawa on behalf of the Garden River reserve. It was ultimately an ineffective gesture, but since the courts refused to hear "Indian" claims, more effective resistance measures were not possible. This attitude did not surprise Chief Shingwauk, who commented that he was very glad he had heard such fine speeches, but was doubtful if they would bring forth any fruit. He went on to say: "Some of you wish to become white men, perhaps you will be like the white man who made this paper (pointing to the Robinson Treaty) and then broke it."[47] The wise chief was aware that mining was the very issue that had led to the original 1850 treaty. Nevertheless, the Grand Council did try to help its members. Dr. Jones and other chiefs frequently met with the Canadian government in order to present the Aboriginal peoples' positions on a variety of topics. The council tried to advance their economic interests by advocating hunting and fishing rights, even when asserting these rights involved active resistance by ignoring Canadian government restrictions.[48]

The Garden River reserve is located in the District of Algoma, situated on the boundary between the Precambrian Shield and the West St. Lawrence lowlands. Chief Shingwauk had not had a chance to read a newly published account of Ontario's mineral resources entitled *The Algoma District,* which begins with the statement "Ontario was a poetic Indian name, signifying a beautiful prospect of hills and waters," although the Aboriginal peoples are never mentioned throughout the remainder of the document.[49] It was the opening gunshot in a renewed struggle between prospectors, surveyors, and miners that would someday include oil and gas exploration. In *The Legacy of Shingwaukonse* Janet Chute describes how Shingwauk and his father, both intelligent and competent chiefs, tried to retain ownership of the resources under their feet.[50]

The president of the Grand Council began the debate on the Indian Act by inviting Dr. Jones to review recent amendments. Jones took the floor and read through the Act, clause by clause. One of the most contentious sections deprived women of the Aboriginal rights they were born with should they marry outside their band. Their children would be affected: they would be denied the right to possess or reside on lands on a reserve, inherit land from parents or others, receive annuity payments, or obtain fishing and hunting rights. The major sacrifice affecting someone no longer considered a Status Indian entailed the loss of the cultural benefits derived from living with friends and relatives and the subsequent loss of identity.[51] A final cruel symbol of their banishment meant that they could not be buried alongside their parents on the reserve. Though many delegates wished to protest such blatant discrimination based on gender, the majority, including Dr. Jones, believed in the traditional principle of descent through the male line.[52] The Grand Council again voted to retain this section. Was Jones's vote prejudiced by his personal situation? He was, after all, a Status Indian because his father had been a Status Indian, and he inherited his father's farm on the New Credit reserve. If he had been a girl, the land would have passed to one of his brothers.

In 1884 the council's focus was primarily on a completely new piece of legislation known as the Indian Advancement Act: "An Act for conferring certain privileges on the more advanced bands of Indians in Canada with a view of training them for the exercise of municipal affairs."[53] Tribal regulations were to be replaced by minor municipal powers in the fields of local taxation, health, and the power to punish those who transgressed the bylaws. The Act was divided into two parts: the first, the appointment of a council of elected councilmen, and the second, the provisions for framing bylaws for the local band government. In "Accounting for Genocide: Canada's Bureaucratic Assault on Aboriginal People," Dean Neu and Richard Therrien argue that the 1884 Indian Advancement Act was important because before that time, their agents decided how each band should spend their annuity monies.[54] The 1884 Act was designed to train band councils by empowering them to raise taxes and acquire expanded powers over police and public health matters, but while this appeared to be a loosening of central government control, it was just a shift in the mechanism of control. The band's Indian agent became the chairman of the council, emasculating the chief councillor, and the election regulations specified the size and functions of Band Councils.[55]

Jones objected to these provisions. Particularly galling was the insistence that the band chief could not even hold a council to address an emergency such as a fire on the reserve. The Indian agent was only a part-time official, often away on private business, but unless he was present, no decisions were valid. Nevertheless, Dr. Jones accepted these setbacks, believing that other elements such as increased control over public health were more important. He made a resolution in favour of limited self-government, which was then put forward and carried by a large majority. Later, in the letter inviting the prime minister to attend the 1886 Grand Council meeting, he referred to the New Credit reserve as "my admirable Baby Municipality."[56]

Dr. Jones made many trips to Ottawa on band business, and in 1886 he met the prime minister himself.[57] The latter was no doubt pleased to hear Dr. Jones's optimistic prognosis on the progress of their campaign to register Aboriginal voters before the 1887 election. Macdonald had met Dr. Jones's father in 1841 when still a young lawyer. He had chaired a meeting of a missionary society that Reverend Jones addressed.[58] Macdonald had never shared Reverend Jones's vision that Aboriginal peoples would someday be capable of competing with "the white race." Now, still smarting from the second "Indian" and Métis resistance in Canada's Northwest, he even wondered whether the Plains Indians required a different, more severe type of Indian Act. He asked Dr. Jones to suggest amendments to update the current act.[59]

Perhaps Jones romanticized his role and took the request more seriously than it deserved, viewing it as a verbal contract or commission. He pored over the earlier federal Indian Acts, which lacked unbiased input from the Aboriginals themselves, and saw to it that on this occasion there would be adequate consultation. This took considerable time and effort. He consulted individual bands, but, most importantly, he managed to have the matter discussed at one of the biennial meetings of the Grand Council. The main issues were band governance and the application of democratic principles to municipal-style governance as outlined by the federal government in 1884.[60] The New Credit Band Council, with Dr. Jones as head chief, had already adopted many of the new measures, but some Aboriginal peoples, such as the Iroquois of the Six Nations, insisted on retaining their system of hereditary chiefs. They maintained the tradition of having a speaker under whose direction discussion of a topic would be prolonged until consensus was reached.

Why did Macdonald entrust Dr. Jones with a potentially vital task? Had he become more cautious following the Riel troubles of 1885? Did he realize how much progress the "civilized Indians" of eastern Canada had made, or was this a political ploy permitting him to claim that the government had consulted the governed? Perhaps he imagined he was consulting a true-blue Tory Aboriginal who would not be overly critical. Whatever Macdonald's reasons, Jones accepted the challenge and sent his report to the prime minister in January 1887, with the following cover letter:

> My dear Sir John
> When in Ottawa last you asked me to give you my suggestions as to amendments I thought necessary to the Indian Acts and I have now the pleasure of sending you the result of my labours in respect to the Indian Advancement Act ... as I have added, struck out, and amended many things in the Indian Advancement Act, my production is more in the form of an Act to replace, than an Act to amend the original.[61]

Jones's suggestions came from the democratically voted resolutions of delegates to the Grand Council and were basically in keeping with established government policy. In the statement of purpose introducing the Indian Advancement Act of 1884, he proudly substituted the phrase "conferring certain privileges on the more advanced Indians of Canada" for the pejorative phrase "training them in municipal government."[62] Jones tried by means of subtle suggestion and some humour to reduce the Aboriginal peoples' dependency within what Morantz describes as a "wardship system."[63] His non-confrontational approach was far too polite, however, and the government just as politely ignored his suggestions.

Jones also reported a resolution passed by the Grand Council that property ownership rather than residence should be the qualification for electors and councilmen. Jones noted that it was unwise to reduce the number of councillors to six, as traditionally the Mississaugas were anxious to include as many families as possible and were used to having a large council. In the margin of the document adjacent to individual sections of the Act, Jones inscribed his suggestions and boldly informed Macdonald, himself a distinguished lawyer, that "throughout this section and this Act, generally ambiguous words and Latin terms are left out and the meaning conveyed in more simple language."[64]

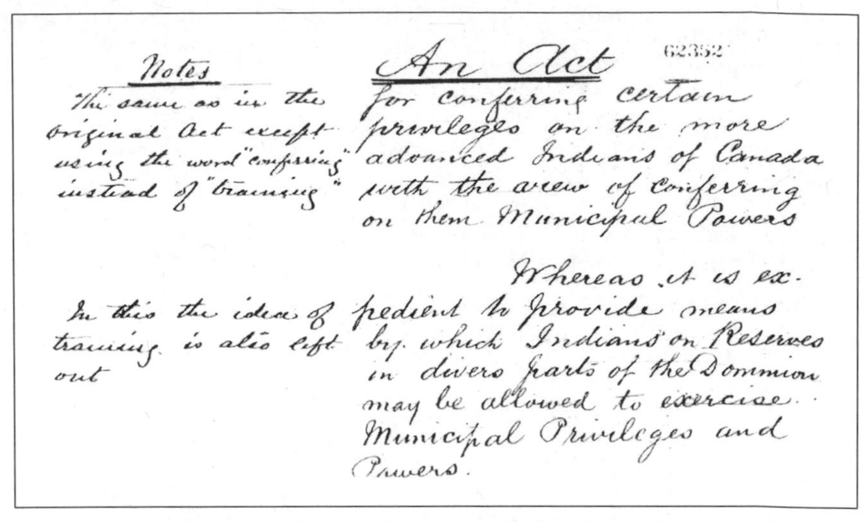

Notes

The same as in the original Act except using the word "conferring" instead of "training"

In this the idea of training is also left out

An Act

62352

for conferring certain privileges on the more advanced Indians of Canada with the view of conferring on them Municipal Powers

Whereas it is expedient to provide means by which Indians on Reserves in divers parts of the Dominion may be allowed to exercise Municipal Privileges and Powers.

Figure 9 Dr. Jones suggests that the prime minister replace the word "training" by "conferring" as he believed the eastern Indians no longer required tutoring. (*Source:* Courtesy of the Macdonald Papers, Library and Archives Canada, MG 26A, vol. 152, part 2, 62344–69)

One suggestion was to grant a modicum of power to the Band Council in emergencies when the Indian agent, only a part-time government employee, was unavailable. As secretary of the Grand Council, Jones asked the Department of Indian Affairs to alter the recent Act so that the band chief could also have the power to "call councils, to preside over them, and record the proceedings." Deputy Superintendent General Lawrence Vankoughnet refused to consider this request, saying that he feared mischievous events could occur if the Indian agent was not present at all council meetings.[65] The Grand Council had shown little patience with band members who failed to pay taxes on the assessed value of their land. They suggested that the penalty for non-payment of taxes be raised from one and one-half percent to ten percent. Head Chief Dr. Jones concurred and could not resist adding in his marginal note on the penalty: "The original [rate] is absurd!!!" although this was a comment that was unlikely to endear him to the prime minister, who had been responsible for the original version of the Act. Jones was far ahead of his time in preparing a new section designed to supply the electors with the information of the doings of the council. Jones's version of Section 15 reads:

> It shall be the duty of the Council of the Reserve to publish the Minutes of each meeting of the Council in some newspaper published in

> the neighbourhood of the Reserve, or otherwise, for the information of the electors, and the expenses connected with such publication shall be paid out of the funds of the tribe.[66]

Even though he had no written contract, Jones considered himself a government consultant. While waiting for a reply on his edits to the Advancement Act, he began working on Macdonald's request for his own ideas on how to design two Indian Acts: one to apply to the so-called civilized bands of eastern Canada, the other to the troublesome bands in the Northwest. The prime minister's original wish had been to grant the franchise to all Aboriginal peoples as part of his lifelong effort to assimilate them into the dominant Canadian culture, but this proved to be impossible. Even though the Electoral Franchise Bill of 1885 limited voting rights to qualified Status Indians residing in the eastern part of Canada, the bill was strongly opposed by Parliament and the public. Following the murder of a government agent who hailed from Ontario at the start of the Northwest Resistance, Aboriginals living in Ontario faced increased discrimination, especially from Jones's fellow Orangemen, even though Dr. Jones and Dr. Oronhyatekha were openly supportive of the actions taken to suppress the Riel rebellion. Oronhyatekha bluntly expressed his sentiments in a letter when he described the uprising as "senseless and wicked."[67] Macdonald needed a separate Northwestern Indian Act to appease public opinion and to help him gain control of land in the West so that he could make it available for new settlers.

Jones spent much time preparing outlines of two Indian Acts and completed the first twelve pages before putting it on hold because, as he later wrote, his work respecting the Advancement Act had not been recognized. Jones responded to a second request by the prime minister in early 1887 when asked to draft a set of questions for the Aboriginal bands with a view to obtaining their wishes regarding future legislation. He forwarded the results to Macdonald's residence at Earnscliffe on 25 June 1887. Receiving no reply, Jones wrote to Joseph Pope, the prime minister's secretary, a month later to request confirmation of receipt of his second report, but it appears that his 25 June letter detailing suitable questions for Grand Council chiefs had never reached Ottawa as it is missing from Sir John A. Macdonald's correspondence files.[68] However, a letter Jones mailed on 28 December 1888 survives and the prime minister's blunt response to his request appears in his marginal note: "My Dear Vt, Will you see what Jones has done for the Dept. He made a report or two, but not I think of much virtue. [signed] JamD."[69]

Dr. Jones's months of concerted effort to make modest improvements to the Indian Act were in vain. The prime minister accepted none of his suggestions, even though they were the progressive views of the Grand Council, intelligent leaders and successful politicians in their own right. What Jones didn't realize was that while Macdonald made great demands on his followers, their only reward was to be greeted by a nod of the head and little else. As his contemporary William F. Maclean observed in *Canadian Magazine*, "Sir John had a wonderful influence over many men ... they served him because they loved him, and because with all his great powers they saw in him their own frailties."[70] Judging from his four decades in power, the technique worked even if it seemed unfair to those like Jones.[71]

Six
Aboriginal Rights Advocate

Soon after becoming head chief, Jones made it his priority to obtain compensation for lands the Mississaugas had owned before they were forced to move to the New Credit reserve. In early nineteenth century, the Crown Lands' Department of the Province of Canada had sold much of the Mississaugas' ancestral lands around Port Credit, Oakville, and Bronte without first obtaining the required surrender document from the band.[1] Band leaders had long complained about the injustice, and no doubt Dr. Jones had learned the details as a child because his late father had kept the books for Joseph Sawyer, head chief of the Mississauga band at the time of the sale.[2]

With access to his father's papers, Jones was in a unique position to advance the claim. He appears to have carried out most of his research into the land claim himself, travelling to government offices in Ottawa and Toronto in order to examine official records and accumulate forceful evidence. He paid lawyers in Brantford and Hamilton $200 for consultations and, as was customary at the time, the band agreed to pay a fee of three percent of the money collected to reimburse him for the time he expended on the claim.[3] Based on his findings, Jones filed a land claim for $68,672, including accrued interest at six percent per annum. He had to calculate the capital and interest payments for each parcel of land based on the date of sale. Though the colonial government had made the transaction some sixty years before Confederation, the matter had been referred to a special commission, which issued a report favouring the New Credit band in 1858. At first, the two new political entities, the Dominion of Canada and the Province of Ontario, denied responsibility for withholding the monies, but Dr. Jones insisted on dealing with the federal Department of Indian Affairs. The department refused, again stating it was a provincial matter, but the British North America Act of 1867 specified that Aboriginal affairs were a federal responsibility. Dr. Jones travelled to Ottawa and presented his case.[4] At the time he was actively campaigning for the Conservative party, and no doubt this helped influence Macdonald to pass the order in council on 30 June 1884, authorizing payment of $68,672 to the capital account of the Mississaugas of the New Credit band. The order in council noted that: "The lands were sold but no record could be found of any of the above amounts having passed to the credit of the Mississauga Band according to a reply received from the Province of Ontario on 6 May 1884."[5]

The funds derived from the sale were credited to the General Revenues of the Province of Upper Canada and not used to settle the valid claim of the Mississaugas. The Department of Finance and the auditor general received copies of the order in council, and the order in council was amended on 8 October 1884 by substituting the words: "that authority be given to transfer the amount above shown to the credit of Indian Funds with a view of the Mississauga Band receiving the benefit thereof and of which they have been so long improperly deprived, and that amount transferred shall be included amongst the items of account to be considered in the forthcoming settlement between the treasurers of Ontario and Quebec respectively and the Dominion of Canada."[6]

Unbeknownst to Dr. Jones, the Department of Finance did not accept the transfer of these funds to the Mississaugas on the basis of the order in council. As a result, the money was never officially transferred from the government's general account to the Department of Indian Affairs. The auditor general agreed with the Department of Finance's opinion, but did not actively pursue the matter. As the prime minister was also the superintendent of Indian Affairs, the department followed his orders and began making interest payments on this additional capital, believing that the actual transfer of funds had taken place.[7]

Curiously, although Dr. Jones's three percent commission was approved by the Band Council of which he was a member and head chief, the Department of Indian Affairs declined to release the money in spite of repeated requests. Always short of funds to support his family and keep his stepsons at school in Toronto, Jones wrote an urgent personal letter to the prime minister, followed by a telegram stating: "Creditors with judgment threatening execution. Relieve my mind respecting requisition. P.E. Jones."[8] The appeal was effective. The Band Council signed the required requisition to the Department of Indian Affairs, and shortly afterwards Jones received a cheque for $2,000. He later wrote: "With this money, we paid most of our debts and built a farm house upon the reserve."[9] In future Jones would be able to spend more time on the farm.

His wife Charlotte, however, preferred to live in Hagersville to be close to her sister Drusella.

Following Macdonald's death in 1891, the Department of Indian Affairs was reorganized by the Hon. Thomas Mayne Daly, who was appointed to the Cabinet as minister of the interior, which meant he served as well as superintendent general of Indian Affairs.[10] Daly was a westerner with experience in managing Aboriginal problems in the North-west. His first goal was to enforce the Conservative government's effort to reduce costs after the economic downturn of 1893. Duncan C. Scott, then the departmental accountant, scrutinized the ledgers and found Dr. Jones's $68,672 land claim, which had been paid in 1884. The settlement was summarily cancelled, and the capital reclaimed along with compound interest for the eight years, which amounted to $29,161. A total of $97,000 was removed from the band's capital account in the Indian trust fund. Now Scott's ledger agreed with the books of the Department of Finance, and the auditor general was satisfied.[11] The one-time infusion of new capital into their trust fund had nearly doubled their annual interest payments, which, apart from modest sales of timber, accounted for the community's sole source of revenue.[12] The Mississaugas were distraught because their chief and Band Council were now hard-pressed to maintain what had been regarded as a model Aboriginal community up to that point. Aboriginal bands used their interest money wisely, first supporting essential community services such public health, education, and providing pensions for widows and the disabled, before distributing the residue to individual members. Sadly, in his last report as Indian agent in 1896, Dr. Jones was to write:

> For many years the members of this band had considered that they had a claim against the Government for a large sum of money, as a result of the sale of their reserves at Port Credit, Oakville and Bronte. During the past year the case was laid before the Dominion and Provincial Board of Arbitrators, and the matter was argued at Quebec in November 1895. The decision was against the Indians' claim, and as a consequence, the capital account of this band has been reduced about one-half.[13]

Aboriginal bands were allowed to send representatives to the Quebec City meeting of the board of arbitrators charged with evaluating claims in dispute between the Dominion of Canada and the provinces, but because they were unable to retain their own lawyer, the New Credit

Band Council had been forced to rely on a hastily appointed government lawyer, who had no time to prepare their case. In the end the arbitrators rejected their claim. The report of the deputy superintendent general smugly noted that "the arbitrators in this gave judgment adverse to the Indians, and, while it may have been a great disappointment to them, it showed them that no further hopes, in the way of recovering anything on their claim, should be entertained."[14]

The Mississaugas of the New Credit stood their ground, however, and the Band Council voted to contest the arbitration board's decision. On Dr. Jones's advice, the band hired someone who had successfully negotiated the claim of the Oneidas of the River Thames reserve. Jones turned over all the relevant supporting evidence to John Chechock, a fellow member of the Mississaugas of the New Credit First Nation, who would work with the new negotiator. Additional negotiators became involved with the result that there was more discussion about how much they would be paid than about what they were planning to do to help the band reverse the arbitration board's decision.[15] Dr. Jones found himself in the peculiar position of being a paid agent of the Department of Indian Affairs and forced to defend the department's position in the dispute. Many years later he recalled the events in a letter to the superintendent general of Indian Affairs: "While most deeply interested in the case for the plaintiffs! I thought this matter should be further attended to, but did not wish to appear as Principal in the movement."[16] Jones found himself caught between his loyalty to the members of his own band and his loyalty to his oath to follow the orders of his employer, the government of Canada. The band's second appeal fell on deaf ears, but Jones continued to press the Mississaugas' land claims by providing interested parties with important documents he had acquired over the years. On 4 March 1899, he sent Miss Catherine Merritt, a member of the family who built the Welland Canal, two recently published government books that he had found on a visit to Ottawa. These revealed that government officials were well aware of the Mississaugas' treaty rights and had failed to properly account and pay for the lands acquired:

> What is now called the "Toronto Purchase" shows, I think, a glaring piece of fraud upon the part of the Govt. See No. 13, page 32. In 1787, a blank Indenture of surrender was made and purported to have been signed by three Chiefs. There is no record that any consideration was given to the Indians. Then after 18 years, in 1805 along came another batch of white men and by showing the unfinished

> surrender, paying 10 shillings, and no doubt a keg of rum, get the three living Chiefs to sign an absolute surrender! Toronto you will see is in this valuable tract.[17]

The Mississaugas of the New Credit Band Council had lost faith in the board of arbitrators most of which were stalled by underlying federal/provincial conflicts that they had no power to adjudicate.[18] Many years later a research report commissioned by the federal government, entitled *A History of Native Claims Processes in Canada, 1867–1979*, would conclude that Aboriginal bands had little opportunity to influence the manner in which claims were presented or argued.[19]

In 1884, Macdonald had most likely agreed to sponsor Jones's proposed New Credit financial settlement because he wished to have his support once the Aboriginals were granted the vote. The country's two political parties were fighting over control of voter qualifications and the boundaries of individual ridings in federal elections.[20] The Constitution Act of 1867 stated that provincial laws governing the election of members of Parliament would prevail until the Parliament of Canada otherwise provided.[21] The prime minister, the principal father of Confederation, was very interested in this issue, and in 1885, the Electoral Franchise Bill would replace provincial voting lists with those prepared by the federal government, thus promoting Macdonald's dream of a strong central government. Following the American Civil War, he had become wary of any political process that vested great power in individual provinces at the expense of the federal government.[22] Five federal elections were held under provincial franchise, but when certain provinces disenfranchised federal employees, they interfered with the Conservative party's patronage appointments. The politically savvy prime minister also knew that he could not win the next election with voters lists prepared by the provinces, most of which were controlled by the Opposition and skewed in their favour. The federal government wanted to establish electoral boundaries in a manner advantageous to them and saw an opportunity to increase Conservative support by extending the franchise to the Status Indians of eastern Canada.

During a divisive debate on the merits of the Franchise Bill, Macdonald insisted that the Bill state that an Indian shall not be excluded from the definition of the word "person."[23] This was a rebuke directed at those who clung to the belief that Indians were not people because they were biologically inferior. William Paterson, a brilliant orator much respected by the Iroquois, replied: "I think we must conclude that by this provision of the Bill it is not intended to uplift the Indian in the social scale. If his [Macdonald] desire is to benefit the Indians, let him give them greater facilities for them to attain the full status of their rights and liberties."[24] Macdonald immediately stood up and expressed his dismay that the proposal to put the word "person" in the bill would result in what he called the blatant indignation of the Opposition party and move them to make such an exhibition of themselves in discussing the question of whether or not an Indian is a person. Importantly, the prime minister also emphasized an oft-forgotten point:

> The annuities paid to the different bands are their own monies and they go to them as their right. Their lands have been sold; the proceeds have been funded at a certain rate of interest, which the government pays; and the Indian has the same right to his annual payment out of that fund as if he were a shareholder in a bank receiving a dividend.[25]

In the debate that followed, David Mills, who was coordinating the Liberal filibuster of the Electoral Franchise Act, had strong words for the prime minister. He implied that Macdonald had paid the Mississaugas of the New Credit land claim in order to curry favour with future Aboriginal voters. He had looked into the matter carefully and tabled a demand that the government furnish him with a list of all payments made to Dr. Jones in the previous four years. In harsh words he accused Macdonald of paying the Aboriginal peoples' claim in order to ensure that when they obtained the right to vote, they would help insure the election of the Conservative government's candidates. This would be particularly important in ridings such as South Brant, which encompassed the large Six Nations territory, as Macdonald's fiercest critic, Liberal MP William Paterson, represented this riding.[26]

The Liberals fought the Franchise Bill tooth and nail. In May 1885, they advertised for men willing to solicit signatures for their petition against the Bill. Men were offered $1 a day, for which they were expected to procure about six hundred signatures. This was no mean feat given the small population of most towns at the time. In Parliament, David Mills, the Opposition's critic, was waiting to pounce, remarking that "The Hon. Gentleman is perfectly willing to give the Indian the vote, to treat him in this particular as a white man, so long as he will vote the Tory ticket."[27] A journalist and law professor, Mills was well aware of the definition of a person. He was also not hostile to Aboriginal peoples. In fact, he had served as the Cabinet minister in charge of Indian Affairs when the

Liberals had been in power, and he later rose in the House to condemn the execution of Louis Riel against the wishes of other Ontario Liberals.[28]

In the same month, an article in *The Toronto Mail* cited Dr. Jones as a strong advocate of the Indian voting Franchise Bill.[29] In nineteenth-century Canada newspapers were widely read even though they were small in size. *The Mail* proudly proclaimed that it had twelve pages. At that time, daily papers carried few advertisements so they could not be influenced by business interests threatening to place their ads elsewhere if they failed to praise their products. A daily paper could survive on subscriptions of $1 per year. The presses derived their support from readers interested in the objectives of the political party they fearlessly supported. In Toronto, *The Globe* was fiercely Liberal and *The Mail* Tory, so the publication of Dr. Jones's opinion in *The Mail* can be regarded as an early piece of Aboriginal political writing. It is interesting to see how Peter Edmund skilfully used the text of his father's 1843 submission to Sir John Bagot's commission of inquiry into Indian affairs in support of granting Status Indians the franchise. Jones wrote:

> Indians at the present time enjoy no political rights or advantages. They cannot vote ... nor act as jurors; however qualified they may be, simply because they have no deeds for their lands. I feel confident that these things act as a powerful check on their advancement in the arts of civilized life.... I know of no legal impediment to their possessing such rights; the difficulty lies in the tenure by which they hold their lands.[30]

Dr. Jones observed that his father did not suggest that land titles be conferred individually on Aboriginal peoples but rather on the tribe as a whole with provisions for individual families. Despite the wonderful progress of the Indians living in eastern Canada, he complained they were still waiting for the right to vote in federal elections. Emboldened by the article in *The Toronto Mail*, Jones bravely attended political meetings in various southern Ontario towns. He soon realized that a Bill offering qualified "Indians" the vote would be a hard sell because all the towns were Liberal strongholds where the notion of granting the vote to Aboriginals was anathema. Jones himself was always the only Aboriginal face in the audience and would record the proceedings with particular attention to the speeches of Opposition members.

On 22 May 1885, Jones's rebuttal was published in *The Toronto Mail* under the heading: "The Indian Franchise, Views of a Head Chief on the Current Topic." Perhaps because Jones was a physician trained in anatomy, the editor added: "He Dissects Grit [Liberal] Meetings and Exposes the Falsehoods of Grit Speeches, His Defence of the Indian."[31] Dr. Jones's differential diagnosis consisted of responses to several hypothetical criticisms. He responded to the Opposition's claim that granting Indians the vote was a political dodge to get rid of certain Liberal members of Parliament whom the government feared. This, Jones stated, was untrue as the prime minister had told the Opposition in Parliament that he also planned to grant voting rights to Status Indians living in the Northwest. Responding to the claim that because "Indians" received interest money, they would be dependent politically on Indian agents and therefore obliged to vote for the government, Jones made it plain that their interest monies were derived from the sale of their lands at below market prices. Jones also tackled the often-heard criticism that Aboriginal

Figure 10 Sir John A. Macdonald in 1883, the year he first tabled the [Indian] Franchise Bill. Following two years of rancorous debates and filibusters, Status Indians acquired voting rights. (*Source:* Courtesy of Topley Studio and Library and Archives Canada, Reference no. C-005332)

peoples don't pay taxes, particularly because in the nineteenth century, the government's only sources of revenue were from customs duties, excise fees, the Post Office, and land sales. Jones countered: "Every particle of dutiable goods and every postage stamp we have bought since Confederation has been a tax."[32]

The Electoral Franchise Act was finally passed at one o'clock in the morning of 4 July 1885.[33] It had been a long battle: briefly introduced in 1883, the Bill had been tabled in 1884, but was withdrawn before it could be criticized. Macdonald had tabled it once more in 1885, superseding an urgent Bill calling for the relief of the Canadian Pacific Railroad Company. The prime minister even considered the introduction of closure to end the rancorous debate in the House of Commons.[34] The prime minister was not nicknamed "Old Tomorrow" without reason. He deliberately held up discussion until just before vacation time so that members of Parliament would have to choose between passing his Bill or remaining in Ottawa during the summer months.[35] This Electoral Franchise Act granted the federal vote to all adult male Aboriginals in eastern Canada without the loss of their existing rights as Status Indians. In his insightful biography of Canada's great statesman, Richard Gwyn praises Sir John's "imaginative initiative that extended a kind of citizenship-plus to Indians."

The Liberals had not been alone in their opposition to the Franchise Act. The Six Nations considered themselves a sovereign nation, and many of their members did not wish to vote. Some traditional members of other eastern Canadian bands, including the Mississaugas, also regarded the Electoral Franchise Act with suspicion. Would it bring assessors to register qualified voters who would then be subject to municipal or provincial property taxes? To clarify these issues for his people before the election, Jones decided to write the prime minister and tell him that many of the Aboriginal peoples had been told that if they were to vote, they would endanger their treaty rights. They had also been told that the granting of voting rights was a scheme to impose direct taxation upon them. These claims had succeeded in inducing many Aboriginals to vote against the government or not to vote at all. The prime minister was urged to express his opinion on these two subjects immediately.[36] Politics were Macdonald's forte, and Jones was sure he would wish to handle this matter himself.

Jones's fears were soon realized. On 12 August a grand picnic was held on the Six Nations' reserve in aid of Saint Paul's church. During the afternoon Iroquois delicacies, prepared by the ladies' committee, were laid out on long tables. The Six Nations brass band kept everyone entertained until the picnic's main event was announced. Liberal and Conservative members of Parliament were to debate the New Franchise Act for the enlightenment of the Six Nations, who had always resisted federal government interference in their traditional affairs. Liberal MP William Paterson, a former Brantford mayor well liked by the Iroquois, was the most eloquent. Sympathetic to Aboriginal concerns, he had opposed the Franchise Act because he believed that Aboriginals would not benefit from the vote. His most powerful argument was the suggestion that the Act had the potential to endanger Aboriginal treaty rights. Nothing could be more important to the hereditary chiefs of the Six Nations, or any other First Nation, than the treaty rights to their lands.

Even though he was not a member of the Six Nations, Dr. Jones had been invited to express a vote of thanks to the speakers. Speaking in English, he noted that the Grand Council had supported the right to vote. Warrior Hill then spoke in Mohawk to second Jones's motion of thanks, which was carried amid wild cheering. *The Toronto Mail* published a detailed account of the event. It had been prepared by their own correspondent, who supported the government, as one might expect from a strongly Conservative paper.[37] The last Conservative speaker warmly congratulated the Indians on their rise to the rank of citizen. Paterson objected, but, according to this biased account, was shouted down and accused of telling a friend that "the Indians were a lazy lot; they will go fishing but won't work and will sit on the fence and boss the squaw."[38] Fortunately, few if any Aboriginal peoples read *The Toronto Mail*. This scurrilous remark had no effect, and in the subsequent election Paterson was re-elected.[39]

At the end of August, Macdonald picked up his pen and wrote a four-page personal letter to Jones to declare that "The object I had in extending the privilege of the franchise to the Indians was to place them on a footing of equality with their white brethren."[40] The Franchise Act had been in force for a year, and the Indians must have observed that their treaty rights had not been affected in the slightest since it became law. Jones was instructed to reassure his people that the Franchise Act would not in any way affect or injure the rights secured to them by treaty or by the laws relating to the "Red men of the Dominion." Macdonald hoped that someday the "Indian Race" would be represented by one of themselves on the floor of the House of Commons. Until then they should vote for White men who would, of course, attend to their interests in Parliament or risk not being re-elected by the "Indians."[41]

Jones pursued the matter by inviting the prime minister to attend the September meeting of the Grand General Indian Council, which was to be held on the Saugeen reserve near Southampton on the shores of Lake Huron.[42] He knew well that most of the more moderate Ojibwe (Anishinabek) bands expected to attend would support the Franchise Act. Macdonald, however, had already scheduled a visit to the thirty-six-hundred-member Six Nations band near Brantford in the hope of garnering support for the new Indian Voting Franchise Act. He was to be disappointed because the spokesmen for the Six Nations, speaking in Mohawk, flatly denounced the measure. The hereditary chiefs who governed the Six Nations also condemned the Indian Advancement Act of 1884, which introduced elected municipal Band Councils.[43]

Despite disparate views on the major issues, Dr. Jones continued to work toward harmonious relations between the Six Nations and the Mississaugas of the New Credit. When tensions arose over land ownership in 1886, Jones took steps to help settle the conflict. The Mississaugas' occupation of their territory was in question because they had settled there in 1847 on land given to the Six Nations, who had fought for Britain in the American Revolution. The Mississaugas had been forced to give up their own land on the shores of the River Credit to the settlers and had nowhere else to go. The Six Nations permitted the Mississaugas to occupy 2,000 hectares, but as their agricultural skills improved, the Mississaugas began to farm an additional 400 hectares. At a council of the Six Nations held in 1865, David Sawyer, then chief of the Mississaugas, admitted that his band had no written agreement beyond a verbal assurance from the council of the Six Nations granting the land. He wanted to obtain a confirmation in writing. Chief John Smoke Johnson was the Grand Council's speaker and, after a fitting reference to the old minutes, which had been read, he agreed that the Mississaugas were quite right to bring their case before the council. The old chief spoke at some length to the historical recollections of their respective peoples and the lands they had previously occupied. He noted that the Six Nations had left New York state and travelled westward after finding insufficient land near the Bay of Quinte. The Six Nations acknowledged that the Mississaugas' lands had once extended from the head of Lake Ontario to the River Thames. Though the occupancy of the additional 400 hectares was not confirmed in writing, Johnson and some of the older chiefs present remembered the oral evidence well. The Six Nations council unanimously reaffirmed its agreement for the 400 hectares.[44] The official from Indian Affairs had quietly sat through the three-day meeting, but he finally said the chiefs had acted justly and wisely as usual and it was only right that the Mississaugas should understand that the lands they had occupied so long were secure for them and their successors. He noted that the lands were to be enjoyed by members of the band and could not be sold without the consent of the Six Nations.[45]

When Dr. Jones became New Credit's head chief, he wrote the Six Nations council, asking if the Mississaugas of the New Credit could be regarded as proprietors of their lands located in the southwest corner of the Six Nations reserve rather than just occupants.[46] By this time, however, the population of the Six Nations had risen to the point where they could no longer provide farms for their own members. They had also lost money on investments, including the now-bankrupt Grand River Navigation Company. Investigation showed that the Mississaugas had not made their promised payment for the improvements made by the former occupants of their farms, such as erecting fences, constructing shelters, and clearing the land they received in 1847. The Six Nations now expected them to pay this account.[47]

The Six Nations had been granted their lands by the Haldimand Proclamation of 1784 "In Consideration of [their] early Attachment to His Majesties Cause." The scholarly writings of Sally Weaver justify their request for the repayment of a portion of the monies they had paid out in 1844 to European squatters, in order to evict them from their territory. Having cleared small patches of land and built log houses, the squatters did not wish to leave the farms they had worked so hard to improve. They appealed to the courts, which failed to recognize the legitimate interests of the Six Nations, so they were forced to reimburse the squatters. Some £8,000 ($32,000) came out of their band funds; the chiefs did not actively force their members to pay their share of the eviction costs.[48]

Funds were short, tempers flared, and the Six Nations Band Council sent a letter in October 1886, giving the Mississaugas notice to leave their reserve by 1 November 1887. Jones immediately wrote his mentor, Sir John A. Macdonald, asking him to use his influence and persuade the Six Nations to drop the matter. Jones claimed that certain Six Nations members were anxious to use the controversy to take over the comfortable homes his band had established over the years. He wondered why the claim had lain dormant for forty years. He also raised the spectre of politics, pointing to the fact that their member of Parliament, William Paterson, was a prominent Liberal. Sir John solved both problems with a single stroke: He separated the Mississauga and Six Nations' agencies and appointed Dr. Jones as the first Indian agent to be placed in charge of the New Credit band.[49]

The deadline for the Mississaugas to vacate the land passed uneventfully, but in an attempt to force a decision, the Six Nations council convened a meeting of the two bands in their Council House in 1889. The traditional opening by the speaker of the Fire Keepers included a warm welcome for the deputation from the Mississaugas of the New Credit.[50] The senior government official present was Superintendent Cameron, of the Brantford Indian office. He stated that the Six Nations' demands were simply that the Mississaugas should fulfill the decision of their forefathers. Agent Jones then addressed the conference, reminding those present that when his band had moved to the New Credit reserve in 1847, Chiefs Joseph Sawyer and Reverend Jones desired that the Six Nations take a monetary payment so that their occupancy of the reserve might be more than a gift. This did not mean that they were afraid of the current generation, but they feared trouble might possibly arise thereafter. Dr. Jones then impressed his audience by drawing a parallel between the 1847 transaction and that related in the twenty-third chapter of Genesis. When his wife Sarah died, Abraham, who was a stranger in the land, asked the local people to sell him a burial site. Holding him in high regard as a man of God, they offered to give him the land, but Abraham insisted that he pay four hundred shekels of silver, the value the Hittites had placed on the land. As a result, Sarah was buried in a cave in Machpelah, facing Hebron in Canaan.[51]

The population of the Six Nations was thirteen times greater than the Mississaugas, who were invited to assimilate and become one people. The government favoured this approach because it would reduce operating costs. The superintendent noted that there had been significant intermarriage between the two bands. The alternatives proposed by the Six Nations were either to pay the money owed with accrued interest or pay for the land at its assessed value. Otherwise, they threatened to surrender the land to the Crown. The Mississaugas would have to deal with the government then.[52]

The Mississauga Band Council felt that it was neither proper nor in good taste to leave the great Ojibwe nation to which they belonged, and Jones emphatically presented this view. The Ojibwe language was completely different, and the New Credit's Band Council was composed of elected, rather than hereditary, chiefs. The loss of interest money would be a severe financial blow, and the relatively small size of their band meant that they would have little influence on the amalgamated council. Dr. Jones said the Mississaugas of the New Credit were prepared to pay the Six Nations $10,000 for a full discharge of all liabilities and for a clear deed of the land they occupied. What was important was the brotherly spirit that existed among Aboriginals; a serious dispute would lower their race in the estimation of Euro-Canadians. Jones complimented the Six Nations on their friendly report and concluded by encouraging the councillors to do all in their power to come to an amicable settlement.[53]

Despite Jones's eloquence, the matter dragged on. A June 1892 government report showed that the situation had deteriorated.[54] It seemed unlikely that anything less than the surrender of the lands would satisfy the Six Nations, but this outcome would involve payment of a large sum to the Mississaugas to cover the value of the improvements they had made to the over 2,400 hectares they occupied. Dr. Jones and the Band Council had worked hard to improve reserve conditions. They built roads and bridges, renovated the Methodist church, and constructed a brick Council House, complete with a gallery and imposing chandeliers. If the Mississaugas surrendered their farms, the land would have to be sold to members of the Six Nations, but as the people were poor, the cost would ultimately be taken from the capital in the trust fund of their band. The resulting reduction in annual interest payments would be a serious matter for every member of the Six Nations. To assess the consequences, government officials recommended that the actual value of the improvements be determined in the hope that it would precipitate an agreement. The Six Nations and Mississauga councils continued to exchange letters and hold joint meetings over the next few years. It was, as most land claims are, a complicated business, but Aboriginal peoples have a long history of peacefully dividing hunting grounds. In 1903, the council of the Six Nations generously voted to accept the $10,000 Jones had first offered in 1889.[55]

Seven
Canada's First Aboriginal Publisher

The urgent need to inform Aboriginals on the reserves of their right to vote and encourage them to register with election officers gave Dr. Jones the motivation he needed to launch his newspaper. He dedicated it to the interests of all the Aboriginals of North America, especially the Aboriginal peoples of Canada.[1] Prior to the arrival of the Europeans, Aboriginal peoples had a communication system covering much of the continent. By establishing an Aboriginal newspaper, Dr. Jones was revitalizing his band's tradition in which runners carried these messages.[2] The Mississaugas living at the foot of the "Carrying Place," now Toronto, were responsible for transmitting information about the fur trade on the Great Lakes. One of their wampum belts, featuring an eagle perched on a pine tree beside the Credit River, even represents the band's "watching and swiftness in carrying messages."[3]

Aboriginal media was a means to unite the various bands. The first Aboriginal newspaper in North America had been the *Cherokee Phoenix*, a weekly published by the Cherokee Nation's council in 1828. Cleverly formatted, it featured adjacent columns in English and in Cherokee syllabic text.[4] The editor hoped to unite the scattered tribes by providing news, editorials, official notices, short works of fiction, and articles encouraging the "arts of civilized life."[5] At the time, the Cherokees faced exile from their ancestral lands in Georgia and surrounding states to the wilderness west of the Mississippi in what would become Oklahoma. The Indian Removal Act of 1830 divided the Cherokee population. Although many were adamant against being uprooted, others favoured negotiation as the government demanded. The newspaper became increasingly supportive of the resistance movement and, reflecting this position, its name was changed to the *Cherokee Phoenix and Indian Advocate*. The newspaper was successful in eliciting widespread public support for the plight of the Cherokee Nation in many parts of the United States and abroad.

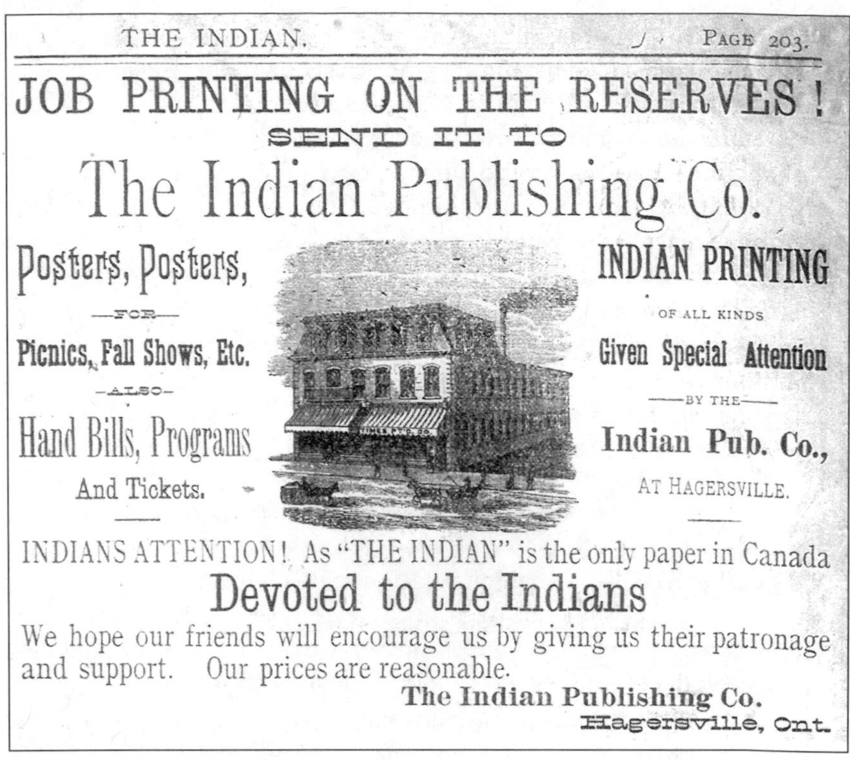
THE INDIAN. PAGE 203.

JOB PRINTING ON THE RESERVES!

SEND IT TO

The Indian Publishing Co.

Posters, Posters,

—FOR—

Picnics, Fall Shows, Etc.

—ALSO—

Hand Bills, Programs

And Tickets.

INDIAN PRINTING

OF ALL KINDS

Given Special Attention

—BY THE—

Indian Pub. Co.,

AT HAGERSVILLE.

INDIANS ATTENTION! As "THE INDIAN" is the only paper in Canada

Devoted to the Indians

We hope our friends will encourage us by giving us their patronage and support. Our prices are reasonable.

The Indian Publishing Co.

Hagersville, Ont.

Figure 11 The Indian Publishing Company as pictured in advertisements placed in their newspaper. (Source: Courtesy of the Toronto Reference Library)

The speeches of US senators condemning the government's "Indian removal policy"—including those by the fiery orator Daniel Webster—were printed verbatim. Local officials decided that the *Cherokee Phoenix* had to be silenced, and a Georgia guard unit destroyed the press in 1834. In 1838, after the thousands of Cherokees opposing removal signed a petition, the United States army entered Cherokee territory, took the protesters captive, and started the infamous "Trail of Tears," the sixteen-hundred-kilometre march to what is now Oklahoma, during which some four thousand men, women, and children perished.[6]

While Dr. Jones probably was not looking to foster violent resistance to government, he did want to provide a forum for communication among Aboriginal peoples that would encourage political participation. The Indian Act had segregated his people on isolated reserves, effectively blocking any communication that could inspire organized resistance, and as the first Aboriginal paper in the Dominion of Canada, Jones's work tried to overcome this disadvantage. Prime Minister Macdonald believed his tough policy was succeeding, as proven by the progress made by the Six Nations and the Mississaugas of the New Credit bands. He believed that they could soon safely be allowed more freedom under his government's program of "tutelage," while other Canadian Aboriginals, especially in the Northwest, would continue to be treated like children.[7] Macdonald never made good on this promise, however. The Six Nations and Mississaugas of the New Credit remained firmly under the thumb of their Indian agent. If the prime minister or one of his many deputies had attended even one Grand Council of Ontario meeting, he may have realized that a great many bands had made significant progress and that their leaders were sophisticated adults, but Jones knew that the time had come to work toward educating his people and acquiring more political

Box 1 Prospectus of *The Indian*, 30 December 1885

"A paper devoted to the interests of the Aborigines of North America, and especially to the Indians of Canada"

1 To be a bi-monthly paper until the subscription justifies a weekly issue.

2 To furnish news from the Indian reserves in Canada and the United States.

3 To publish a general epitome of news from all parts of the world.

4 A thorough discussion from time to time of the legislation respecting Indians.

5 Correspondence upon subjects affecting the affairs of Indians.

6 Statistics as to the financial and other conditions of the Indian Bands.

7 Biographical sketches of noted Indians' characters, past and present.

8 Papers and correspondence upon American archaeology.

9 Editorial articles in the Ojibway and Mohawk languages.

10 Reports of the Grand General Indian Council and other meetings of Indians.

11 Sketches of Indian history and more, especially of the tribes of Canada.

12 If found practicable, a continued story upon an Indian subject.

13 Notes upon hunting, fishing and the game laws and a market report of fish, furs and game. With natural history sketches of the fur bearing animals and game fish as observed by Indian hunters.

14 Notes upon agriculture and religion.

influence. His paper, *The Indian*, would enable the widely scattered reserves to communicate with each other and meet these new challenges.

Jones travelled to Toronto in hopes that *The Toronto Mail*, the Conservative party organ, would supply its weekly edition to the Aboriginal reserves at no cost.[8] When this effort failed, he had no alternative but to go it alone. Jones contacted the prime minister's office and Conservative party officials, seeking financial support and help from government departments and advertisers. Members of the Liberal Opposition kept themselves well informed about his plan to make Aboriginal peoples aware of the importance of exercising their newly acquired voting rights. The Liberals violently opposed the idea; they feared a change in the status quo because they already controlled the ridings close to the Ontario reserves. William Paterson, the Liberal member of Parliament for South Brant whose riding encompassed the Six Nations reserve, feared interference by Dr. Jones. On 9 November 1885, Jones published his prospectus along with an advertising poster, which noted that the newspaper's editor would be Chief Kahkewaquonaby M.D., the secretary of the Grand General Indian Council.[9] The Liberal Opposition decided to attack Dr. Jones before he had the opportunity to print the first issue of his newspaper. The very next day this scurrilous article appeared in their official newspaper, *The Toronto Globe*:

> Chief Kah-ke-wa-quo-na-by, alias Dr. Jones of Hagersville, an almost full-blooded white, announces that a paper to be known as *The Indian* is about to be published. Presumably Chief Kah-ke, &c., is to be the editor, and presumably therefore, the organ will be Tory. The fact that a journal is to be published in the interest of the Indians will be hailed with pleasure. That it is launched clearly with the object of capturing the Indian vote is no doubt true.[10]

The words "an almost full-blooded white," coming from an editor who knew very well that Jones bore unmistakable signs of his race, would signal the first of many petty attacks by the Opposition's press. Eventually these oft-repeated aspersions got to Jones, who had been raised as a proud Status Indian, and he wrote Macdonald: "You have noticed how the *Globe* and its followers are treating me. I feel myself able to cope with them, but not with the apathy of a party who should give me a whole solid support and tangible assistance."[11]

Enthusiasm is a powerful force, however, and Jones was not to be deterred. On 30 December 1885, the first edition of *The Indian* appeared on the newsstands. It was the birth of Canadian Aboriginal journalism, the pioneer of the host of Canadian Aboriginal newspapers in the years to follow. Jones proudly maintained a high standard for his newspaper. It was quite free of typographical errors, and the quality of the prose met Victorian standards. On the front page of the first issue of *The Indian*, he welcomed his Aboriginal readers:

> Upon sending out the first number of a newspaper it is usual for the editor to tell his readers the reason he has for printing such a journal. This we will try to do in as few words and in as plain language as we can reasonably use. It will be the first object of this paper to strive, with what means and ability we may have, to educate the Indians and by advice and suggestion, to elevate them step by step to the same position in the social, agricultural, and commercial world, which is now enjoyed by their White brethren. We are well aware that the White population has the advantage over us of many centuries in the march of progress and civilization. We appreciate the example set by them to us in their many proper habits and customs. The principal changes they have established are—Christian Religion, Agriculture and Industry. These then will be strongly advocated and urged by *The Indian*.[12]

The third page included an editorial in Ojibwe, but the most important of the paper's objectives, set forth in the prospectus (see Box 1), would be to provide a thorough discussion of legislation respecting Aboriginal peoples.[13] The terms of the act granting Status Indians in eastern Canada who met the qualifications voting rights would be clearly explained. Hamilton barrister Edward Furlong was one of Jones's long-time supporters, and he contributed explanations of the Indian Act and the workings of the electoral system.[14] Although Jones did not forcefully encourage the teaching of Aboriginal languages, he tirelessly persuaded readers to submit articles and poems in their native tongue. Since few of his readers could write, he had limited success, but was able to reprint hymns translated by his late father.[15] *The Indian* is, therefore, very different from contemporary Aboriginal publications, which often make a point of demonstrating their linguistic traditions. The publication included little in the way of Ojibwe or Mohawk texts, and nothing was written in Cree.[16]

In his bid for excellence, Jones enlisted the help of the intellectual elite such as Professor Daniel Wilson, principal of Toronto University, and James Bain Jr., the founding librarian of the Toronto Public Library. Anthropologist and archaeologist David Boyle, the curator of the

Canadian Institute (a forerunner of the Royal Ontario Museum), became an enthusiastic supporter. He contributed a learned article in which he pleaded that traditional Aboriginal names be retained, noting that the original name of Lake Simcoe was "Toronto" or "Deonda." He thought it was marvellous that Niagara Falls had escaped the "Europeanizing craze."[17] The paper also reprinted an appeal from Reverend Dr. Henry Scadding, a noted historian and president of the Pioneer Association of Ontario, a group promoting the preservation of original Aboriginal and French names.[18] The paper featured learned articles on American archaeology and Aboriginal artifacts, and Jones commented that "just now this subject is greatly occupying the attention of Canadian scientists and it is hoped the columns of the *Indian* will be freely used to encourage this good work."[19] The articles pleaded with Aboriginal peoples to turn over artifacts of their early civilizations to David Boyle in Toronto. This was an urgent matter; numerous artifacts from southern Ontario were being bought up by American and European collectors, including Andrew Carnegie and the Smithsonian Institution. The Aboriginals, especially the Iroquois of the Six Nations, co-operated as they wished to prove that their territory was located on land long occupied by Aboriginal peoples. Charles A. Hirschfelder of Toronto, an archaeologist who collected prehistoric Aboriginal artifacts like Jones and his father, contributed a three-part article entitled "Gi-Ye-Wa-No-Us-Qua-Go-Wa," Iroquoian for "The Sacrifice of the White Dog." Six Nations Chief George H.M. Johnson had invited him to observe the sacred festival marking the event and served as his translator, ensuring that the description was accurate.[20] The actual name of this festival literally means "the most excellent faith" or "the supreme belief." The Iroquois believe that in ancient days there was a covenant made by their forefathers with the Great Spirit to the effect that every year they should sacrifice a white dog. White is the emblem of purity and goodwill so that by sending up the animal's spirit, the Iroquois acknowledge their faith and loyalty to the Great Spirit, who would open his ears and hear their petition. The dog was probably selected because of his great fidelity to man and his companionship in the chase—he would be the most trustworthy animal to carry their petitions. Today the live animal has been replaced by a symbolically decorated basket.[21]

With a political organizer as loyal as Jones, the prime minister was certainly keen to support the new paper, and federal bureaucrats were asked to provide essential assistance by placing advertisements for public works. It made scant difference that the ads were calls for tenders to deliver provisions to Mounted Police posts in the Northwest or build a railway on Cape Breton.[22] Those placing the ads seemed blissfully unaware that Aboriginal peoples were not permitted to work for the railways or the post office and were offered only menial jobs elsewhere. Their bravery and skill as ironworkers had yet to be appreciated. Jones published both favourable and critical reviews; he was pleased that the Euro-Canadian press took note of his publication. The Opposition party organ, *The Toronto Globe*, was quick to point out the taint of political patronage, however, commenting:

> The first number of the *Indian* has appeared. It is published at Hagersville, and edited by Chief Kahkewaquonaby. The initial number is a creditable one. The supply of federal advertisements is up to the average. A few months will probably determine whether it is to be run in the interests of the aborigines or in the interests of Toryism. And it might be observed that "Old-To-Morrow" [Sir John A. Macdonald] has now as many journals as the country can now afford to support.[23]

The Globe's prediction was correct because articles favourable to the Conservative government appeared in every issue. On 23 June 1886, for example, a column announced a grand Conservative picnic at which the present government would explain why certain Aboriginal peoples had been granted the privilege of voting for members of the Dominion House. The article goes on to say:

> It is a grand thing for our race that the whites have now to come upon our reserves, explain the politics of the country, ask for our support, and promise us their assistance in the management of Indian affairs in Ottawa. The Conservative party who hold this picnic fought hard to give us this right, and the other party fought hard to keep it from us.[24]

The correspondent of the Conservative *Toronto Mail* also submitted a partisan account titled, "An Indian Picnic: A day among the Six Nations on their reserve; the Franchise Act discussed: Speeches by prominent White men from Brantford and by Indian Chiefs." In it, the reporter notes that, "Head Chief Kah-ke-quo-na-by, of the Mississaugas of the New Credit, was warmly welcomed by his red brethren in recognition of his efforts to elevate the Indians in a social scale, and more especially their enfranchisement as citizens."[25]

Although he most certainly did favour Macdonald's Conservatives, Dr. Jones's primary interest was in gaining respect and a modicum of political advantage for his people by helping to elect a sympathetic member of either party. Under the heading "Editorial Notes," he replied to the Opposition party's criticism with humour on 3 March 1886:

> *The Globe* calls the editor of this paper "The Dominion Government's Authorized Franchise Agent Among the Indians." What an extensive title this is! It beats the editor's Indian name all to pieces! The *Indian* with our English name have [*sic*] been long enough, so with the *Globe*'s permission we would suggest an abbreviation. How would this do—H. Chief K.—P.E.J., M.D., T.D.G.A.F.A.A.T.I? It will help us both, in our busy editorial work, to have this distinguished name boiled down.[26]

In the same column, however, Jones went out of his way to encourage his people to vote for good candidates of either party:

> Several of the Indians of the Kettle Point and Stony Reserves have written to say they "strongly object to having anything to do with voting as we do not see that we are to be in any way benefited by it, and further if compelled to vote, we will vote for a Reform or Liberal Government not Tory." ... It is a great pity that these bands of Indians should have obtained the idea that they can be "compelled to vote." Such is not the case. You have the same liberty as a white man. You may vote or not as you wish. You may vote for Tory or Reformer as you see fit. By all means get your names upon the voters list. Who knows but that, by the time another election takes place in your community, a nice Reform or Liberal candidate may be thankful for the assistance you can give him towards election, and for this he will likely promise you that he will pay particular attention to any business you have in Ottawa. Then, if he is an honest man, you have certainly derived a benefit by having a person in Parliament to whom you can very properly appeal in case of necessity.[27]

Dr. Jones's Mohawk colleague, Dr. Oronhyatekha, a strong Tory supporter, also encouraged his fellow Aboriginals to take advantage of the newly won franchise so they might influence both political parties. The 26 May 1886 edition of *The Indian* reported:

> Dr. Oronhyatekha addressed a large meeting of the Mohawk Indians at the Council House, Belleville, on Wednesday of last week, explaining to them the provisions of the new Franchise Act as they affected the Indians. He advised them to form an organization and to work harmoniously and united to make themselves respected by both parties.[28]

The Conservative party's organ *The Toronto Mail* published a very encouraging review, noting that *The Indian* was a "neat publication of twelve pages devoted entirely to the interests of the Indians of this country."[29] Under the header "Hagersville—A Laudable Enterprise," the Anglican journal called the *Churchman* observed, "*The Indian* was devoted chiefly to the interests of our fellow red subjects. Dr. Jones, one of themselves, is editor. He is a skilful practitioner in medicine, and for many years a delegate to the Synod of Niagara." The same review concluded by pointing out that the editor believed the progress of the Aboriginal peoples was very largely due to the missionaries who laboured among them.[30] Dr. Jones supported the missionaries, but was careful to steer clear of favouring a specific denomination.[31] Jones also supported the government-sponsored industrial schools, which were still small and run by the Church in those years. Strict Victorian discipline, the banning of Aboriginal languages, poor nutrition, and exposure to tuberculosis were common, but the expansion of the residential school system and its similar or worse abuses occurred long after Jones's newspaper had ceased publication. Most of the new institutions were located in the recently settled Canadian Northwest.[32] By the advent of the twentieth century when the government's assimilation policy was in full swing, children would be routinely taken from their homes and placed in schools, usually in remote areas. Moreover, they were stripped of their language and culture and frequently suffered physical and sexual abuse. Roughly one-third of Aboriginal children, again mainly from the West and North, attended a residential school. When they eventually went home, they could no longer speak their language, dance, fish, or hunt. They felt isolated from the very people that normally would have nurtured them and suffered greatly.[33]

The New Credit reserve was relatively unique in that the Band Council still had funds derived from the sale of its old reserve and was motivated to support a local school. The Band Council selected the teachers, maintained the building, and encouraged the children to attend. Jones reported that the daily attendance was about forty children, which was quite an accomplishment considering the total population averaged 250 souls.[34] Dr. Jones took his role seriously, checking the sanitary facilities and soliciting a council grant so prizes could be awarded at the end of term. The day school was also inspected annually by an approved educator at the Band Council's expense. Dr. M.J. Kelly, school inspector for the County of Brant, charged the band $14 for his 1894 report.[35] Jones had hoped that some students would proceed to the high school in Hagersville, but this would be a long time in coming. The more populous Six Nations had a dozen day schools, some run in collaboration with various religious denominations.[36]

Jones's support for education manifested itself in his newspaper again and again. One of the paper's stated aims was to publish sketches of Aboriginal history and more especially of the separate "Tribes of Canada." This was a long-time passion of Dr. Jones and a legacy from his father. *The Indian* proudly announced that "the editor possesses one of the largest private Indian Libraries in Canada, containing nearly all the Principal Works of Indian History."[37] There were several articles by Aboriginals and reports from outlying reserves, but the general tenor of the paper was that of White people writing about Aboriginal peoples, often in glorious terms. *The Hamilton Spectator*'s columnist was quick to observe that "the paper before us is full of interest for White readers."[38]

Apart from history and news of current interest, *The Indian* reprinted articles and stories from books published elsewhere. For example, it serialized J. Fenimore Cooper's novel, *The Last of the Mohicans*, a White man's narrative that portrays the "noble savage."[39] This inappropriate choice was probably made by Eliza Jones, who had enjoyed reading the romantic novel in England while awaiting the sea voyage to New York City to marry her future husband.[40] As a heroic account of noble Indians written by a White man, it was unlikely to impress Aboriginal readers forced to live in cramped quarters on reserves. Far more appropriately, each issue of *The Indian* contained an excerpt from Eliza Jones's biography of the renowned Six Nation's leader, Captain Joseph Brant. She used her Ojibwe name, Ke-che-ah-gah-me-qua, as a byline.[41] One edition reprinted an article from *The Ottawa Citizen*, which reported a speech to an Ottawa medical society describing the range of Aboriginal medicine that Peter Edmund's former medical school teacher, Dr. Robert Bell, observed in Canada's northern regions.[42] Though a competent writer, Dr. Jones did not contribute articles on health issues, except for an article entitled: "How Do Indians Know? Indian Medicine and Women," which extolled the wisdom of traditional healers."[43] Jones preferred to write editorials on his pet subject, the Indian Advancement Act of 1884.[44]

Unlike modern Aboriginal newspapers, there were few accounts of traditional foods. In spite of this absence, Jones was also proud that the settlers had borrowed culinary terms such as *succotash* from the Algonquian language, and his mother had often defended the culinary skills of Aboriginal women, saying "they far exceed us in the variety and abundance of the table."[45] A column bearing the one-word heading "Recipes" offered traditional British fare such as rice pudding, ham cooked in cider, cracker barrel apple pie, cold catsup, and steamed bread-and-butter pudding.[46] When receptions or musical evenings were the subject of social reports, the fare included sandwiches and tea rather than traditional Aboriginal food. George S. Conover (Hy-We-Saus), however, contributed a column entitled "Indian Delicacies—Nut Oil, &c." as an indication of how the Aboriginal peoples' domestic economy once used various articles of food "not for sustenance only, but to gratify the palate as well."[47] The article cites early European reports that "the butternut, black walnut and shag bark walnut or hickory nut were much prized by the Indians as articles of food, especially the extracts made from them for seasoning."[48] It goes on to describe the way the Aboriginal peoples prepared the nuts: "They pound in wooden mortars and, boiling the paste in water, collect the oily matter which swims upon the surface, to season their aliments."[49] By publishing these accounts, Dr. Jones employed the new medium of the newspaper to document valuable elements of Aboriginal oral history. His people had survived and were maintaining their cultural identity, albeit in modified form.[50]

The paper regularly carried news items from various reserves throughout Ontario, including both Mohawk and Ojibwe bands. Jones was a politician who was not averse to using the newspaper to advertise his own accomplishments:

> During the past two or three weeks much has been done to beautify the Council House grounds of the Mississaugas of the Credit. A fine gravel pit was found upon the Reserve and opened out. The sidewalks upon each side of the driveway have been covered with six inches of fine gravel, and the circle in front of the Council House and the driveway to the road, have also received a coat, and the approaches to this beautiful council house now looks very neat and tidy.[51]

Despite its diverse content, by the beginning of August, Jones could no longer afford to pay his printer and was forced to take drastic measures. A desperate plea appeared in the next issue: "Having assumed the business management of *The Indian*, we propose to give all our profits away for the first year to reliable energetic canvassers."[52] Jones appears to have been obliged to take over the production side of the paper as he began to solicit orders to print pamphlets, posters, and other items for the bands. He had already hired his stepson, Alph Dixon, to the new post of special agent, and announced that Dixon would visit as many reserves as he could, engaging contributors and establishing a regular network of correspondents.[53] Dixon had some success. Interesting reports were received from both Ojibwe and Mohawk reserves, but Jones's ambitious plans were thwarted by illiteracy on a massive scale. Band documents show that many of the otherwise well-informed and capable farmers on his reserve were still unable to sign their names.[54] *The Indian* was a sophisticated newspaper, published quarto style with its twelve pages bound and beautifully typeset, but, like a typical Victorian journal, it had reprinted articles from Ontario's major cities without making an effort to adapt them in order to reach readers with limited education. It is, therefore, unlikely that this newspaper influenced many Aboriginals to use their newly gained right to vote, despite being distributed to all the reserves in Ontario. Jones claimed to have 15,000 readers, which is doubtful, but he printed sufficient copies to warrant purchasing a steam press.[55]

Perhaps if Dr. Jones had abandoned his political agenda and allied himself with one of the missionary movements, the paper might have been able to survive, as the clergy would have found the paper a useful tool. Perhaps, however, Jones's open mind kept him from taking this step. Writing in the *Haldimand Atlas* of 1879, he had admired traditional "Indian" spirituality, including the practices of "pagan" members of the Six Nations who continued to hold ancient feasts and ceremonies such as the green corn dance and the sacrifice of the white dog. Bravely Jones remarked that many believed that the pagans were superior to Christian Aboriginal peoples in morality and sobriety.[56] The Protestant missionary's son dared to express a surprisingly secular viewpoint:

> The temporal welfare of our people, however, has not had the proper attention. The laws respecting Indians, their rights to lands, their position in respect to treatment and their financial standing with the Government are all subjects which it is the duty of *The Indian* to pay immediate attention to. The worldly affairs of our people must

have the larger part of our attention for several months. Matters of grave importance to our temporal welfare are now before us. We have been granted the privilege to vote (after paying fifty years taxes without it), and now we must make it a study to use this franchise in a proper way.... *The Indian* is the first paper published solely in the interests of our people. We have the franchise now, and must look sharp and quick after our worldly interests as persons fully qualified to take advantage of the privilege due us from the taxes we pay."[57]

Still, in spite of the financial problems, Jones's paper remained a point of pride for the band. On 18 October 1886, four important Cree and Salteaux head chiefs from western Canada visited the New Credit reserve for the inauguration of the Brant memorial in nearby Brantford. These chiefs felt comfortable visiting the Mississaugas, who spoke an Algonquian language like their own.[58] The next morning, Mr. A. McDonald, the Indian agent in charge of the western visitors, called on Dr. Jones in Hagersville and was conducted through the press room of *The Indian*. McDonald later reported: "During their visit to the Six Nations and Mississauga reserves, the visiting chiefs witnessed the progress made by the majority of those Indians in agriculture. They also have seen what education is doing for their brethren in the East."[59]

The Globe, however, then watchdog of the Liberal Opposition party and critical of Jones's newspaper, was thrilled to publish a letter from an Aboriginal chief from Tuscarora of Six Nations, dated 13 February 1886, stating that "the Indians down here do not take much stock in the little doctor's paper or his person," and that the sum of $2,000 had been paid to this Mr. Jones by the Dominion government out of the "Indian Funds" for the express political purpose of establishing the Aboriginal newspaper.[60] Dr. Jones replied that "the Dominion Government had not given him one dollar, much less $2,000, towards the publication of *The Indian.*" Nonetheless, Jones did admit to receiving payment of $2,000 for negotiating the land claims settlement when he became head chief, the agreed fee being three percent of the settlement. The payment was to cover legal fees and other expenses incurred in order to thoroughly examine the documents, and he had spent the money in question long before he had even thought of publishing his newspaper.[61]

As the struggle to finance *The Indian* intensified, however, Dr. Jones seems to have had second thoughts about his initial scruples and allowed advertisements for proprietary medicines to appear in his pages, although he always excluded the purely magic cures promoted by the travelling medicine shows. At first, *The Indian* had carried no advertisements for what are now called over-the-counter and patent medicines. Perhaps the advertisers believed that the Aboriginal readers would not use their products, although vendors of phoney medicines, such as those made by the Kickapoo Indian Medicine Company, carried out a brisk business on the reserves.[62] Their high-powered salesmen found the Aboriginals eager to try the White man's novel medicines even when the cough syrup contained Jamaica rum and New Orleans molasses. In his own practice, Dr. Jones rejected any medication that did not identify the ingredients on the label and prescribed only those listed in an official compendium of drugs or pharmacopoeia. *The United States Pharmacopoeia* (USP) had created a system of standards, quality control, and a national formulary with its foundation in 1820.[63] Only 217 drugs that met the criteria of "most fully established and best understood" were admitted. In Canada, the amended *British Pharmacopoeia* of 1864 was regarded as the standard.[64] Jones explained his willingness to move away from this standard in his paper's advertisements one of *The Indian*'s last issues:

> A visit to Dr. Green's Laboratory at Woodbury, N.J., has considerably changed our views and especially our prejudices in regard to what are generally known as "Standard Patent Medicines" ... Being a physician, I had the curiosity to know how such a sale of two medical preparations could be sustained for so many years.... August Flower for Dyspepsia and Liver Complaints, and Bouchee's German Syrup, for Throat and Lung Troubles, were for the complaints they are recommended, most excellent remedies, and only regret that in much of our practice, medical ethics prevent us from prescribing them without making the formulas public.... I feel like endorsing Dr. Green's suggestion that the Government accept such valuable formulas, and license them for general use by giving protection to the inventor same as patents generally.[65]

Dr. Jones was well aware of the need to insist that ingredients be listed to protect the public against adverse reactions. The country doctor was ahead of his time; pharmaceutical firms would not be compelled to reveal their secret ingredients for many years to come.[66]

The most frequent advertisers were the Dominion government, the railways, and many of the local merchants. They regularly placed box ads or business cards in *The Indian*. Daniel J. Lynch's One Price Cash Store, for example, announced that all orders on interest money would be taken in exchange for goods if approved by Chief Kahkewaquonaby.[67]

The general store proclaimed in its advertisement that "Indians dealt with and waited upon in the same manner as White people."[68] Towns located near an Indian reserve greatly benefited from their contribution to the local economy, and beyond advertising in Jones's paper, some stores accepted corn mats, baskets, and other crafts in exchange for goods. They paid attention to the Aboriginal trade.

Despite all the advertisers, government and private, it was clear that Dr. Jones was spending a lot of his own money to keep this high-quality publication afloat. He had even taken out a mortgage on his property to help with the financing. As evidenced by his letter to Prime Minister Macdonald to express his disappointment, the government had failed to support the newspaper:

> Do not be vexed at the length of this letter. There are several matters of importance I would desire you to pay immediate attention to. Of importance because I wish your Government to retain the zealous attachment of my people who now have the franchise.... As Superintendent General of Indian Affairs, I think I should expect from you a recognition of the only periodical devoted to Indian matters in the Dominion. I know *The Indian* does not come up to the press you could wish. Still, it is very young, and needs encouragement and advice, especially advice, would not only stimulate me to greater exertions.... To carry on, I have had to obtain a second mortgage upon my property. I have received from the Government cash subscriptions from each of the Departments (except the Post Office which refused it), and several advertisements which I have printed but not been paid for.[69]

Dr. Jones, who was obviously having cash-flow problems, would never see the message that the prime minister would write in spite of being busy with armed resistance in the West, the building of the transcontinental railway, and the Opposition's demand for free trade to aid the faltering economy. Macdonald did take up the letter and ask his deputy to deal with it. He was, after all, a gentleman and surprisingly polite. He wrote, "My dear Vt, I found this letter in my basket unanswered. Will you read it and return it with remarks. JamD."[70] Some time later, Lawrence Vankoughnet wrote a reply to Sir John, but evidently no further action was taken on this matter. The struggling Aboriginal editor in small-town Ontario was too far from the mind of the busy prime minister. Twelve months and twenty-four issues after launching *The Indian*, Jones abruptly ceased publication. The final instalment of *The Last of the*

THE INDIAN.

—A PAPER DEVOTED TO—

The Aborigines of North America,

—AND ESPECIALLY TO—

THE INDIANS OF CANADA.

SUBSCRIPTION $1.50 A YEAR IN ADVANCE

Will be published by THE INDIAN Publishing Company, of Hagersville, and for the present will be issued Fortnightly, and until further notice.

ADVERTISING RATES.

A limited number of advertisements will be received at the rate of $4.00 per inch per annum solid measure. Contracts for shorter periods at proportionate rates. Special contracts with large advertisers at a reduction of 10 to 20 per cent. off above rates.

The Indian Publishing Co.

Hagersville, Ont. Canada.

Head Chief Kah-ke-wa-quo-na-by,
(DR, P. E. JONES) Managing Editor.

BIRTHS. MARRIAGES AND DEATHS.

Insertions under this head for Indians will be 25 cents. For other than Indians 75 cents each insertion

NEW CREDIT RESERVE.

A very pleasant and largely attended tea meeting was held in the Council House, of this band, on the evening of January 27th. The tea, and a plentiful supply of the choicest kinds of cakes, pies and sandwiches were distributed with a lavish hand and were greatly appreciated and praised by the large audience. The proceeds were in aid of the New Credit Cornet Band and realized the respectable sum of $36.00. The distinguished visitors Chief Tecumseh, (John Henry) of the Caradoc Reserve and Mr. N. H. Livingston, Manager of the Hagersville Branch of the Bank of Hamilton, a nephew of the celebrated explorer Dr. Livingston. Everything passed off satisfactorily, Chief P. E. Jones, of the Messissaugas, occupied the chair. The following is the program :—Chairman's address ; Music by the N. C. C. B. ; Speech, by James Tobicoe ; Duet, by Chief Herchimer & Elliott ; Music, by the N. C. C. B. ; Ex-Chief Sawyer ; Bass Solo, by Chief Tecumseh ; Music, by the N. C. C. B. ; Speech, by Chief Herchimer ; Music, by N. C. C. B. ; Speech, by Rev. Mr. Weaver ; Duet, by Messrs. Herchimer & Elliott ; Address, by Mr. Livingston ; Music, by the N. C. C. B. ; Address, by Chief Tecumseh ; God Save the Queen, by the N- C. C. B.

JOHN H. HAGER, GENERAL MERCHANT,
Cor. King and Main Sts., Hagersville.
The Old Post Office Store. Never forget the Old Reliable Place when in Town.

B. QUIDER, - HAGERSVILLE,
Manufacturer of and Dealer in
ALL KINDS OF HOUSE FURNISHING GOODS.
A large stock kept constantly on hand at lowest prices.
A Specialty made of Undertaking. Public Orders from the Head Chief of the Mississaugas accepted and Indians liberally dealt with.

DAVID ALMAS, - HAGERSVILLE,
—GENERAL DEALER IN—
Staple & Fancy Dry Goods, Hats, Caps, Boots, Shoes,
CHOICE FAMILY GROCERIES, ETC.
Indians dealt with and waited upon in the same manner as other people.

Figure 12 (A) The masthead, (B) news items, and (C) advertisements from *The Indian* newspaper. (*Source:* Courtesy of the Toronto Reference Library, Toronto)

Mohicans ended with a prophetic remark: "Let us go, said Cora"—the date was 29 December 1886.[71] Jones's property was mortgaged to the hilt, his printing business a failure.

Some years later he tried to revive *The Indian*, but he never succeeded in this endeavour. Dr. Jones had enjoyed the role of editor and was once referred to by a professional journalist as a "clever writer."[72] In a letter written to Thomas Mayne Daly Jr., then superintendent general of Indian Affairs, on 3 May 1894 Jones wrote: "I had a fine lot of contributors to this journal and it is a question if it would not be wise to have it revived by Government assistance.... I would like to give up my whole time to such a work."[73] Government assistance was not forthcoming and he would never again publish a newspaper. *The Indian*'s flame died down, but like a traditional council fire, the embers retained life. In 1963 Lloyd S. King and Andrew Jamieson were instrumental in launching a weekly newspaper named *Tekawennake: Two Voices: Six Nations & New Credit News*.[74] Then a full century after the demise of *The Indian*, the Union of Ontario Indians began publication of the *Anishinabek News*, which they distributed across the province and placed on the Internet. The prospectus of this newspaper lists objectives that are almost identical to those proclaimed by *The Indian*.

What changes would Dr. Jones notice if he were to read these newspapers? At first glance he would probably be impressed by colour printing, and photographs in place of woodcuts. The most important difference since 1886, however, would be the stories of Aboriginal women now serving as chiefs, band councillors, professionals, administrators, and business people. Women were barely ever mentioned in his newspaper and Aboriginals were mere customers, not vendors of a wide variety of goods and services. Jones would be sad to learn, however, that his goal to elevate his people to the same level as their "white brethren" had yet to be attained; many of the political wars his Grand General Indian Council fought so vigorously in the nineteenth century have yet to be won.[75]

Eight
Federal Indian Agent

In 1886 Dr. Jones found himself in difficult financial circumstances, and he sought new opportunities. Having worked tirelessly to support Macdonald's Conservative party by inducing a significant number of his fellow Aboriginals to register with the voting authorities, Jones set his sights on obtaining a post in the Ottawa office of the Department of Indian Affairs. He could remember how, when he had looked on as a ten-year-old boy, the late Dr. Egerton Ryerson had tried to convince the department to hire his father.[1] Like Reverend Jones, Dr. Jones believed that an Aboriginal could serve as a bridge between the Ojibwe people and the government.

With his medical, political, and journalistic accomplishments, Jones felt his curriculum vitae were impressive enough to apply to the civil service.[2] He raised a petition in order to demonstrate that he had the support of Hagersville's merchants and notable citizens. Signatories included his stepson Alpheus Dixon, the manager of his newspaper, and Dr. Robert McDonald, a former town mayor who was also his brother-in-law. A neighbour, Robert Henry of Hagersville, said that the doctor was very able and much liked by his people. Independent signatories such as Thomas Elliott, president of the Conservative Association of South Brant, and M.M. Livingstone, a local official, also recommended Jones.[3] In the recent Haldimand County by-election, the doctor had aided W. Hamilton Merritt, the Conservative candidate. This had been the first election in which Aboriginals could vote, and Jones had encouraged band members to register and to cast their ballots. Though the Liberals retained the seat, Merritt appreciated Jones's help and immediately wrote a personal letter to his good friend, the prime minister.[4] Doubtless the most persuasive recommendation came from William H. Montague, a prominent Conservative, who wrote that Dr. Jones's services to their party "have been faithful and valuable as he could personally testify. The Doctor had in every way possible forwarded our interests and had done considerable work in connection with the Indian Act."[5] Not surprisingly, there were no letters from Mississauga band councillors or Elders on the New Credit reserve. The Aboriginals could have had no say in who managed their affairs, so their recommendation would have been counterproductive.

Deputy Superintendent General of Indian Affairs Lawrence Vankoughnet, who appears to have supported Jones's application, wrote to the prime minister on 15 November 1886: "This Band has never before had a local agent to administer its affairs. The Indian Superintendent at Brantford embraces in his sphere of duty the Mississauga Band and the Six Nations Indians and his salary has been regulated accordingly."[6] Meanwhile, unaware of Vankoughnet's appeal on his behalf, Dr. Jones decided to write the prime minister a personal letter dated 16 November 1886:

> I hope you will not forget my application for a situation in the Department of Indian Affairs. My long experience as Secty. of the Grand Council, as head chief of my Band, and the opportunity I have had of observing the practical working of the laws respecting Indians, should have made me a person who would be useful in the service. In addition to this, I have the further qualification of being an educated Indian who made a study of the characteristics of his people. Politically, you know my life has been one of loyalty to the Crown and to Conservative principles. I have practised medicine for over twenty years and now find that my health suffers by the irregular life and the exposure which a country medical man is obliged to endure. I desire a position in which my employment is day work, and I have a certainty of the nights for rest.[7]

It is possible Dr. Jones alludes to suffering from what is now known as post-polio syndrome, whereby a combination of muscle weakness and severe fatigue returns in later life to cause further disability. The severity of his initial illness strongly favours this diagnosis, and it should be kept in mind when judging the events that transpired in his latter years.[8] In the same letter to Macdonald, Jones suggests the names of several people he could replace, including Jasper T. Gilkison, a long-time local superintendent who, he brazenly suggested, might be superannuated before the general elections:

> A change in the officers of the Department may take place which would give an opening for me. I would not however desire the Superintendency over the Six Nations.... Although I would like an office in the inside service at Ottawa, still I think I would be of more use if brought in contact with the various bands, especially of the Ojibway [*sic*] speaking Indians. I will send you shortly the petition of my Band praying for the establishment of a local agency for them at Hagersville. The salary for a local agent here, however, would be so small that I could not be justified in giving up my practice for it and any Indian work would be circumscribed and local.[9]

It should be noted that since 1878, in addition to being prime minister, Macdonald had kept the portfolio of minister of the interior and superintendent general of Indian Affairs for himself.[10] In 1885, however, a rapid decline in the buffalo population, resulting in widespread starvation among Aboriginal peoples and the troubling effects of the second Métis resistance, created an urgent need to deal with the West before it was lost.[11] To that end, Macdonald appointed a newly elected Conservative, the popular and capable Thomas White, to be minister of the interior and superintendent general of Indian Affairs in October 1887. White was one of his few associates whom Macdonald addressed by their first name.[12] He had been educated at the High School of Montreal and served as an apprentice in the grocery trade before settling in Ontario. Though he later studied law, White was a journalist at heart, having learned the printing trade at the Queen's Printers in Ottawa. Later he took over the *Hamilton Daily Spectator and Journal of Commerce*, an influential Conservative daily paper.[13] Widely admired as being the right man in the right place, White wasted no time after he was appointed and immediately travelled west to try and repair the lingering damage left in the wake of the troubles of 1885. One of his duties was to sponsor legislation giving the Northwest parliamentary representation.[14] White's appointment marked a turning point in Dr. Jones's efforts to become Indian agent. Like White, Dr. Jones was a member of a Hamilton Masonic Lodge, and Hagersville was a mere forty-five kilometres southwest of Hamilton where White worked. The Department of Indian Affairs, however, was surprisingly small: Some thirty people, including clerical staff, attended to the needs of some 100,000 Aboriginal peoples, and a glance at the annual reports reveals that there was little turnover.[15] Having a Status Indian on staff at the head office was likely too risky an innovation, especially if he were a medical doctor.

To Jones's delight, however, the new superintendent general decided to create an independent New Credit Indian agency with Dr. Jones as the local Indian agent. On 4 January 1888, he telegraphed Jones to announce: "You have been appointed Indian Agent, Happy New Year."[16] Jones also appreciated receiving a very friendly letter of advice. He and his wife entertained Thomas White when he visited Hagersville. During the visit, Jones recalls that he "took great interest in the conversations which naturally arose reflecting Indian Affairs."[17] Dr. Jones had previously been a visitor to the offices of the Department of Indian Affairs, hidden away in a corner of the Parliament buildings' East Block in Ottawa, but he was now welcomed as an officer of the department's "outside" service. Virtually all of the several hundred officers and staff of the outside service were part-time employees; some, particularly in the Maritimes, were clergymen.[18] The stipends of Indian agents reflected the size of the band(s) administered so Dr. Jones was paid $600 per annum, near the bottom of the scale and insufficient to allow him to give up his medical practice. By comparison, T.S. Walton, the local Indian agent of the Parry Sound reserve on Georgian Bay, was also a physician, and he received an annual stipend of $900, plus $60 to cover his administrative office's rent. One of Walton's fringe benefits was his right to a commission of five percent on all timber sales by the Aboriginal peoples.[19]

White was a mere twelve years older than Jones and was seriously considered as a possible successor to the prime minister, but to the shock of the nation, he died suddenly of pneumonia on 18 April 1888. The aging Sir John Macdonald collapsed in tears, and Parliament was adjourned on a motion seconded by the Liberal leader, Sir Wilfrid Laurier.[20] The very next week, Dr. Jones wrote a letter of condolence to the prime minister, expressing his sadness at White's untimely death and noting that "this feeling is intensified because I believe I am the last appointment he made in the Indian Branch of the Government and from the friendly way he made it." Soon after, Edgar Dewdney, a close friend of Macdonald, was named to succeed White.[21]

In reality, the day-to-day operations of the Department of Indian Affairs were firmly in the hands of the deputy superintendent general, a position held for some twenty years by a career civil servant, Lawrence Vankoughnet. Vankoughnet was seven years older than Jones, a graduate of Toronto's Trinity College and a dedicated Tory. His family had migrated from the German province of Alsace in the eighteenth century after it was acquired by France, and members of the family included military officers, naval commanders, and a director of Molson's bank.

Many were friends of the MacDonalds, and one of Lawrence's nieces, Gertrude Agnes Vankoughnet, would later become the second wife of the prime minister's son, Hugh John Macdonald.[22] When Macdonald first elected to retain the portfolio of minister of the interior and superintendent general of Indian Affairs, he knew he could count on Vankoughnet as a hard-working assistant who would not only carry out his orders but anticipate his wishes. Macdonald, a prodigious worker, stayed up much of the night reading his correspondence and then, for issues dealing with Aboriginal peoples, he could simply jot down his comments and instructions to Vankoughnet in marginal notes.

Macdonald also relied on Vankoughnet to supervise the seven or eight administrators, thirty-odd clerical workers, and additional temporary clerks, who would be hired at $2 a day during peak periods, when band interest payments or presents were being distributed.[23] Since the office's

Figure 13 Lawrence Vankoughnet, deputy superintendent of Indian Affairs, who managed the department singlehandedly from 1874 to 1893. Photo dated September 1873. (*Source:* Courtesy of Topley Studio and Library and Archives Canada, 1936-270 NPC)

inception, the Department of Indian Affairs' operations were highly centralized. Agents in the field merely transmitted their recommendations to Ottawa by mail. Instructions were also sent by mail because telegrams were considered too expensive. Often the crisis was long past before orders arrived, which must have been a contributing factor in the blatant mismanagement of both the "Indians" and the Métis during the troubles of 1885. Dr. Jones, however, could gain faster access; his role as one of Macdonald's political promoters enabled him to write directly to Earnscliffe, the prime minister's residence, bypassing the lower echelons of the department.

On the reserves, agents were responsible for the distribution of interest money and could authorize certain local stores to furnish household items or winter clothes to band members. Seeds for planting were a major expense each year. Local agents were also responsible for selecting the supplier and calling for tenders when construction such as fencing the band's cemetery was required.[24] Aboriginal peoples were not permitted to market their farm produce, relying instead on their agent. Although in theory they were being trained to run their elected Band Councils as municipalities, it was their agent rather than the head chief who chaired their meetings. For the most part, the agents appear to have been genuinely concerned with conditions on their reserves, and some took a true interest in agriculture, housing, education, and health.

Unlike non-Aboriginal Indian agents, Jones was aware of how important hunting for game to augment their food supply was to his people and strongly defended their right to leave the reserve for several weeks during the hunting season. When the Department of Indian Affairs threatened to punish Edward Spencer for joining a Mississauga party that went north to hunt in the Muskoka region, Jones wrote Ottawa and defended him, saying that it was his traditional right. By supporting the Aboriginals' resistance he risked losing his government job.[25] In the nineteenth century New Credit housed a small community, but had the advantage of being adjacent to the Six Nations reserve, home to thirty-six hundred people. Both communities farmed arable land, had medical attendants, and benefited from competent Band Councils. Their band physicians could request medical consultations and, in some instances, patients were sent to hospitals in Brantford, Hamilton, or even as far away as Toronto.[26] Very few children from families living on the Grand River reserves were sent to a residential school as both bands had good local day schools that were as good as those in rural Euro-Canadian communities. Jones was proud to observe in his last agent's report that the Mississaugas' day school was ably run. By means of properly managed examinations, the children were moving up in their classes, and two of them, Effie Wood and Regie McDougall, having passed the entrance examinations, were attending high school in nearby Hagersville.[27] Indian Affairs agreed that in Ontario, there were many Aboriginal day schools in which the public school inspectors had reported that the work done and results obtained equalled those of the common schools of the rural districts. In the Northwest, however, they felt that lasting good could not be expected from day schools owing to the fact that "home influences interfered." The department was closing day schools as soon as accommodation became available in their residential schools.[28]

The total Canadian Aboriginal population was roughly 100,000. The majority of the communities were located in Manitoba, the Northwest, and British Columbia, and their share of the annual departmental budget amounted to more than $1 million. By comparison, $65,000 was allocated for the Indians of Ontario, Quebec, and the Maritime provinces.[29] Indian agents in the eastern part of the country were entrusted with simply maintaining the status quo on the reserves, whereas in the Northwest, new reserves and schools were being established. Agents had to submit a detailed annual report about the reserve along with ledgers itemizing every expenditure and receipt. These reports formed the basis of an executive summary prepared for the superintendent general and presented each year to the governor-general of Canada in council.[30] These detailed documents provide a unique record of individual Indian bands.

On 15 August 1888, Dr. Jones's first report noted that the census taken in October 1887 showed a population of 245, including eleven births and six deaths and giving a net increase of five over the preceding year. A review of the census over the past eight years showed a net increase of thirty-seven members. The death rate was lower than the average for Aboriginals, but far higher than the Euro-Canadian population. Dr. Jones was proud of these statistics, and with the unjustifiable optimism that pervades virtually all his Department of Indian Affairs reports, he explained:

> This very satisfactory condition is due to several causes; the heads of families are in much better financial condition than in previous years; poverty, requiring the exercise of charity by the council, is of rare occurrence; their homes are more comfortably furnished and more cleanly kept; they appreciate the value of early medical advice in sickness, and understand more fully the benefit of prophylactic or

> preventative treatment. They have been remarkably free of contagious diseases, and habitual drunkenness is now unknown amongst them.[31]

Dr. Jones's public health measures on the reserve included vaccination against smallpox, quarantine for infectious diseases, ensuring that potable water was available, and preventing the accumulation of garbage, especially near the houses.[32]

Edgar Dewdney, the new superintendent of Indian Affairs, included words of praise for Dr. Jones in his first report to the governor-general:

> The Mississaugas of the Credit, who were previously included in the same Superintendency with the Six Nations, were in the early part of the past year, separated there from and assigned to the care of an agent. A member of the band, Dr. Jones, who is a medical man, being a graduate of Queen's College, Kingston, and who was for a number of years the head chief of the band under his Indian name of Kahkewaquonaby, was appointed to the position.... Under the management of a resident agent, and with the control over local matters exercised by the council elected annually in accordance with the provisions of the Indian Advancement Act, there is no doubt that this band will make further and more rapid progress.[33]

Lurking behind these progress notes, however, lay a statistic that seems to have been accepted by the Department of Indian Affairs—the alarming number of cases of consumption, the term then used for pulmonary tuberculosis. It was routinely listed as the most frequent cause of death in Canadian Aboriginals, but no funds were specifically allotted for the prevention and spread of tuberculosis until well into the twentieth century.[34] It often presented as scrofula, an old-fashioned term for enlarged cervical lymph glands filled with pus, which frequently required incision and drainage. This form of the disease is most often seen as an acute infection contracted under poor living conditions. Other patients presented with symptoms of pulmonary disease, such as the coughing up of blood, indolent fever, loss of appetite, and severe weight loss. The eponym "consumption" was coined to describe this form of the disease because this progressive wasting illness appeared to be actually "consuming" the body.

Tuberculosis is not a highly infectious disease like measles; transmission usually requires close, frequent, and prolonged exposure to an active case. It has always been an ancient and worldwide health problem, existing in North America long before the arrival of Europeans.[35] It is almost always transmitted when microscopic droplets containing the bacilli are catapulted into the air by coughing and remain airborne for some time. When the Aboriginal peoples lost their land base and were crammed into small reserves, the disease became a major health problem.[36] Extended families occupied small cabins and sleeping accommodations were frequently cramped. The number of patients per room, today referred to as housing density, along with a high-carbohydrate diet and the presence of silent carriers, no doubt amplified the spread of the disease. The association between overcrowding and an increased incidence of tuberculosis in children has long been recognized.[37] Another important risk factor was the indoor combustion of wood for both cooking and eating, which exposed the inhabitants, especially women and children, to dense smoke. When wood burns, it releases toxic chemicals such as benzene, which irritate the facial sinuses and respiratory tract. Chronic sinus infections were very common because the toxic chemicals slowed the rate whereby the cilia in these passages work to eliminate secretions.[38]

The population of the Mississaugas failed to rise significantly during Dr. Jones's tenure as agent; each year he was forced to report the death of several young children. Indian Affairs expressed concern over the poor ventilation and foul air of their charges' cabins. The youngest children, who always accompanied their mothers, were continuously exposed to the smoke of cooking fires or inadequately vented wood stoves. Only recently have scientists discovered that wood fires emit ultra-fine wood particles so tiny that they are carried by the inhaled air deep into the lungs, where they damage the walls of the respiratory passages. Infection soon follows, leading to bronchitis and often fatal pneumonia. In Dr. Jones's time, this likely accounted for as many as half of all deaths among children less than five exposed to indoor air pollution.[39]

Indian agents' reports frequently note that nineteenth-century Aboriginal diets were overly rich in corn, an imperfect carbohydrate lacking in key vitamins and other nutrients. A diet rich in cornmeal and low in protein tends to reduce the function of the immune system, making both children and adults more susceptible to tubercular infections.[40] Pork became the main source of protein when the Mississaugas, traditionally a fishing community, were displaced from their customary locales near rivers and lakes. No longer were they able to follow their migratory lifestyle in which they would successively visit the sugar bush, fish, harvest wild rice, collect nuts and berries, and hunt for deer, moose, and small animals.[41] Given these circumstances, there was little Dr. Jones could do to halt the march of this dreaded disease. When five band members died of tuberculosis during the 1890 epidemic of influenza or *la grippe*, Jones expressed the medical opinion that influenza aggravated a latent tendency to tuberculosis.[42] Though he was aware that Robert Koch had discovered the causative agent, mycobacterium tuberculosis, in 1882, he lacked the laboratory tests and chest X-rays needed to identify such patients. There was no way he could isolate his patients in order to protect their relatives; effective antibiotic therapy for this unusually resistant micro-organism would become available only in the 1940s.[43]

Consumption, as Jones called the dreaded disease, was always the most frequent cause of death in his annual reports to the government.[44] The Department of Indian Affairs was able to neglect this statistic because it was erroneously believed that Aboriginals were biologically inferior regarding their natural immunity to this infection. As the nineteenth century drew to a close, Indian agent E.D. Cameron and physician Dr. L. Secord of the Six Nations were ahead of their time in realizing that this pejorative theory was flawed. In his 1893 report, Cameron declared, "The physical development of the people is high, their average weight, particularly among the females, is much greater than their white neighbours and though contrary to the prevailing opinion, I do not believe they are more prone to consumption than the latter."[45] In *Medicine and Politics among the Grand River Iroquois*, Sally Weaver cites Secord's opinion: "The character of disease affecting the Indian is in no way different from what would be experienced among a similarly situated white population; but we have at times been particularly struck with a wonderful recuperative power shown in some cases."[46]

Despite the dramatic impact of dismal living conditions, even those with superior accommodations did not escape the disease. One such case was Dr. George Bomberry, a chief of the Cayuga tribe of the Six Nations. As the first Aboriginal physician in the area, Jones was a role model for George, five years his junior. An exceptionally bright student, Bomberry had attended a private school in Toronto on a scholarship provided by the New England Company, a charitable arm of the Church of England.[47] He was fluent in English, well versed in the classics, and had even studied French, which helped him land a job in the Montreal office of the Grand Trunk Railway. Nevertheless, he found that his absence from the Six Nations reserve debarred him from his rights as a band member. Hence, he no longer received his annuity payments nor could he take his seat in the council of hereditary chiefs. On his return to Brantford, he was approached by Dr. Robert H. Dee, the long-serving medical officer of the Six Nations, who needed an assistant. Dee convinced the Mission to award the promising student a grant of £60 annually for four years, provided they remained satisfied with his conduct and progress. Although Bomberry intended to study at Trinity University in Toronto, several of his old schoolmates were going to McGill University in Montreal. It was agreed that Bomberry would benefit from switching to McGill, where he would derive support from his familiar mentors. He passed his preliminary exams and was admitted to McGill in 1871, just in time to see the microscopic slides from William Osler's thesis on display.[48] Tuberculosis, however, was the "silent killer" of medical students, and Bomberry became one of its victims. Despite frequent bouts of illness, he obtained his degree in 1875 and was hired by the Six Nations.[49] Later Bomberry applied to sit the licensing examination, which he had missed due to illness. The province had no control over health care on federal "Indian" reserves, but like Dr. Jones, Bomberry would need a licence to treat patients living in the White community.[50] He was granted a special examination and obtained his licence without difficulty in June 1878. A natural leader and skilled physician, Bomberry somehow managed to find the strength to continue practising until he passed away from pulmonary tuberculosis in 1879.[51]

Clergymen officiating at funerals on the New Credit reserve in the latter part of the nineteenth century carefully transcribed the cause of death section of the physician's certificate. A search of these burial records revealed the causes of death of thirty-eight people older than twelve years of age and buried between 1887 and 1901. Consumption was listed as the cause of death in eighteen cases (forty-seven percent of all cases), the median age at death being twenty-six years (thirteen to seventy-five years). In contrast, other causes were responsible for twenty deaths (fifty-three percent of all cases), the median age of death being forty-seven years (fourteen to ninety-nine years).[52] Seven additional records were retrieved from the registrar general's files in the Archives of Ontario.[53] Of these, three deaths were ascribed to consumption, the median age being twenty-three years; four deaths were ascribed to influenza, cancer, uremia, and angina pectoris respectively, the median age being sixty-four years. Tuberculosis was also the most common cause of death in the non-Aboriginal population of Ontario between 1871 and 1882 (ten percent of all deaths), but the above data, although admittedly meagre, suggest that the incidence was five times greater on the New Credit reserve.[54] The incidence of fatal tuberculosis was likely augmented by patients returning to the reserve when seriously ill. Jacalyn Duffin reviews the detailed daybooks of Dr. James Miles Langstaff, who had an extensive practice among the White townsfolk living in nearby Richmond Hill, Ontario. He listed nineteen of 317 adult deaths (six percent of all deaths) as the result of tuberculosis, but this was probably low as Duffin notes that the kindly doctor wished to spare families from the social stigma attached to the disease.[55]

The review of the thirty-eight deaths on the New Credit reserve, however, also uncovered encouraging data supporting Dr. Jones's claim that the overall health of the band had been good.[56] Just one death was attributed to childbirth, likely because many traditional Aboriginal practices were still observed and experienced Aboriginal midwives took charge of the deliveries. Only one death—that of a thirty-five-year-old woman—was blamed on diabetes. Many band members lived to what would be considered an advanced age in that era. Dr. Jones's uncle, Chief David Sawyer, died of pneumonia at seventy-eight years of age, while his Mississauga grandmother Tuhbenahneequay was ninety-four when she passed away.[57]

Beyond his concern for his patients' health, Dr. Jones was responsible for enforcing the Indian Act like any other Indian agent, and he evidently took his job seriously. The government forbade the sale of intoxicating liquors to Aboriginal peoples and had recently introduced stiff penalties for non-compliance. Thus, in 1888, the *Hagersville News* reported: "Dr. P.E. Jones, Indian agent, is exhibiting to the public a printed copy of the Indian Act respecting the furnishing of intoxicants to Indians.... We trust it will be the means of preventing drunkenness amongst these people, which is so apt to occur after receipt of their interest money."[58] The proclamation was posted on the wall of the Indian office located in Dr. Jones's frame house on the corner of Main Street at David Street in Hagersville. Ironically, Jones's home directly faced the site chosen years later for the local outlet of the Liquor Control Board of Ontario.[59]

When Superintendent General Edgar Dewdney visited the counties of Brant and Haldimand in October 1889, Dr. and Mrs. Jones were proud to have the opportunity to entertain him at their Hagersville home. Dr. Jones used the chance to discuss the problems Dewdney had encountered while lieutenant governor of Manitoba.[60] Armed with this background information, Jones felt confident enough to apply for a position as an Indian agent in the Northwest, but his application was not entertained. He had to be content with his present appointment. By 1889, the Mississaugas of the New Credit numbered 253 and occupied eighty-nine houses. They were successful farmers. Half of the reserve's land was under

NOMINATION AND
ELECTION OF
FIVE COUNCILLORS.

NOTICE IS HEREBY GIVEN that the undersigned will attend at the Council House of th
MESSISSAUGAS OF THE CREDIT
Between the hours of Ten in the Fo-enoon and 12 at Noon, upon
MONDAY 7th SEP. '96
For the purpose of receiving nominations of Candidates for the election of 5 Councillors for the ensuing year, and in the event of more than 5 electors being nominated
THEN A POLL WILL BE OPENED
At the same place between the hours of Ten in the Forenoon and Four in the afternoon on
MONDAY 14th SEPTEMBER '96
For the purpose of ELECTING 5 COUNCILLORS from among those nominated.

INDIAN OFFICE
Hagersville.
29th August, 1896.

P. E. JONES,
INDIAN AGENΓ.

Figure 14 Poster calling for nominations for the Mississaugas of the New Credit Band Council. (*Source:* Courtesy of Library and Archives Canada, C-97585)

cultivation with the aid of a few oxen and many horses. The band raised cows, sheep, and pigs, and it produced wheat, oats, hay, and vegetables.[61] Dr. Jones managed his own farm, assisted by his stepson Sylvanus, who returned to live with the Jones family after a sojourn in Philadelphia. Band members resented Sylvanus's continuous presence on their reserve; Euro-Canadians were not supposed to farm on the Mississaugas' land. Though he was a capable carpenter, Jones, in his capacity as the Indian agent, should not have allowed him to receive the contract to move the old schoolhouse to the Council House grounds.[62]

Jones carefully noted any changes in the population and state of the band in his reports as an Indian agent. In his annual report for 1890, Dr. Jones noted that the population of the band had increased by three. Despite eleven births, there were eight deaths five from consumption, one from exposure while intoxicated, one from old age, and one from brain disease.[63] Sanitary conditions were also addressed by then Deputy Superintendent General Hayter Reed. His 1892 report took aim at the badly ventilated and overcrowded one-room houses on the reserves. He wrote that on moral and social grounds, these should be replaced by buildings sufficiently commodious to allow for separation of the sexes and a separate kitchen area, but he was forced to admit that the department had as yet found no remedy.[64] The Mississauga band census for 1892 had shown a decrease by one due to four deaths from consumption and two other youngsters who had died from "infantile complaints." On a happier note, Dr. Jones reported that otherwise the general health of the band was remarkably good. Moreover, the band had built a new brick schoolhouse that was situated so as to improve sanitation. Jones boasted, "The Band Council was doing its job and paid the teacher, caretaker and supplied all books and material needed. The average daily attendance had more than doubled as parents were fined if they did not send their children to school...."[65] (Now that there was a high school in the village of Hagersville, Dr. Jones believed there was no reason why young Aboriginals should not acquire as good an education as rapidly as their White neighbours.) The following year saw three deaths due to consumption, but in 1894 the overall health of the Mississauga community was very good, with the exception of an epidemic of measles. Jones poignantly had to report that the single adult death was that of his brother George, who had died very suddenly.[66] The 1895 census showed a net decrease of three—two adults died from consumption and there was one infant mortality. Meanwhile the land was being well cultivated, and a substantial amount of good fencing had been completed. Always interested in farming, Jones mentioned that a band member, Allan Sault, had purchased a new threshing machine.[67]

Dr. Jones's yearly stipend of $600 per annum as agent was insufficient to enable him to give up his medical practice among the people of Hagersville, but he was understandably suffering from fatigue after so much service to the community. A country doctor in solo practice had no choice but to make house calls in all types of weather, and Dr. Jones had made himself available to both his Hagersville and Aboriginal patients for twenty-eight years. In recent years, he had been forced to split his workdays between his post as a part-time Indian agent and the demands of his practice. He was fifty years of age and subject to recurrent upper respiratory infections and chronic fatigue, but retirement was not an option. In the modern era he would have likely been evaluated to determine whether he was suffering from post-polio syndrome, but the medical community lacked knowledge of such a condition during Jones's lifetime.[68]

Townsfolk now referred to Jones as the "old doctor" because Hagersville was becoming a commercial centre. There was no longer a doctor shortage. Among the most prominent doctors was his brother-in-law, Robert McDonald, who had married Mrs. Jones's younger sister Drusella and moved to Hagersville from a nearby town in 1877. Dr. McDonald was born in 1840 in Oxford County, Upper Canada, attended teachers' college, and then taught school for two years. Then in 1868 he obtained a medical degree from one of the eclectic medical colleges in the United States and was granted a licence to practice in Ontario the following year. Eclectic physicians were a phenomenon of nineteenth-century American medicine based in large part on observations of how the Aboriginal peoples employed their traditional botanical remedies and physical therapies. The term "eclectic," derived from the Greek "to choose from," was selected because these physicians preferred to administer whatever safe herbal or physical therapy would benefit their patients. These doctors opposed the excessive bloodletting, purging, and toxic inorganic chemical therapies then in vogue. The eclectic medical colleges, however, also taught basic and clinical medical skills. As medical science progressed, these schools were unable to afford the scientific laboratories required by the American Medical Association, and one by one they were forced to close and were almost all gone by the end of World War I. Dr. McDonald, however, had received a good training and would practise conventional medicine, obstetrics, and surgery for many years to come.[69] The local newspaper reported that he was "indefatigable in the discharge of his duty, relieving the sick regardless of road or weather conditions." Civic-minded McDonald entered politics, serving first as the reeve (mayor) of the town and later chairman of the school board. Jones had to acknowledge his rival's popularity and success, but was compensated somewhat by assuming the role of substitute doctor for McDonald whenever the latter was busy with other duties, including his responsibilities as coroner. Dr. Jones never had the luxury of turning down an opportunity to treat a paying patient. He was always in need of money to support his wife, who held herself in high regard.

In 1888, Jones, who had borrowed money in order to print and distribute his ill-fated newspaper, was sued by the Bank of Hamilton for $250, plus $50 in costs. He only obtained temporary respite by borrowing the funds at ten percent interest.[70] He had never been paid for the work he had done reviewing the Indian Act for Sir John A. Macdonald, and on 28 December of that year, Dr. Jones penned the prime minister a letter from "The Indian Office, Hagersville," detailing the work he had performed and asking for some form of payment:

> I do not write to ask you for either a gift or a loan.... I will be as concise as possible. I married a widow with three little boys; the youngest is now 18 years old. The past four or five years, I have used all the money I could spare from my earnings to give them a good education in Toronto and the High Schools. I must also say that I did more than this; I borrowed money to keep them at school, expecting that the sale of Mrs. Jones' farm would relieve me. But legal processes thwarted that. When I did the work mentioned I expected I would be remunerated for the labour expended, and I spared no pains to do it as well as I could and secured the assistance of a legal friend, and was obliged to go to Brantford to consult him. My salary as Agent is forty-nine dollars per month, but this is not sufficient to keep my family and pay my debts and from my inability to attend to it, my white practice has left me.[71]

Jones then asked the prime minister to "review the work I have done and pay me what you think proper."[72] He ended his letter on a depressive note: "Mrs. Jones joins me in wishing Lady Macdonald and yourself all the compliments of the season, which to most persons is so joyous and festive."[73]

Unfortunately for Jones, Sir John A. Macdonald was not a micromanager and was interested only in political matters, even when acting as superintendent general of the Department of Indian Affairs. He still always relied on Lawrence Vankoughnet for day-to-day operations. Jones's letter was marked "personal," and Macdonald took the time to read the letter himself. However, he then handed the reply over to Vankoughnet with a condescending marginal note: "My dear VT, Will you see what Jones has done for the Dept. He made a report or two, but not I think of much virtue? JamD."[74] Macdonald, who had invested in land, banks, Great Lakes shipping, and other business ventures, had suffered serious financial setbacks on a number of occasions. During the depression of 1857, he had to make payments on his land holdings and later ran up debts because of his law partners' reckless deals. After spending a lifetime in politics and incurring many expenses such as the renovation of Earnscliffe, the stylish Ottawa home he first rented and then purchased, Macdonald was never free of debt.[75] Dr. Jones could not expect any more compassion or relief from the penny-pinching deputy superintendent.

Vankoughnet was the man who had cut the food rations of the starving Cree in half in order to save funds.[76] In fact, Vankoughnet likely believed the prime minister had honoured Dr. Jones simply by asking for his opinion. His work would have been considered a voluntary act performed in order to help his people. The Department of Indian Affairs would not have realized that although he was a physician, Jones's practice had shrunk, in part, because he had spent so much time ensuring that the prime minister was re-elected. Vankoughnet also remembered that Jones had received a commission of $2,000 in 1884 for his work on the Mississaugas of the New Credit's land claim and currently received a stipend of $600 per annum as local Indian agent and another $250 from the band for his work as a medical attendant. This compared favourably with the average stipend of the twenty physicians employed as band doctors in Ontario and Quebec, about $384. Times were hard, the Department of Indian Affair's budget was stretched to the limit, and Vankoughtnet's own salary had been set at $3,200 per annum for years.[77]

Shaky finances inevitably contributed to Dr. Jones's distress. He was unable to finance the lifestyle to which he and his wife were accustomed. Charlotte was a proud lady who entertained well. Her guests included notables like William Blair Bruce, the Hamilton-born Canadian abstract painter, and his wife, Caroline Benedicks, a Swedish sculptor of aristocratic birth. She also hosted Sir Charles Tupper, a father of Confederation, and other artists and writers, some of whom left her copies of their works.[78] However, as noted in Peter Edmund's letter to the prime minister, Charlotte never did receive her first husband's $1,100 estate and was unable to contribute to the high cost of educating two of her children in private schools.[79]

By this time, Dr. Jones had begun to imbibe excessive quantities of alcohol on a regular basis. Most disturbing were episodes in which he would consume large amounts over short periods and become grossly intoxicated.[80] Though he likely began using alcohol in college along with his medical school classmates, Dr. Jones would have had no problem getting alcohol. Ethyl alcohol was an important therapeutic agent in the nineteenth century. It often took the form of brandy, gin, beer, cider, or whiskey. It was then frequently mixed with honey, milk, or raw egg and administered as a therapeutic punch. The detailed records of one of Dr. Jones's contemporaries, James Langstaff, offer a snapshot of nineteenth-century medical practice.[81] Dr. Langstaff, though he was a strong advocate of temperance, purchased alcohol from the general store and left a supply of punch with patients after visiting them at home. It was his fourth most frequently prescribed medication in the 1870s, and he considered it a stimulant. This view of alcohol persisted well into the twentieth century.[82] Should the patient become flushed or agitated, the administration of alcohol was discontinued, but Langstaff found it was usually well tolerated by the sick. Even diehard abstainers would take alcohol when prescribed by their physician, and Dr. Jones would have had no compunction prescribing alcohol-laced medicine to the settlers in and around Hagersville. The sale of alcohol to Aboriginal peoples was a crime under federal law, but an exception might be made in the case of a valid prescription. According to Indian Affairs' records, Dr. Jones did purchase alcohol on behalf of his Aboriginal patients and, like many doctors of that era, was subjected to temptation.[83]

Dr. Jones's drunken behaviour first came to light in 1889. David Almas, a prominent Hagersville businessman, told the deputy superintendent of Indian Affairs that he would no longer act as his surety or be responsible for Jones's debts: "The doctor was frequently under the influence of liquor and was not a person who could be safely entrusted with the care of the money of the Indians."[84] The department then checked up on Jones, who claimed he had stopped drinking and even offered to have some of his neighbours sign a certificate to this effect. Deputy Superintendent Vankoughnet asked Jones to find another reliable citizen to act as his bondsman. This was quickly done so Jones was able to keep his job. Vankoughnet also asked Department of Indian Affairs Inspector C.A. Dingman to investigate the charge of alcoholism, but he appears not to have filed a formal complaint. However, Dr. Jones's reputation was obviously severely compromised both in Hagersville and on the New Credit reserve, which was strongly Methodist and proud of its successful fight to prevent alcoholism. The doctor's home life was also in disarray. The 1891 census reveals that his wife Charlotte had taken refuge in the home of her sister Drusella, the wife of Dr. McDonald. Dr. Jones was likely closeted on the family farm.[85]

Matters did not come to a head until 1895, when the Band Council forced Dr. Jones to relinquish his appointment as their physician.[86] Next, Hayter Reed, the new deputy superintendent of Indian Affairs, received a letter from two leading band members, Chief Nicholas McDougall and George Henry Jr., asking him to remove Jones from the post of Indian agent "because he was so addicted to drinking that he was utterly unfit to efficiently perform the duties of his office."[87] The chief complained that it was extremely difficult to find Jones sober enough for the proper transaction of business. He complained that while presiding at the distribution of interest money, Jones had "exposed himself to everyone that he was too far under the influence of liquor to conduct himself in a manner befitting his position."[88] Meanwhile Charlotte Jones and her son Sylvanus secretly informed the department that Jones could not be trusted with money. In fact, Sylvanus had to "make good" money for which the doctor could no longer account. Ottawa soon had a firsthand view of Jones's sorry state when he visited the departmental offices. Hayter Reed explained to Minister Thomas Mayne Daly that "he showed evidence of being pretty much the worse for liquor."[89]

An order in council on 25 January 1897 indicated that Dr. Jones's services as an Indian agent were eventually dispensed with because his work had been performed carelessly. His conduct of the financial affairs of his agency had been irregular, and he had been so derelict in attending to communications from the department as to render it exceedingly difficult to properly direct the affairs of the band. Jones was so addicted to intemperance as to interfere with his usefulness as an Indian agent.[90] The order in council was necessary because Dr. Jones had been appointed by Sir John A. Macdonald's Tory government, a decision the new Liberal government would publish in the press. Prior to the June 1896 election, the Liberals under Sir Wilfrid Laurier, desperate to gain power after eighteen years in Opposition, had offered their supporters patronage appointments, and once they took power, many long-term Tory appointees to the Department of Indian Affairs were dismissed. Dismissing Jones suited party purposes and was not unusual even without his problems. In historian Peter S. Schmalz's opinion, if a band wished to have its agent removed, the only opportunity was right after the party in power had fallen.[91] An agent's work was complex, and as they were part-time employees, it was not difficult to find errors or omissions that could be used to justify a firing done for political reasons. Another agent, Thomas Walton, M.D., of Parry Sound, was dismissed after thirteen years' service, losing all his contributions to the superannuation fund. The local Ojibwe band had accused Walton of irregularities in the granting of a lumber contract. Though exonerated by an inquiry that showed he did not benefit personally from the move, he was replaced by the son-in-law of the newly elected local Liberal member of Parliament.[92]

Jones did not appear to recognize that he had been fired for just cause or that the Department of Indian Affairs had looked the other way for years. Instead, he seemed to blame Liberal leader Sir Wilfrid Laurier, who was now prime minister. In a letter to his old friend, archaeologist David Boyle, he sadly complained:

> Since the new Government decapitated me, I have had nothing to do, and am only waiting to get some money. I expect to move down South. I am very poor just now. Mrs. Jones joins me in kind regards.
>
> —Kahkewaquonaby, M.D.[93]

In his last report, written in 1896, Dr. Jones had revealed how dependent farmers were on the government for help when crops failed. Earlier that year, severe frost and subsequent drought kept the hay crop from maturing. The Aboriginal peoples were seriously short of both hay and straw to feed their animals over the winter. When the council asked for relief, the department furnished baled hay from eastern Canada. The hay was initially paid for by the band and was then refunded by the individuals receiving it.[94] This prevented what no doubt would have been a calamity, and only a few head of stock died during the following winter, which was severe. Despite these hardships, the band's population remained the same as the previous year, the number of births making up for the losses. The report concluded with the good news that children were attending the high school. On a more philosophical note, Jones recorded that "the health of the people has been good. Peace and quietness reign amongst the council and the band."[95]

Perhaps Jones's disappointment in the loss of his position as an Indian agent was misplaced because after his firing, the good doctor finally had the chance to find his own peace and quiet, devoting himself to his small medical practice, family, friends, and his farm. Still respected by the community, there were no further complaints relating to alcoholism. He stuck to the sidelines, but continued to busy himself with the band's quest to obtain a just settlement of their land claim, played chess by mail, and displayed his taxidermy, much to the enjoyment of the townsfolk.

Nine
The Later Years

With the loss of his jobs as Indian agent and band physician, Dr. Jones's major sources of income disappeared at the same time. He made up his mind to practise medicine in Washington, DC, believing his career in Canada was over. His mentor, Sir John A. Macdonald, had died in 1891, leaving a disorganized political organization that was soon defeated by Wilfrid Laurier's Liberal party. Dr. Jones's medical replacement was his brother-in-law, Dr. Robert McDonald, who by now was officer of health for Hagersville and president of the Haldimand County Medical Association.[1] Perhaps because of his stature in the community, the band increased the band physician's stipend to $350 per annum, $100 more than Dr. Jones had received.[2] McDonald was later assisted by his own daughter, Minnie Alice, a 1901 graduate of Trinity University in Toronto, working from the office in their home. Reportedly, Dr. Minnie, as she was affectionately known, was "very successful in the treatment of children's and women's diseases."[3] Following her father's death in 1915, she stayed in Hagersville until she passed away on 26 September 1954.

Before he left Hagersville, however, Dr. Jones treated a child named Rose Hoover, and many years later she recalled the event in a letter dated 12 July 1962 to Harold Senn, a descendant of Augustus Jones and his Mohawk second wife Tekarihogen:

> I am 78 years of age and the youngest of nine children of Eliza Sturgis and Archibald Russell. There was a Dr. Peter Jones practising in Hagersville when I was a kid in school. He was the official doctor for the Chippewa but we employed him. The last time he treated me for an inflamed eye was when I was ten or eleven years old. He was a cousin of my father's. He had one short leg and walked with a cane. He left town not long after that.[4]

Dr. Jones left for Washington in May 1898.[5] While there, he spent time in the Division of Ethnology of the Smithsonian Institution, where he was already recognized as an expert, having provided them with English translations of Ojibwe place names.[6] He also pursued his interest in Aboriginal archaeology, and in August 1898, the Smithsonian Institution asked him to don Reverend Jones's traditional Aboriginal costume for a series of photographs in which Dr. Jones bears a remarkable resemblance to his late father.[7] The museum then purchased and catalogued a number of his artifacts, including the beaded deerskin coat, sash, pouch, and feathered bonnet in which he had been photographed. The Bureau of Ethnology considered the collection to be of more than usual interest, and ethnologist W.J. McGee later described the items in the *American Journal of Anthropology*.[8] In subsequent years, the artifacts have been loaned for display in other American museums. One item that Jones retained, however, was the steel peace-pipe tomahawk presented to his father in 1838 by Queen Victoria's cousin, Sir Augustus d'Este. This same pipe was lit and smoked by Iroquois and Mississauga chiefs in the 1840 reaffirmation of the one-hundred-fifty-year-old treaty of friendship between the Mississaugas and the "People of the Long-House."[9]

Dr. Jones had often criticized the American government's policy of reappointing Indian agents after each federal election, noting that many rushed to "feather their own nest" during their four-year tenure.[10] He felt that American Aboriginal reservations would benefit if the government could be persuaded to adopt the Canadian model and employ career civil servants. In a letter written to Mr. W.L. Stone, of Jersey City, New Jersey, he had already expressed a strong desire to move to Washington some day to help depoliticize the governance of American Aboriginal peoples: "Can such a system be established under your Republican Government? I think it is the only salvation for the Indian tribes and I have had it in my mind, that as soon as I feel able financially to go to Washington, I will do so, and herd the lion (or Eagle) in his den, or eyrie."[11] It is unclear whether or not he followed up on this 1882 promise, or whether he met members of the fledgling Aboriginal peoples' movement during his sojourn in Washington.

Dr. Jones intended to set up a medical practice in Washington, but there is no record of whether he was successful in this endeavour.[12] As a licensed graduate of a well-known Canadian university who had previously worked in New York City, Dr. Jones would likely have been allowed to practise in Washington. In that era, doctors advertised for patients, and the fact that Jones was Aboriginal would have enabled him to attract those believing in the magical powers of Aboriginal healers.

Records indicate that he acquired funds by selling many of his valuable artifacts to the Smithsonian Institution and Carnegie Museum, which were pleased to enhance their collections.[13] A few months later, however, the doctor appears to have drifted back to his farm on the New Credit reserve, which had been run by Charlotte, Sylvanus, and their hired hands in his absence. After his return to Hagersville, Dr. Jones continued to build up and classify his collection of Aboriginal artifacts. He also continued to indulge in taxidermy, an activity imported to the New World by Europeans but vigorously rejected by the Aboriginal peoples.[14] In the 1840s, A.D. Ferrier, of Fergus, asked one of their Mississauga hunters why he did not kill more wolves as the bounty was so high. His answer was: "Indians no care to kill wolves, they hunters as well as Indian."[15] In this way, he expressed the ancient belief that the thinking processes, emotional reactions, and relationship with the environment were much the same for animals and human beings. Traditional Aboriginal peoples would always apologize to the animals they were forced to kill, and because they disapproved of taxidermy, many would blow tobacco smoke at a stuffed moose, deer, or other animal. This gesture was intended to be a conciliatory offering since they believed that the spirit of these animals must be offended by the indignity shown to their remains.[16]

Dr. Jones respected his Christian teachings, but, like many physicians of his era, he was intrigued by Darwin's recently published work, *On the Origin of Species*.[17] He had been trained in anatomical dissection and was able to figure out how to stuff and preserve animals and birds. In a letter to Dr. Lyman Draper of Madison, Wisconsin, he commented: "I am very fond of Natural History and have built a place in my house for a private museum. I understand taxidermy and prepare all my own specimens and these with my collection of Indian relics [artifacts]—insects, fossils, coins and library, will eventually make my home a pleasant one for friends to visit who have a taste for such things."[18] Jones also described his library of Aboriginal works that he and his father collected, including Henry Schoolcraft's classic 1851 work, *The History of the Indians of the United States, a Gift of the Author*.[19] In June 1899, Dr. Jones was one of three collectors invited to display their artifacts in the "Indian room" at the first exhibition of the Ontario Historical Society in Toronto.[20] The little museum, filled with taxidermy specimens on the first floor of his home on Main Street, had also become an attraction in its own right. One contemporary writer noted, "It was a pleasure for many to stroll past his windows or enter his abode to view the fascinating array of wild creatures so cleverly mounted."[21]

Dr. Jones's life continued to be a full one, and he still treated his old patients and their families, though he most likely restricted the number of house calls. His family always received priority treatment, and when his late brother Charles's widow, Hannah Ellis Jones, became ill, the doctor invited her to live in his home, where Charlotte cared for her until her death in May 1902. A train then carried her to Brantford, where Jones had reserved a place at her late husband's side.[22] Work was never Peter Edmund Jones's sole activity, and his hobbies and outside interests served him well in his later years. He was the long-time secretary of the Hagersville Chess Club and remained a gifted player who took part in local competitions. In those days the dense rail network ensured surprisingly rapid mail delivery, which enabled him to play chess via correspondence. His memorabilia include a number of penny postcards to and from colleagues in the United States, each bearing a series of moves for two simultaneous games.[23] There is no doubt as to when and where he acquired knowledge of the fine points of the game. A few months before she sailed for New York to marry Reverend Jones, an entry in his mother's diary states "I worked a little at my chess board."[24] When mother and invalid son lived in their big home in Brantford, this was likely an enjoyable way of passing the time.

Jones continued to farm, though his stepson Sylvanus continued to do much of the work with the aid of hired hands. They still had financial difficulties, however, and on several occasions Jones was obliged to ask for government assistance. Many in the Department of Indian Affairs recognized his abilities and his important contributions, and they tried to help. The deputy general of Indian Affairs, Hayter Reed, supported Jones's application for funds to buy some brood mares, and he wrote A.E. Forget, the assistant Indian commissioner in Regina, saying that it was a good idea because the reserve was a splendid place for horses. Reed suggested that the Aboriginal peoples, who were becoming more sophisticated farmers, could then use work horses instead of oxen. Jones also requested $200 to buy a threshing machine; although his own farm was too small to justify such a machine, he planned to thresh the grain for other farmers.[25]

Neither of these attempts at improving his family's financial situation proved fruitful. The department was able to help Jones in one small matter, and that was to support him in his battle to recoup his pension fund contributions. In those days, contributions to the civil service superannuation fund were returned only when the employee reached sixty-five years of age, and Jones was only fifty-four. However, Hayter Reed asked the government to refund the abatements from his salary amounting to $110: "In view of the fact that Dr. Jones is reported to be in a delicate state of health and unable to support himself and family."[26] Reed was able to point out that such a refund had just been authorized by an amendment to the Superannuation Act passed by the very last session of Parliament. Deputy Superintendent General Hayter Reed went out of his way to help Dr. Jones. When Reed served as Indian agent in Manitoba, he was disliked by the Cree, who referred to him as "Iron Heart." Though no longer active in the activities of the New Credit band, Jones did request the council's aid when high winds destroyed his barn. Jones knew that the Indian Act had just been amended so that Band Councils could now lend money for capital expenditures, such as improvements to buildings, on their reserves.[27]

Charlotte was proud of the benefits conferred upon her as the wife of a member of the Mississaugas of the New Credit. In addition to receiving interest payments, she was entitled to purchase a first-class railway fare at

Figure 15: Dr. Jones, his wife Charlotte, and dog Judge entertain a friend in the garden of their frame house on Maine Street, Hagersville, Ontario. (*Source:* Courtesy of Margaret Sault, Hagersville)

half price. On her frequent trips to Hamilton to attend book readings or art exhibitions, she naturally sat in the first-class carriage as an unescorted lady. In 1875, the Hamilton to Lake Erie Railway had offered this discount "for all time to come" in compensation for a right of way through the Six Nations reserve. By building the rail line across the reserve, they avoided causing serious damage to the farms of Euro-Canadian settlers in the Township of Oneida. The agreement had to be approved by the Department of Indian Affairs, which refused to allow the Six Nations to receive any money or benefits from the railway. Moreover, the then superintendent informed the railway company that there was "no necessity to take a surrender from the Indians as the law authorized the railway company to take all lands needed."[28] The best the Aboriginals could garner from the loss of a thirty-metre swath of land through a portion of their reserve was the miserly privilege of purchasing their tickets at half price. All band members benefited because the price was lower than the second-class fare, and whole families from the Six Nations and New Credit reserves could buy these tickets when journeying to the Niagara fruit belt to work in the orchards. In 1903, however, the railway changed its long practice of selling Status Indians first-class tickets at half fare and began to issue Status Indians special tickets called "Indian tickets," which were sold at half of the first-class fare, but purported on their face to be second-class tickets (half the first-class fare, however, was not the same as second-class fare). On 18 May of that year, when Charlotte purchased an Indian ticket from Hamilton to Hagersville, she was not aware of the new rules, nor did she examine her ticket and observe the words "second class."[29] When the train pulled in to the little loading platform, she noted that it was comprised of the engine, coal tender, and two carriages. A well-dressed passenger, she was helped into the first-class carriage and given a seat among the other passengers, many of them women. The train chugged off, and the conductor made his way down the narrow isle and asked her for her ticket. When he glanced at the ticket, he briskly exclaimed that something was amiss. It was a second-class ticket fare, and to remain in the first-class car, she must pay the 40-cent difference between the second- and first-class fares. He insisted very firmly that if she would not do this, she must travel in what he said was a second-class car. Humiliated in front of the other passengers, as a refined Edwardian lady and the wife of a physician, Mississauga chief, and former federal agent, Charlotte refused to do either. The other carriage did not offer proper second-class accommodation; it was a smoking car, which she referred to as a "cattle car" in her anger. The argument ended at the very next stop when she was unceremoniously ejected from the train. Alighting on the platform in fighting form, she observed through the windows of the other carriage a number of people with pipes in their mouths, contentedly smoking.[30]

When Dr. Jones heard of the indignities Charlotte had endured, he was aghast. Had the conductor picked on Charlotte because she was the wife of a Status Indian? In view of the long practice of issuing first-class tickets to Aboriginal peoples at half price, there should have been some special warning. The doctor refused to take these affronts lying down. When the train next stopped at Hagersville, he undertook a detailed examination of the carriages, accompanied by the brakeman. The car that Charlotte had refused to enter was not marked as second class, and he found that the word "Smoking" was painted on the inside walls. There was a small compartment with a small square of paper posted over the door with the words "No Smoking" printed with pen and ink that could substitute as second class. The conductor only checked this compartment when there were women present and had not informed Charlotte of its existence. On other occasions this compartment was also used by smokers and exuded an offensive odour like the rest of the carriage.[31]

The Joneses retained a lawyer, A.G. Chisholm, of London, and sued "to recover damages for being ejected from a train of the defendants, the Grand Trunk Railway Company."[32] There were two parts to their action: the right of Status Indians to purchase first-class tickets at half price, and the refusal of a passenger to travel in a smoking car. The case was heard before Judge J. Britton, of the Ontario High Court, on 3 June 1904. While the judge felt it had been wise to get the consent of the Six Nations before taking the lands in their reservation, he found that the railway had the right to restrict the cheaper Indian tickets since the Six Nations were not able to obtain a formal contract, though he thought that the railway was inconsiderate in not giving advanced warning. This branch of Charlotte Jones's action was dismissed, essentially because Status Indians were not, strictly speaking, "legal persons" but merely government wards deprived of a contract even when they were being cheated.[33]

A jury was then convened to hear evidence concerning Charlotte's claim that there was no second-class carriage but only a smoking car. The conductor claimed there was a second-class car, but the brave brakeman, backed up by Dr. Jones's meticulous notes, convinced the jury that his superior was wrong. The jury awarded Charlotte damages of $10, plus costs for rudeness and inconvenience, noting that the damages would be the same whether she had had the right to travel first or second class.[34] The Grand Trunk Railway Company recognized that this ruling set a legal precedent for their dealings with Status Indians, and an appeal dealing with Charlotte's claim that the accommodation offered was unsuitable was heard on 12 April 1905. The railway's lawyer, W.R. Riddell, who had been honoured by an appointment as King's Council (K.C.), cited both common law and the Railway Act. The younger Mr. Chisholm, speaking for Dr. and Mrs. Jones, replied that the question involved in the appeal was really very simple. The appeal court had ruled in 1903 that "a railway is bound to take reasonable means to prevent one passenger from assaulting another," and "there is really in principle no difference between an actual assault and the puffing of tobacco smoke in the face of a fellow passenger."[35] With this statement, advanced thinking for its time, the appeal was dismissed, and the Grand Trunk Railway Company was ordered to pay Charlotte Jones $10, plus her legal fees. The spectre of this and other cases in which Aboriginals fought for their rights alarmed the federal government so the Indian Act was amended to prevent them from raising money, organizing associations, or hiring lawyers. Though this restriction ended in 1927, it took until 1985 for the Six Nations to regain the 105 hectares of reserve land appropriated by the Grand Trunk Railway Company.[36]

Shortly after his victory in court, Dr. Jones was diagnosed with carcinoma of the tongue, an organ that is relatively resistant to tumours because its tissues have evolved to withstand salivary acids, food, and microbes. The main risk factors for cancer of the "oral tongue," as the forward two-thirds of the organ are called, are the heavy use of alcohol and tobacco.[37] These were the days before surgical excision, followed by radio and chemotherapy, so the tumour grew steadily, causing great pain. He obtained some relief from opium, the drug that renowned Canadian physician Sir William Osler considered "God's own medicine."[38]

A short time before his death, Dr. Jones was injured in a carriage accident involving a runaway horse. In later life, Charlotte's nephew, McDonald Holmes, of Edmonton, recalled visiting Dr. Jones around that time:

> Had to go by horse and buggy from Oshweken, 10 miles to Brantford, 10 miles to Hagersville. Dr. Jones, short, swarthy. I'd be about eight the last time I saw him. Dying of cancer; died about eighteen months after the run-away incident. Had a broad face, high cheekbones, jaws a little wide, nose narrow, straight, thin lips. Peter was confined to his den, used laudanum, a great sedative. I just knew

> him as a kid, called him Dr. Jones, didn't regard him as anything else than an Indian. When Charlotte Jones wanted groceries she put a note in a basket around dog Judge's neck, he'd take it into town. Aunt Charlotte was very good with poultry, White Orpingtons, Large white birds—roasting fowl, maximum nine pounds.[39]

Even now Dr. Jones was still trying to recoup the funds that had eluded the New Credit band when Parliament had voted to repay just the $29,161 representing their interest payments removed from their account in 1893 rather than the $68,672 capital payment he had obtained in 1884.[40] Dr. Jones's last letter to the Department of Indian Affairs, stamped "Accountants Branch Feb. 10, 1909," ends on a personal note. In tremulous cursive script he wrote: "I cannot write with pen and ink. My sickness is a very painful and tedious one, carcinoma of the tongue, and I may last many months or one or two years for my body is not otherwise much affected. I have to take great quantities of opium, and need money to keep me through my sickness."[41]

The local Indian agent, W.C. Van Loon, wrote the department that "the doctor is now very poorly and will require some assistance before spring."[42] The cancer eventually prevented Jones from speaking or swallowing anything but liquids or semi-solid foods. The old doctor, once a familiar figure on Hagersville's Main Street, was confined to his den with his beloved stuffed animals and birds.[43] The respected Aboriginal Elder was too weak to visit old friends on the reserve, which he once proudly referred to as his "Baby Municipality."[44]

Dr. Peter Edmund Jones died on 29 June 1909.[45] His funeral was organized by the Masonic Lodgers of Hagersville and Hamilton, Ontario, and held at his home, with the rector of the Anglican church in Hagersville officiating. He was buried in Greenwood Cemetery in the plot purchased by his father, Reverend Jones, a few years before his death in 1856. Curiously both men died on 29 June, and the tall slender monument erected in honour of Reverend Jones still marks the spot they share. Unfortunately, marble is not a weather-resistant stone. Time has erased all the names but one of Dr. Jones's sisters-in-law, nor are there head markers to mark the exact location of Dr. Jones's grave or those of other members of this close-knit family.[46]

Charlotte remained in the family home in Hagersville. It does not appear as if she ever involved herself with the women of New Credit whose activities revolved around the Methodist church. Sylvanus continued to run the Jones's family farm, but once Dr. Jones died, the fact

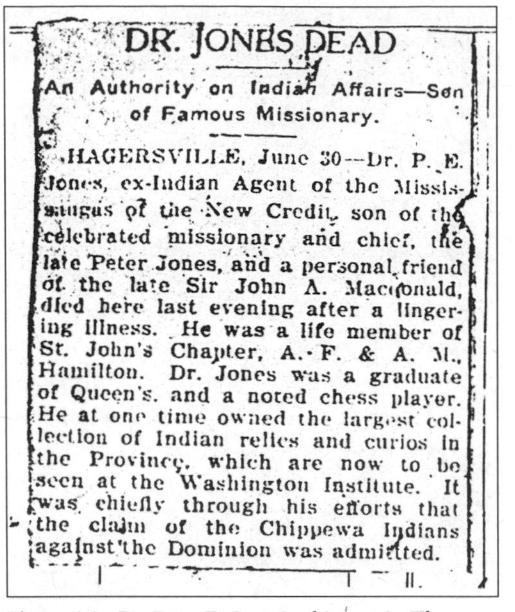
DR. JONES DEAD

An Authority on Indian Affairs—Son of Famous Missionary.

HAGERSVILLE, June 30—Dr. P. E. Jones, ex-Indian Agent of the Mississaugas of the New Credit, son of the celebrated missionary and chief, the late Peter Jones, and a personal friend of the late Sir John A. Macdonald, died here last evening after a lingering illness. He was a life member of St. John's Chapter, A. F. & A. M., Hamilton. Dr. Jones was a graduate of Queen's, and a noted chess player. He at one time owned the largest collection of Indian relics and curios in the Province, which are now to be seen at the Washington Institute. It was chiefly through his efforts that the claim of the Chippewa Indians against the Dominion was admitted.

Figure 16 Dr. Peter E. Jones's obituary in *The Toronto Globe*, 30 June 1909. (*Source:* Courtesy of the Haldimand County Museum and Archives, Cayuga, Ontario)

that both he and his mother were non-Aboriginals was unacceptable to band members. They had had enough of Sylvanus, who, though registered as living with his mother in Hagersville, spent most of his time on the reserve.[47] After working as a farmhand for most of his life, Sylvanus was now out of work. The land belonged to the Crown, and it had long been a sore point that the Jones family held location tickets for sixty hectares, three-times more than the usual twenty hectares per family. As the property was on Crown land, the heir's stake was limited to the value of improvements such as fences, buildings, and the like. Charlotte told the Band Council that her price was $1,500, but she appears to have eventually accepted considerably less.[48]

Widowed and penniless a second time, Charlotte, like so many disillusioned farm folk from the East, decided to move with Sylvanus to Alberta, following the death of her sister Drusella in 1912.[49] Drusella was Charlotte's last family tie to Hagersville. Fortunately, her nephew had moved to Edmonton. This was none other than Dr. Charles Holmes, physician to the Six Nations, who had previously lived in the nearby town of Ohsweken. The Holmeses were in the habit of visiting their relatives in Hagersville, Dr. and Mrs. Jones and Dr. and Mrs. McDonald. They helped Sylvanus and his mother move to Edmonton, Alberta, and always looked after them there. One year after moving to Edmonton, Charlotte and Sylvanus moved to Peers, two-hundred kilometres further west, where Sylvanus found work as a hired hand.[50] Charlotte stayed in Alberta until 1919, when she suffered a "stroke of paralysis" and left to join her youngest son, Elvin Dixon of Vernon, British Columbia, a Hudson's Bay manager and one of the town's early pioneers. She was seventy-seven when she reportedly died of a "haemorrhage in the brain" on 9 October 1921. Charlotte retained proud memories of her years in Hagersville until the end of her life.[51] Her second son, Alpheus, Dr. Jones's right-hand man when he published his newspaper, became assistant commercial editor of *The Toronto Empire*. Later he owned and edited the *Orchard and Farm* magazine in California, and in 1902 served as an officer of the San Francisco Press Club. He died a few months before his mother in 1921.[52]

The Jones family's papers, books, and Aboriginal artifacts, along with Dr. Jones's later additions, were preserved by his stepson, Elvin Dixon, of Vernon. They were subsequently donated to the Vernon Museum and Archives.[53] Later some of Reverend Jones's books and papers were turned over to the United Church Archives in Toronto. Other books on American Aboriginal peoples were sent to the Indian Program Department of the Smithsonian Institution in Washington, DC. Dr. Jones's collection of stuffed birds found a home in the Vernon public school system. His collection of prehistoric artifacts, including 325 stone projectiles, knives, and other four-thousand-year-old stone implements, are now held at the Woodland Indian Cultural Centre and Museum in Brantford.[54] Items from the collection can also be found in the Royal Ontario Museum, Toronto, and the Smithsonian Museum of the American Indian in Washington, DC.

The historic steel peace-pipe tomahawk, smoked by Mississauga and Iroquois warriors in 1840 at a special Grand Council held on the Credit River, however, was unaccounted for. This ceremony had ratified the treaty of friendship between these former enemies dating from about 1700, and the pipe had likely also played a role in the opening ceremonies of the Grand Council meeting organized by Dr. Jones at the New Credit reserve in 1882. Donald Smith had been looking for the pipe for more than a decade when he was able to solve the puzzle in 1982. He found it in the keeping of Reginald Campion, of Manitoba, who had received the pipe from Sylvanus Dixon, Jones's last surviving stepson. Sylvanus had moved to Manitoba following his mother's death to work as a farmhand,

and he took his father's pipe and Masonic medals with him as souvenirs of the Hagersville days. He later left them to Campion. On discovering its significance, Campion wished to find a home for the steel peace-pipe tomahawk in an appropriate museum. It is now displayed in the Mississaugas of the New Credit First Nation section of the Woodland Indian Cultural Centre and Museum in Brantford, Ontario.[55]

Today, Peter Edmund Jones's name remains virtually unrecognized by Canadians despite his many accomplishments, foremost of which were his contributions to Aboriginal journalism and self-governance. He believed that effort and education would enable Aboriginals to compete with their Euro-Canadian neighbours, and he tried to act as a bridge between them. Jones felt particularly let down when a new government in 1898 abrogated the Indian Franchise Act, which had enabled eligible Aboriginal voters to cast their ballots in federal elections.[56] Suspended between two hostile shores, Dr. Jones was buffeted by alternating successes and failures.

Dr. Jones had made the mistake of trying to act as leader of his people from outside the reserve. Doubtless, his decision to live in an adjacent White community was strongly influenced by his wife and the educational needs of her three children, but it is no wonder that his band regarded him as an outsider. Jones appears to have been a romantic who felt his early success would carry him ever onwards, and he failed to realize the harsh consequences of dependency on a single source of support—in this case, the Conservative party. His newspaper failed, leaving him with an unpaid mortgage on his house. He received neither kudos nor the desperately needed payment for his work on behalf of the Indian Act. Moreover, his Hagersville patients deserted him for younger physicians. Dr. Jones must have been grievously disappointed by this turn of events. After a problematic childhood, he had found success and reward in his early career, only to experience rejection and failure in later years.

Nevertheless, in hindsight, Jones's contributions to Aboriginal self-governance are considerable. As secretary of the Grand General Indian Council of Ontario and Quebec, he brought resolutions passed by the head chiefs at their biennial meetings to the federal government's attention. Invited by Prime Minister Macdonald to suggest changes to the Indian Act, he attempted to remove paternalistic wording and introduced greater band self-government. He fought assimilation with the Euro-Canadian society and, like his father, fought for the electoral franchise without any loss of their treaty rights. By publishing and editing the first Canadian Aboriginal newspaper, *The Indian*, Jones promoted democracy by educating his people on the importance of their newly acquired right to vote in federal elections. The biweekly newspaper aimed to unite the widely scattered tribes while recognizing their individual traditions and languages. Contacts were established between all North American Aboriginal nations. As head chief and band physician of the Mississaugas of the New Credit First Nation, Dr. Jones instituted public health measures and promoted education. During his tenure, the federal Department of Indian Affairs recognized the band's success in agriculture, sanitation, and municipal governance. Appointed to the civil service as his band's Indian agent, Jones risked losing his job by encouraging Aboriginal resistance when the government refused to allow his people to leave the reserve in order to hunt for food.

Jones was an accomplished archaeologist, and his collection of Aboriginal artifacts, some dating back thousands of years, now grace several major museums. Soon after being elected head chief in 1874, Jones identified long forgotten land claims of the Mississaugas and throughout his life fought for a just settlement. Though a Tory supporter, he encouraged qualified Indians to vote for the candidate of their choice in the hope of influencing government policies. Unfortunately, when the government's interest in the Aboriginal peoples of eastern Canada waned after the troubles of 1885, their attention was then directed toward managing the larger western Aboriginal population so that the land could be settled. Nonetheless, Dr. Jones's pioneering work in the fields of Aboriginal governance, journalism, and public health helped lay the foundation for future relations between Canada and the First Nations.

Appendix
Effective Herbal Therapies of Aboriginal Women

Careful people, who noted what had best helped the sick, then began to prescribe them. In this way medicine had its rise....
—Aulus Celsus, *De Medicina* (c. 50 BC).[1]

Peter Edmund Jones's graduating thesis, entitled "The Indian Medicine-Man," is, unfortunately, lost to posterity.[2] It would have offered a fascinating glimpse into the lifestyle of Aboriginal peoples. No doubt his professors would have insisted that he ridicule non-Christian medical practices. North American physicians abruptly abandoned Aboriginal remedies in the mid-eighteenth century even though they knew many were effective. Licensed physicians feared being confused with quacks and salesmen who sold worthless cures, actually alcohol and colouring, at so-called Indian medicine shows. If Peter Edmund were to write his thesis today, he would realize that Aboriginal herbal therapy, acquired over the millennia by means of chance observations and trial and error, was in many ways more scientific than the bleeding, blistering, and purging advocated by his professors. A century after his death, he would be proud of the resurgence of traditional Aboriginal medicine. It is appropriate to honour Dr. Jones by reviewing literature that demonstrates the efficacy of traditional Canadian Aboriginal herbal therapy.[3]

Peter Edmund would have acquired knowledge of Aboriginal herbal therapy from his father. Reverend Jones had been one of the last Mississaugas to take part in the seasonal migrations of the hunter-gatherers. While travelling through the once dense forests of southern Ontario, his childhood illnesses would be managed by his mother and grandmother. In the spring and fall he would have attended the elaborate ceremonies of the professional healers, members of the Ojibwe Grand Medicine Society, or *Medewiwin* who combined traditional spirituality with secret herbal therapies. At fourteen years of age and educated to be a warrior,

Reverend Jones went to live with his American father and his Mohawk second wife near Brantford. There he was exposed to the sophisticated herbal therapies of the Six Nations. Then as a missionary, Jones had a second exposure to Aboriginal herbal medicine. The energetic preacher visited most of the Ojibwe bands in Upper Canada, including some that had yet to be placed on a reserve. Unlike his British confreres, who insisted that their new converts discard traditional therapies, Jones respected Aboriginal herbal medicine and was knowledgeable enough to prescribe them. A box containing his herbs, along with a knife and pharmacy scale dating from 1838, survived the shipwreck of the *Colborne* on a reef near Port Daniel, Quebec, in 1838.[4]

As a teenager, Dr. Jones helped his mother edit his late father's missionary diaries and complete the manuscript of his seminal work, *The History of the Ojebway Indians*, which includes a table listing their principal medicinal plants (see Table 1, pp. 35–36).[5] They were aided by an article he had published in a Toronto magazine fifteen years before his death, entitled "The Indian Nations."[6] In describing the medicines used by the North American Aboriginal peoples, he proudly stated that "they had an abundant variety of remedies, every way suitable for the diseases common to their country and climate." The book was published in England the year before Peter Edmund went off to medical school. Reprinted many times, it is still readily available.

Women had always played an especially significant role in meeting the health needs of their families. As ethnobotanist Judith Sumner observed, they frequently possessed more accurate information about reproductive complaints and pediatric problems than their male counterparts.[7] According to Christina Clavelle, most plant-gathering and processing activities among the northern Saskatchewan Cree were the domain of women. Those few plant-related activities that men engaged in would have involved collection and preparation of species for medicinal-spiritual uses.[8] Following the First World War, when botanist Jacques Rousseau surveyed the medicinal plants employed by the Mohawks living on the Kahnawake Territory near Montreal, he was struck by how effectively the missionaries, supported by the Indian agents, had stigmatized the professional Shaman. According to Rousseau, "Once the medicine-men had been banished, the women healers took the stage. In reality, these women were not newcomers to the scene, but the descendents [*sic*] of midwives who had plied their profession for as long as women had given birth."[9] Men had quietly respected women's role in healing as they treated sickness by means of warmth, fluids, nutrition, and simple remedies. Moreover, girls, then as now, required the help of their mothers, aunts, and grandmothers, as well as Elders with experience in herbal medicine. These women were the carriers of oral traditions concerning health care, which had long maintained the circle of family life.

Ojibwe historian Professor Cary Miller has re-examined the role of women in eastern woodland Aboriginal societies.[10] Though the authoritarian role of women was more visible in matrilineal societies like the Iroquois, the Ojibwe recognized and honoured women as mothers of the nation, particularly for their ability to grow crops. Ojibwe women's work groups were organized under the authority of the *ogimaakwe* or chief woman. Their animated discussions led to a consensual opinion that the chief woman would present at Band Council meetings, which all the women attended. While only the men stood before the government negotiator's desk in treaty negotiations (the Aboriginals were never allowed to sit), the women found a way to have their say. During breaks in the meeting, everyone rushed to visit the women's cooking fires, which surrounded the area. Once they arrived, the women were able to express their political opinions freely to the officials.[11]

In the Prairies there were many women herbalists, usually women past child-bearing age. Sarah Carter's work illustrates the important role they played in the early reserve years.[12] Many of the elder women proved adept at diagnosing ailments and prescribing the correct herbal tea. In this way they replaced the water and salt lost via the sweat during a febrile illness. For example, babies, fretful because of colic, responded positively to tea brewed from the leaves of the catnip (*Nepeta cataria*); the fruit of the horsenettle (*Solanum carolinense*) contained enough scopolamine (an anticholinergic drug) to sedate sleepless band members; and the boiled roots of lady's slipper (*Cypripedium hirsutum*) alleviated nervous symptoms such as hysteria.[13] According to entries in the ledgers of the fur traders who preceded the agricultural settlers, the women were paid a fee for their "doctoring."[14]

Aboriginal peoples had effective home remedies; each tribe selected barks, leaves, roots, or whole plants that grew in their own hunting region. As chemical constituents are often concentrated in a specific part of the plant, herbalists had to know the location of the active medicinal agents.[15] In some instances particularly important herbal products were imported via messengers sent to barter with distant bands. Some bands used the same herbs, but prescribed them for different illnesses. This was evident when the American government forcibly removed members of the Delaware tribe to what is now the state of Oklahoma in the nineteenth century, and a few escaped and found refuge with the Cayugas of the Six Nations of the Grand River in Ontario. Ethnologist Gladys Tantaquidgeon's research shows that both groups continued to employ the same herbal preparations, but they prescribed them for different situations.[16] In addition, not all herbal practices involved ill health. A Delaware woman herbalist, Touching Leaves (alias Nora Dean), told historian Carl Weslager that her mother, also trained in herbal medicine, would take her into the woods in the early spring in order to find wild grapevines (*Vitis aestivalis*). Cutting the vine to express the sap, she applied the viscous natural liquid to her hair as a cleanser, after which it was shiny and black.[17] Similarly, crushed strawberries (*Fragaria virginiana*), applied to the face, acted as an astringent to remove facial blemishes resulting from exposure to the sun and wind.[18]

Mothers had treatments for different conditions affecting overall health or a particular part of the body. Women spent much time cooking over wood fires in confined spaces, exposing their eyes, nasal passages, and sinuses to hot smoke and flying ash. Subsequent inflammation of the conjunctivae responded to repeated bathing with an infusion of goldenseal (*Hydrastis canadensis*), a poultice prepared from the inner rind of the bark of the witch hazel shrub (*Hamamelis virginiana*), or by applying mesquite (*Prosopis glandulosa*) leaves directly to the irritated conjunctiva.[19] Women also steeped the flowers, leaves, and stalks of yarrow (*Achillea millefolium*) and poured the liquid into aching ears.[20] Insect bites, the scourge of peoples living in the woods, were eased by applying a combination of witch hazel and the leaves of wild tobacco (*Nicotiana rustica*).[21] Aboriginal herbalists also discovered that a decoction prepared from the root and rhizome of black cohosh (*Cimicifuga racemosa*) helped to control menstruation and reduced the severity of symptoms associated with menopause.[22]

Burns and scalds occurred frequently in Aboriginal communities because women stood around cooking fires, boiling water or roasting meat, while others came to warm themselves, and children played nearby. Treatments were readily available: The bark of young trees—white pine (*Pinus strobes*), basswood (*Tilia americana*), or slippery elm (*Ulmus fulva*)—was boiled, and the resulting solution applied to the skin.[23] Aboriginals harvested pumpkins (*Cucurbita pepo*) long before the Europeans arrived. (Jacques Cartier saw them for the first time on his second visit.) They were not just important foodstuffs, however. Pumpkin sap also proved to be soothing when applied to burns. Another manner of easing pain and promoting healing was to cover the burn with the wilted leaves of the Jimson weed (*Datura stramonium*).[24]

Bruises and contusions responded to poultices of fireweed (*Epilobium augustifolium*) or crushed sunflower roots (*Helianthus occidentalis*).[25] Bleeding was arrested by applying moistened roots of the tall cinquefoil (*Clintonia borealis*), which they placed on top of soft duck down.[26] They also prepared a tea from the bark and roots of sumach (*Rhus glabra*). White alum, a soft mineral, was also applied to hasten coagulation and stop bleeding.[27] It was the forerunner of the shaver's styptic pencil.[28] The Seneca tribe is credited with the discovery of petroleum in America, and French explorers reported that they scooped up the viscous liquid as it rose to the top of pools of water. It was employed to ease the pain of burns and as a lubricant for irritated mucous membranes.[29] Bear grease had many uses as well, one being an effective insect repellent when applied to the skin.[30]

The Aboriginal peoples prevented scurvy by means of strong teas brewed from the buds of young evergreen trees, all of which contain vitamin C. Their knowledge saved explorer Jacques Cartier's expedition when, on his second voyage, his crew was ravaged by scurvy in March 1536 while trapped in the ice near present-day Quebec City. Cartier was amazed at the recovery of Chief Domagaya, who a few days earlier had been ill with a swollen knee and bleeding gums, the very affliction his men were suffering from. At the first opportunity he asked the chief what had helped him and, learning that it was the juices of the leaves of a special tree, asked if there was such a tree close by. Thereupon Domagaya sent two women herbalists to help him gather nine or ten branches. They then showed Cartier how to grind the bark and prepare a tea by boiling the bark and leaves in water. When the tea was prepared and offered to the sick men, at first none of them would taste it, but finally one or two decided to risk a trial. They soon began to feel better and when this became known, there was such a demand for the medicine that in less than eight days a whole tree was consumed. The Iroquoian people called the tree *Annedda*, but a grateful Cartier preferred the name *L'arbre de vie*, which means the tree of life. Unfortunately, the captain did not provide a drawing in his otherwise detailed report. As a result later explorers and settlers were unable to identify the tree by its name and in an era before the discovery of vitamins failed to realize that other evergreens could be used. Four and a half centuries later, Quebec historian Jacques Mathieu and colleagues, after a review of the botanical and linguistic evidence, concluded that Cartier's *L'Anneddal/l'Arbre de vie* was most probably the balsam fir (*Abies balsamea*). The foliage and bark of this tree, widely utilized in traditional Iroquois herbal medicine, contains the highest concentration of vitamin C among the evergreens.[31]

Fir trees were not the only sources of vitamin C that were known to North America's Aboriginal peoples. Another example was discovered by Dr. Weston Price, a dentist who sought to identify dietary regimes associated with dental health. In the summer of 1933, Dr. Price and his wife set out from Alaska by boat with the expressed goal of finding more information on the health of the Aboriginal peoples. Crossing the Rocky Mountain divide, they finally reached the headwaters of rivers flowing into the Arctic Ocean. Their objective was to examine a group of Aboriginals who could not obtain the animal life of the sea (not even the running salmon could enter the waterways draining to the Arctic). In the Yukon Territory, Price and his party made contact with a group of Aboriginals who had just emerged from the Pelly Mountain country to sell their furs at the Hudson Bay Company outpost. These wandering tribes followed moose and caribou herds, and their diet was almost entirely limited to these animals. During his visit he examined eighty-seven individuals; only four teeth had been attacked by dental caries. The Aboriginals' knowledge of the use of different organs of the animal's body as a source of essential nutrients surprised Price, who asked an Elder why his people did not suffer from scurvy. The prompt reply was that scurvy was a "white-man's" disease; "Indians" knew how to protect themselves. When the chief learned that the doctor had come to advise them not to eat the food sold in the White man's store, the Elder was allowed to reveal their secret. When the Aboriginals shot a moose, they took care to remove two balls of fatty tissue located just above the kidneys. They were cut into as many pieces as the family required and eagerly eaten by adults and children alike. They also enjoyed a portion of the wall of the second stomach. Price recognized that the cap-like organs sitting on top of the kidneys were the adrenal glands, and the production of hormones released as a response to stress depends on a supply of vitamin C. The Aboriginal peoples had discovered the richest source of vitamin C in the animal kingdom.[32]

The Aboriginal peoples also utilized many non-medicinal therapies to relieve muscle aches and rheumatism, including visits to hot springs to soak in the mineral waters, which soothed skin and relieved rheumatism.[33] The sweat lodge used by western tribes cleansed the skin, relieved muscle aches and rheumatism, calmed the nerves, and engendered a feeling of well-being. Women built the fire, rolled burning-hot stones into the enclosure, and closed the flap. The occupants poured cold water on the stones, exposing themselves to extreme moist heat for some twenty minutes in a lodge, which was usually set up on the side of a lake or stream so the participants could later jump into the cold water. They were then rubbed with oil, wrapped in a blanket, and put to bed. The womenfolk had their own sweat lodges some distance away.[34]

Upper respiratory infections were a frequent occurrence in harsh northern climes; colds, coughs, and fever required attention either in the encampment or on the trail. A medicine prepared by boiling liquorice roots (*Glycyrrhiza lepidota*) was employed as a decongestant.[35] Aboriginal peoples also boiled wild cherry bark (*Prunus serotina*) to prepare a bitter solution, which they drank hot to treat a heavy cold; adding wintergreen (*Gaultheria procumbens*) made the medicine more palatable.[36] The dried inner bark of the white pine, containing oil of turpentine, is still a widely used expectorant first discovered by the Aboriginals.[37] The bark of the slippery elm (*Ulmus fulva*) contains an abundance of mucilage, a gummy secretion, which has a soothing action on all mucous membranes so it makes an effective cough remedy.[38] Marsh marigold (*Caltha palustris*) is another cough remedy common among the Ojibwe, while small children with croup responded to tea prepared from wild garlic (*Allium reticulatum*), known by some tribes as wild onion.[39] Resin obtained from the leaf buds of the balsam poplar (*Populus balsamifera*) was an expectorant cough medicine, and Canada balsam, derived from the balsam fir, is an effective decongestant that stops runny noses.[40] The bruised roots of Virginia snakeroot (*Aristolochia serpentaria*) were held against the nose to relieve the soreness caused by constant blowing of the nose. The European newcomers appreciated this particular remedy's effectiveness, and it continued to be an official drug until 1955.[41] For the treatment of nasal congestion, dried herbs or a mixture of dried flowers were placed on small heated stones. The patient could wrap a blanket around the stones and his head and inhale the fumes.[42] This herbal medication, described in Dr. Jones's 1865 textbooks, remained an official drug for more than a century.[43] Another practical remedy was prepared from the bark of the red oak (*Quercus rubra*); singer-drummers performing at powwows always kept a container of the liquid close at hand to prevent hoarseness.[44]

The Aboriginal peoples were prone to gastrointestinal problems, due in part to the vagaries of their food supply. They started the day with breakfast, but the next meal depended on their craving for food or its availability. Hunters were willing to fast, but they overate if their efforts were successful. If need be, vomiting was precipitated by inserting a strip of slippery elm bark in the throat or swallowing a tea prepared from the white hellebore plant.[45] Cascara sagragada (*Rhamnus purshiana*), also called "sacred bark," and American senna (*Cassia marilandica*) were mild laxatives, but a decoction of May apple root (*Podophyllum peltatum*) was a much more drastic cathartic.[46] A tea prepared from the inner bark of high-bush cranberry (*Viburnum opulus*) or the bark of the black walnut tree (*Juglans nigra*) soothed stomach cramps. Diarrhea responded well to a tea prepared from the dried bark of the rhizomes and roots of low blackberry plants (*Rubus canadensis* and related species); the settlers adopted this Aboriginal cure and Blackberry® was a popular home remedy throughout America until the twentieth century.[47] North American Indians had also independently invented a rectal syringe by tying the neck of a deer's bladder about a short piece of hollow rush.[48] They were able to provide nutrition, treat constipation or diarrhoea, and even apply astringent pastes to relieve hemorrhoids.

Intestinal parasites' infestations, most commonly various types of worms, were a common complaint, especially in children who acquired the fertilized eggs or larvae from contaminated soil or food and from exposure to wildlife. By far the most common parasite was the pinworm: The female pinworm migrates into the perianal region during the night, causing itching and scratching that disturbs sleep. An even more serious problem was posed by the much larger roundworm. Adult worms up to twenty-five centimetres long maintain themselves in the small intestine by virtue of their muscular activity and feed on undigested food. Unnoticed at first, they eventually cause cramps, abdominal distension, vomiting, nutritional deficiency, and fatigue.[49] Thousands of years ago the Aboriginal peoples of America identified certain weeds that enabled them to rid the body of these unwelcome parasites. For example, the leaves, fruit, and seeds of chenopodium or wormwood (*Artemisia absinthium*) yielded oil that effectively eliminated intestinal worms. Prehistoric peoples of Utah, Colorado, and Arizona not only had access to chenopodium but commonly consumed it as part of their diet. Botanist Eric Callen and parasitologist Thomas Cameron of McGill University developed novel laboratory techniques to analyze specimens of ancient preserved feces, which they called coprolites. Samples containing chenopodium seeds proved to be free of roundworms; in contrast, there was a high incidence of parasitic infection in the absence of this herb.[50] We now know that the plant produces a potent neuromuscular blocking agent that stiffened and paralyzed the worms with the result that they let go of the intestinal wall and were eliminated in the feces. Aboriginal herbalists generously shared their knowledge with the European settlers, who called the plant "wormseed"; it soon became a doctor's prescription medicine. The textbook used by students in Dr. Jones's day devoted two pages to the action and uses of this plant, but warned that it had a nauseous smell and offensive taste.[51] Aboriginal mothers cleverly fooled their children by encouraging them to lick a mixture of crushed wormwood seeds in maple sugar. Another one of their tricks was to put some hemlock spruce (*Tsuga canadensis*) leaves in medicinal teas to disguise an unpleasant taste. Oil of chenopodium was an official medication in the United States until 1960, when safer synthetic compounds became available, but Aboriginal peoples still deserve full credit for this discovery because the chemists merely carefully analyzed their herbal medicine and produced a synthetic drug that employed the same mechanism of action as its herbal forerunner.[52]

Fish tapeworms, a common problem in all fish-eating societies, can infect humans who eat raw or poorly cooked fish. The fertile eggs of these parasites can be ingested when humans are in contact with infected dogs, brown bears, foxes, and other wildlife. These parasitic infections lead to anemia, which can be severe and lowers resistance to other infectious agents. The fish tapeworm (*D. latum*) grows to an immense length and, when lodged in the terminal portion of the small intestine, can cause pernicious anemia by interfering with the absorption of vitamin B_{12}. Women healers discovered that pumpkin seeds, when ground, pounded in a wooden mortar, and mixed with water to yield a pulpy mass, was such an effective treatment that it was appropriated by the newcomers and cited in Dr. Jones's textbook.[53] A more drastic intestinal irritant employed to eliminate tapeworms was prepared by soaking the leaves or roots of the male fern (*Dryopterus felix-mas*) in water and administering a few hundred millilitres by mouth. The advice of a professional herbalist would be sought out before administering it, however, as this plant is known to be very toxic. Today its use is usually confined to the elimination of worms in domestic animals.[54]

The care of pregnant women was completely ignored by the great medicine men as beneath their dignity and left to the female attendants. In a paper presented to Ottawa physicians in 1886, Dr. Robert Bell used his experiences in practising medicine among the Aboriginal peoples living in northern Canada while serving with a geological survey when he remarked that a profound knowledge of obstetrics was seldom called for because the babies were usually small, which facilitated delivery of the head.[55] The delivery took place in a wigwam set aside for this purpose; the patient was placed on her hands and knees on the ground, with the midwife supporting the abdomen with her hands. Labour would be hastened by the judiciously timed induction of violent sneezing. Women herbalists prepared special medications that provided fluids and perhaps some analgesic effect. The herbalist also applied massage to quicken the third stage of labour and lessen the anxiety of the mother. Aboriginal midwives knew how to manually express the afterbirth by grasping the uterus firmly through the abdominal wall, kneading it, and pressing downward to stimulate contraction. Known as Credé's manoeuvre, it became popular in Europe only in 1854; prior to that, doctors would rush removal of the afterbirth by pulling on the umbilical cord or invading the vaginal tract, inadvertently causing bleeding or infection. Aboriginals also minimized the risk of infection by isolating the new mother and child from the family for a long period of time after the birth. A Belgian who settled in Alberta was grateful that two Aboriginal midwives, accompanied by their children, had set up a tepee next to his cabin in the summer of 1892. They made a liquid out of twigs or roots that "worked like a charm" during his wife's delivery and helped insure that it was uneventful.[56] Dr. Elizabeth Matheson, the band physician on the Onion Lake reserve in Saskatchewan between 1898 and 1918, even called upon an Aboriginal midwife to assist in the births of her own children.[57]

Headaches were eased by the application of a compress of horsemint leaves (*Monarda punctata*) soaked in water or white pine needles to the head. Aboriginal patients also ingested the bruised leaves and berries of red cedar (*Juniperus virginiana*) or chewed willow bark (*Salix alba*). The Montagnais made a mash of red willow bark (*Salix lucida*), which was then bandaged to the head to relieve headache. The leaves were steeped in water that was drunk for the same purpose.[58] Elders knew that the bark of the willow tree was very bitter.[59] Boiling the inner bark yielded an effective medicine for fever, headache, and rheumatism, and chewing the bark was equally effective. We now know that a couple of teaspoons of white willow bark will yield approximately one hundred milligrams of salicin, a drug similar to Aspirin®.[60] More than eighty-five percent of the salicin in willow is absorbed by the digestive tract, providing a therapeutic level for several hours.[61] Other healers preferred to use the inner bark of birch trees or brewed wintergreen leaves. This infusion, called Canada tea, contains methyl salicylate, a precursor of salicylic acid, which is the active ingredient in Aspirin®. Wintergreen oil, which contains methyl salicylate, penetrates the skin and relieves aching muscles and arthritic joints.[62] Aboriginal peoples had discovered that butterbur (*Petasites hybridus*), a member of the daisy family, offered relief from the intense throbbing of migraine headaches. Just chewing the raw root was helpful, though a tea prepared from either roots or the rhubarb-like leaves was more convenient. The efficacy of a purified extract of butterbur in migraine prevention has been confirmed in well-designed clinical trials. Patients should not consume any part of this plant other than a commercial product in which plant carcinogens have been removed.[63] The northern prickly ash (*Zanthoxylum americanum*) was called the "toothache tree." The Aboriginals of eastern North America applied the bark or mashed bark into or around carious teeth. A primitive form of root canal treatment involved thrusting a burning hot splinter of birch wood into the decayed tooth to destroy the nerve. Birch twigs are astringent and contain some methyl salicylate, which would help to relieve pain.[64] Dental extraction involved attaching a sinew or cord about the aching tooth and tying the other end to a branch, and then throwing oneself to the ground.[65]

Trauma was unavoidable so as a precaution, all communities had a number of members who could attend to dislocations or fractures of the limbs. Dr. Jones's Mohawk step-aunt, Catherine Russell (1800–1880), was such a practical doctor. Her daughter recalled her response when a young lad fell and put his shoulder out of joint: "Grandmother Catherine took off her shoe, put her foot against his ribs then pulled his shoulder into place. She then reached into her bag, took out a ball of yarn and placed it firmly in his armpit before bandaging the arm to his side; the shoulder healed perfectly."[66] The practice of the Ojibwe was to wash and grease the skin overlying the fracture and apply a poultice of wild ginger (*Asarum canadense*) with spikenard root (*Aralia racemosa*) once they had aligned the bones. Prolonged fixation of the limb was achieved by means of tightly bound thin cedar splints. They maintained the reduction of more extensive fractures with canoe-thickness birchbark that had been softened by heating before being moulded over the limb. When the bark cooled, it became as rigid as a plaster of Paris cast or a plastic brace. Elders whose limbs or knees were weak often made supports by taking wide strips of fresh basswood bark and binding it around their limbs as a splint. When dried, the bark grew hard and supported their limbs so they could get about.[67]

One of the most widely used fever medicines was an infusion prepared from the bark of the flowering dogwood (*Cornus florida*) tree. This was the North American Aboriginal's best substitute for Peruvian bark, the source of quinine, a specific treatment for malarial fevers.[68]

A weakness of North American Aboriginal medicine was that neither the South American cinchona tree, whose bark contains quinine, nor the opium poppy, which was the source of powerful painkillers and cough suppressants, were available prior to contact with Europeans.[69] It is also unlikely that many Aboriginal peoples ingested medicinal herbs for prolonged periods in part because of their nomadic habits. Interestingly, the women did construct spoons, birchbark measures, and other containers to administer herbs. Dosage was measured in mouthfuls. Larger containers of liquids provided replacement fluids to maintain life in the face of a high fever.[70] As there was no way of telling time, and because Aboriginal peoples had no fixed mealtimes, the ingestion of medicine was largely symptom-driven, especially in the case of gastrointestinal disorders or pain.

Postscript

Once Aboriginal mothers took up residence on reserves, they maintained their traditional approaches and continued to employ many of their effective traditional methods of family health care. Predictions of the demise of Aboriginal healing practices proved wrong; in fact, there has been a resurgence of interest in these practices in healing circles. Therapies such as the sweat lodge are now widely accepted as effective, and Cree First Nations are today sharing their knowledge of plants used to control type II diabetes with the Canadian Institutes of Health Research.[71]

Many Aboriginals also quickly developed a high regard for Western medical technology. Their traditional trust in the Medicine Man was transferred to physicians selected and paid by their own Band Council and approved by Indian Affairs in Ottawa. For example, Dr. Robert Dee, the first physician hired on a full-time basis by the Six Nations, received an annual allowance for purchasing supplies of drugs such as morphine and the anti-malarial agent quinine. The traditional members of the Six Nations who followed the religion of the longhouse, preferred to use their own herbal remedies and curing rituals.[72] In 1876, when the Aboriginals of central Saskatchewan and Alberta signed Treaty Six, they stipulated that the government be bound to keep a "medicine chest." A century later, a lower Canadian court interpreted the provision of a "medicine chest" to be a metaphor implying that Status Indians were entitled to total health care. The issue was partially resolved when all Canadians became eligible for government-sponsored comprehensive medical insurance, though conflicts over non-insured services remain.[73]

Notes

Chapter 1 Peter Edmund Jones's Origins

1 Chief Kahkewaquonaby, M.D., to Sir John A. Macdonald, dated Hagersville, 30 May 1885; Canada, Commons Debates, 48 Victoria, 8 June 1885, 19: 2371, LAC; Canada, The Electoral Franchise Act, S.C. 48 Vict., c. 40, ss. 2, 11.

2 Donald B. Smith, *Sacred Feathers: The Reverend Peter Jones (Kakewaquonaby) and the Mississauga Indians* (Toronto: University of Toronto Press, 1987); Donald B. Smith, "Jones, [Reverend] Peter," in *DCB*, vol. 8, 1851–1860 (Toronto: University of Toronto Press, 1985), 439–43; Kyle Carsten Wyatt, "Rejoicing in This Unpronounceable Name: Peter Jones's Authorial Identity," *Papers of the Bibliographical Society of Canada*, 47, no. 2, Autumn (2009):153–76; Donald B. Smith, "Jones, Peter Edmund (Kahkewaquonaby)," in *DCB*, vol. 13, 1901–1910 (Toronto: University of Toronto Press, 1993), 530–31; William Cochrane, "Peter Edmund Jones, M.D.," in William Cochrane, ed., *The Canadian Album: Men of Canada; or, Success by Example*, vol. 2 (Brantford: Bradley, Garretson, 1893), 262.

3 Minutes of Senate, Queen's University, 27 March 1866, QUA; CPSO, historical register: Dr. Peter E. Jones, licence no. 678, 14 November 1866.

4 No author, *Indians of Ontario: An Historical Review* (Ottawa: Indian and Northern Affairs Canada, 1966), 29.

5 *The Indian*, 30 December 1885, 1–12; 29 December 1886, 1–12 (Toronto: Maclaren Micropublishing, 1974) mfm, TRL; Canada, Dept. of the Interior, RG 15, Series D-11-1, vol. 403, file 104,198, mfm T-13109, LAC; Peter Edmund Jones, "An Indian's View of the Indian Question," *The Toronto Daily Mail*, 16 May 1885; Edward S. Rogers, "The Algonquin Farmers of Southern Ontario, 1830–1945," in *Aboriginal Ontario: Historical Perspectives on the First Nations*, ed. Edward S. Rogers and Donald B. Smith (Toronto: Dundurn Press, 1994), 148.

6 *The Toronto Globe*, 30 June 1909, Jones's obituary mentions that he had been a life member of St. John's Chapter, A.F. & A.M. Masonic Lodge; Orange Directory of Western Ontario, 1871, Part 2, District of Oneida, online at http://www.members.tripod.com/~Roughian/index-410.htm.

7 Canada, Dominion Electoral Franchise Act, S.C. 1898, C. 14, s. 5(a).

8 Ontario, register of deaths, "Peter Edmund Jones," RG 80-8, vol. 8, 1909, no. 12092, AO.

9 Donald G. Jones, "Augustus Jones 1758–1836," in *Head of the Lake Historical Society*," 15 (1988):1–21, reprinted November 1995. Donald G. Jones of Dundas,

ON, is a descendant of Augustus Jones's brother, Stephen Jones, Sr.; Donald B. Smith, "Jones, Augustus," in *DCB*, vol. 7, 1836–1850 (Toronto: University of Toronto Press, 1988), 450–2; "Tuhbenahneequay," in *Eagle Press Newsletter*, Hagersville, ON, The Mississaugas of the New Credit First Nation, 15 May 1997. Tuhbenahneequay was born in 1780 (cited in the Credit Mission Church registry) and died in 1874 (cited in the New Credit Church registry). She is memorialized by a grove of oak trees situated along the ancient Toronto Carrying Place Trail; John Ladell, *They Left Their Mark: Surveyors and Their Role in the Settlement of Ontario* (Toronto: Dundurn Press, 1993), 84–100; J.L. Morris, *Indians of Ontario* (Toronto: Ontario Department of Lands and Forests, 1943), 4.

10 Smith, *Sacred Feathers*, 247; Eliza Jones to John Dunlop, dated Brantford, 22 November 1856, PJC, VUL.

11 Hubert H. Lamb, *Climate History and the Modern World* (London: Routledge, 1995), 433; Smith, *Sacred Feathers*, 41.

12 Smith, *Sacred Feathers*, 43–44.

13 Peter Jones, *History of the Ojebway Indians: With Especial Reference to Their Conversion to Christianity* (London: A.W. Bennett, 1861) reprint (Freeport: Books for Libraries, 1970), 10.

14 Smith, *Sacred Feathers*, 123–26.

15 For a photograph of Jones's costume, see plate 57 in Sara Stevenson, *Facing the Light: The Photography of Hill and Adamson* (Edinburgh: Trustees of the National Galleries of Scotland), or Smith, *Sacred Feathers*, illustration no. 23. Jones complained of having to appear in his "odious Indian costume," Peter Jones's Letterbook, 29 October 1845, PJC, VUL.

16 Smith, *Sacred Feathers*, 127–29; Donald B. Smith, "Field, Elizabeth (Eliza) (Jones; Carey)," in *DCB*, vol. 11, 1819–1882 (Toronto: University of Toronto Press, 1982), 316–17.

17 Smith, *Sacred Feathers*, 136–44.

18 Jennifer Lund, "Eliza Field Jones Carey's Mission to 'Civilize' the Native Women of Early Nineteenth-Century Upper Canada" (M.A. thesis, University of Toronto, 1991), 35.

19 Donald B. Smith, "The Transatlantic Courtship of the Reverend Jones," *The Beaver*, Summer (1997):40–46.

20 Peter Jones to Eliza Jones in Letterbook (1833–1848), box 3, file 4, including a letter from Hamilton, ON, dated 23 June 1843, mfm, PJC, VUL.

21 Smith, "Jones, Peter Edmund (Kahkewaquonaby)"; Smith, *Sacred Feathers*, 189–92.

22 Canada, S.C., R.S., 1985, c. I-5, The Indian Act, definition and registration of Indians, online at http://laws.justice.gc.ca/en/showdoc/cs/I-5/bo-ga:s_5-gb:s_5//en#anchorbo-ga:s_5gb:s_5/; Anishinabek Nation Secretariat—The Union of Ontario Indians, online at http://php?option=com_content&task=viewed=56&Itemid=37/; Dr. P.E. Jones, cited in "The Meaning of Place Names Asked by Mr. H.F. Gardiner, Supplied by Dr. P.E. Jones, 25 May 1898," *Anthropological Archives*, Smithsonian Institution, Washington, DC; James Constantine Pilling, "Dr. P.E. Jones' Biography and His Translations of the Meanings of Place Names," in *Bibliography of the Algonquian Languages* (Washington, DC: Smithsonian Institution, Bureau of Ethnology, 1891), 272.

23 Donald B. Smith, "Peter and Eliza Jones: Their Last Years," *The Beaver*, Winter (1977):16–23.

24 Peter Jones, Letterbook containing copies of correspondence from Peter Jones to Eliza, 1833–48, box 3, files 4 and 5, PLC, VUL. Peter Edmund's parents called him "Popsey"; when he became a physician, his brother Charles referred to him as "Pills"; Charles A. Jones, Charles A. Jones Correspondence, box 5, files 2–3, PLC, VUL.
25 John R. Paul, *A History of Poliomyelitis* (New Haven: Yale University Press, 1971), 17–47. Orthopedic disorders that prevent children from walking, such as congenital dislocation and developmental dysplasia of the hip, cannot be fully excluded.
26 Amalie M. Kass and Edward H. Kass, *Perfecting the World: The Life and Times of Dr. Thomas Hodgkin, 1798–1866* (Boston: Harcourt Brace Jovanovich, 1988), 269–72, 478–80.
27 Michael B.A. Oldstone, *Viruses, Plagues, and History* (New York: Oxford University Press, 1999), 90–102; Paul, *A History of Poliomyelitis,* 17–47; T.E.C., Jr., M.D., "A Case of Poliomyelitis in an English Child Reported in 1835," *Pediatrics* 80 (1987):244.
28 Charles Bell, "Case 183: Case of Wasting of a Child's Leg in Consequence of an Epidemic of Fever in St. Helena," in *The Nervous System of the Human Body as Explained in a Series of Papers Read before the Royal Society of London* (London: Henry Renshaw, 1844), 434–35.
29 Michael A. Underwood, *Treatise on the Diseases of Children with General Direction for the Management of Infants from the Birth* (London: Matthews, 1789); David Hewitt, *Scott on Himself* (Edinburgh: Scottish Academic Press, 1981), 10–15. Scottish author Sir Walter Scott was stricken with a similar paralytic illness, most likely poliomyelitis, at eighteen months of age and, like Peter E. Jones, was determined to lead a normal life.
30 Peter Jones, Letterbook, entry for 4 March 1846, PJC, VUL.
31 Indian Affairs, RG 10, vol. 438, 805; Muncey Mission, 2 December 1848, Peter Jones to Joseph Clench, Indian Affairs, RG 10 vol. 438, 821.
32 Indian Affairs, RG 10 vol. 438, 821, Peter Jones to Joseph Clench, 7 March 1850; Daniel J. Brock, "Clench, Joseph Brant" in *DCB*, vol. 8, 1851–1860 (Toronto: University of Toronto Press, 1985), 161–63.
33 Peter Jones's Diary, 23 June 1832, PJC, VUL.
34 George Dickson and G. Mercer Adam, eds., *A History of Upper Canada College, 1829–1892* (Toronto: Rowsell & Hutchison, 1893), 297. Wilson is listed as Francis Jones.
35 Indian Affairs, RG 10, vol. 1011, entry book 1831–1848, Peter Jones to George Vardon, Port Credit, 8 February 1847, LAC.
36 Ibid.
37 Smith, *Sacred Feathers*, 209, 324, n. 53; ibid., 213–14; Peter Jones, Letterbook, box 3, file no. 10, PJC, VUL.
38 Ibid., 213–14; Peter Jones, Letterbook, box 3, file no. 10, PJC, VUL.
39 Eliza Field Jones's Diary, box 4, PJC, VUL.
40 Smith, *Sacred Feathers*, 215; Eliza Jones Carey's Diary, n.d., p. 1 of 29, box 4 mfm c.1880, PJC, VUL.
41 Smith, *Sacred Feathers*, 213.
42 Mary Byers and Margaret McBurney, "Missionaries Home Has Classical Look," *The Toronto Globe and Mail,* 12 May 1983; Jean Waldie, "Long Colorful Story of Echo Villa," *The Brantford Expositor,* 16 November 1956; Jean Waldie, "The

Romantic Story of 'Echo Villa' Home of Peter Jones," in *Brant County: The Story of Its People*, vol. 1 (Brantford: Brant Historical Society, 1984), 68–70; Donald B. Smith, "Peter and Eliza Jones: The Last Years," 16–23.

43 Smith, *Sacred Feathers*, 216.

44 Ibid., 215–20.

45 Veronica Strong-Boag and Carole Gerson, *Paddling Her Own Canoe: The Times and Texts of E. Pauline Johnson (Tekahionwake)* (Toronto: University of Toronto Press, 2000), 28–30; Smith, *Sacred Feathers*, 228–29.

46 Eliza Field Jones's Diary, 26 March 1854 to 16 August 1854, 19 April 1854, box 4, file 7, PJC, VUL.

47 David Hewitt, *Scott on Himself* (Edinburgh: Scottish Academic Press, 1981), 10–15.

48 Acts 17:30, *The Bible,* Authorized King James Version (AV).

49 Eliza Field Jones's Diary, 26 March 1854 to 16 August 1854, 1 May 1854, box 4, file 7, PJC, VUL; Smith, *Sacred Feathers*, 228.

50 Cunard Steamship Fleet, 1849, online at http://www.ns1763.ca/ponyexpress/ponyex13/.

51 Eliza Jones's Diary, 27 April 1854, box 4, mfm, PJC, VUL.

52 Ibid., entries for 30 April and 1 May 1854.

53 John Walton, "My Great Grandfather's Diary," online at www.personalpages.tds.net/~jonwalton/Diary/. A description of a sea voyage to England in May 1856.

54 Eliza Jones Carey's Diary, box 4, file 7, PJC, VUL.

55 Kass, *Perfecting the World*, 452–53.

56 F.R. Miles, "William Adams (1820–1900), in *Oxford Dictionary of National Biography* (Oxford: Oxford University Press, 2004–8), online at http://www.oxforddub.com/view/article51476/.

57 Eliza Jones's Diary, 12 August 1854, box 4, mfm, PJC, VUL.

58 Smith, *Sacred Feathers,* 139. In the post office London directory for 1832, Charles Field's firm is listed as Wax-chandlers and Bleachers to His Majesty King William IV; Smith, *Sacred Feathers*, 131.

59 Eliza Jones's Diary, 12 August 1854, box 4, mfm, PJC, VUL.

60 Eliza Jones's Diary, 12 August 1854, PJC, VUL.

61 Dr. P.E. Jones to William L. Stone, Esq., Jersey City, NJ, 31 October 1882; Draper/ Brant Papers, 13 F13, Wisconsin State Historical Society.

62 Smith, *Sacred Feathers,* 225–33.

63 Ontario, RG 2, C1, copy of letter from Egerton Ryerson to chief superintendent, Indian Affairs, 21 November 1854, AO.

64 Smith, *Sacred Feathers*, 226–27.

65 Peter Jones, *Life and Journals of Kah-ke-wa-quo-na-by (Rev. Peter Jones), Wesleyan Missionary* (Toronto: Anson Green, 1860).

66 Jones, *History of the Ojebway Indians.*

67 Smith, *Sacred Feathers,* 217.

68 Peter Jones Collection, Victoria University, E.J. Pratt library, online at http://www. library.vicu.utoronto.ca/special/F17jonesintro/.

69 Eliza Jones's Diary, 1845–1854, box 4, PJC, VUL; J. Stewart Cameron, "Milk or Albumin? The History of Proteinuria before Richard Bright," *Nephrology, Dialysis, Transplantation*, 18 (2003):1281–85.

70 Charles M. Godfrey, *Medicine for Ontario: A History* (Belleville: Mika Publishing Co., 1979), 50.

71 Claude E. Doleman, "Bovell, James," in *DCB*, vol. 10, 1871–1880 (Toronto: University of Toronto Press, 1972), 83–85; William Canniff, *The Medical Profession in Upper Canada 1738–1850* (Toronto: William Briggs, 1894), reprint (Toronto: Clarke, Irwin & Co., 1980), 257–58; Michael Bliss, *William Osler: A Life in Medicine* (Toronto: University of Toronto Press, 1999), 40–61.

72 Robert Wynyard Powell, *The Doctor in Canada: His Whereabouts and the Laws Which Govern Him. A Ready Book of Reference* (Montreal: Gazette Printing Company, 1890), 248, 302; Dr. Egerton Griffin is listed as coroner and health officer for Brant County. At the time of publication, twenty-three physicians were members of Parliament and nine were members of the Ontario Legislature.

73 Eliza Jones to Catherine Sutton, Brantford, 25 June 1856. This letter, sent four days before Reverend Jones's death, to his niece is now in the possession of the Owen Sound and Grey County Museum, Owen Sound, ON; Smith, *Sacred Feathers*, 235–37.

74 Smith, "Peter and Eliza Jones: Their Last Years," 22. Donald B. Smith noted that in spite of their acceptance of many of the "Whiteman's" ways, the Aboriginal Christians had maintained their faith in the superiority of their own cures.

75 Smith, *Sacred Feathers*, 237; Ontario, RG 22, box 14, "Probate Will of Reverend Peter Jones," 9 May 1856, AO.

76 Mark D. Walters, "According to the Old Customs of Our Nation: Aboriginal Self-Government on the Credit River Mississauga Reserve, 1826–1847," *Ottawa Law Review*, 30, no. 1 (1998/99):1–45; Gerald R. Vizenor, *The People Named the Chippewa: Narrative Histories* (Minneapolis: University of Minnesota Press, 1984), 66–74.

77 Eliza Jones's Diary, 1 September 1856, PJC, VUL; letter to Eliza Jones from her sister, Mrs. Dowling, of Bristol.

78 Elizabeth Field Carey to John Dunlop, 22 November 1856, manuscripts dept., no. 360/102, National Library of Scotland.

79 Rose Hoover wrote a letter, dated 12 July 1963, in which she recalled that Dr. Peter E. Jones, a cousin of her father, treated her for inflamed eyes when she was ten or eleven years old, c. 1897: "He had one leg shorter than the other and walked with a cane," courtesy of Harold Senn, Victoria, and Donald B. Smith, Calgary.

80 Jennifer Lund, "Negotiating Race and Gender in the Diaries of Eliza Jones, British Wife of an Ojibwa Missionary in Upper Canada, 1823–1883" (Ph.D. dissertation, York University, 2010), 23, 225. Smith, *Sacred Feathers*, 245–47.

81 C.M. Johnston, *Brant County: A History 1784–1945* (Toronto: Oxford University Press, 1967), 84–85; Ontario, RG 2-21, mfm Ms 8339 (Brantford, date range: 1854–1862), AO; Peter Edmund Jones is mentioned in: *Grammar School Trustees Half-Yearly Returns and Annual Reports*; C.M. Johnston, *Brant County: A History, 1784–1845* (Toronto: Oxford University Press, 1967).

Chapter 2 Medical Education

1 Peter E. Jones and Peter Martin are listed in the 1862–63 calendar of the Toronto School of Medicine, and in the *Cumulative List of Students,* published in 1871, UTA.

2 George W. Sprague, "The Trinity Medical College," *Ontario History*, 63 (1996):71; Charles M. Godfrey, *Medicine for Ontario* (Belleville: Mika Publishing Co., 1979), 57–58.

3 Marian A. Patterson, "The Life and Times of the Hon. John Rolph, M.D. (1793–1870)," *Medical History*, 5 (1961):15–33; Peter Jones's Diary, 23 June 1832, PJC, VUL.

4 William Canniff, *The Medical Profession in Upper Canada 1738–1850* (Toronto: William Briggs, 1894), reprint (Toronto: Clarke, Irwin & Co., 1980), 38–49.

5 N. Tait McPhedran, *Canadian Medical Schools: Two Centuries of Medical History, 1822–1992* (Montreal: Harvest House, 1993), 104; Martin L. Friedland, *The University of Toronto: A History* (Toronto: University of Toronto Press, 2002), 126–31.

6 Eliza Field Jones had learned to play chess in England. Peter Edmund eventually became a chess master, as reported by *The Hagersville News*, 3 June 1898, HCMA.

7 Ethyl Brant Montour, *Canadian Portraits: Brant, Crowfoot, Oronhyatekha* (Toronto: Clarke Irwin and Co., 1960).

8 Gayle M. Comeau-Vasilopoulos, "Oronhyatekha (Peter Martin)," in *DCB*, vol. 13, 1901–1910 (Toronto: University of Toronto Press, 1994), 791–95; Keith A. Jamieson, "Mohawk Ideals-Victorian Ideals, the Dr. Oronhyatekha Exhibit," in *Wadrihwa*, Quarterly Newsletter of the Woodland Cultural Centre, vol. 16, no. 1 and 2, (2001):10–14. Tom Hill and Keith A. Jamieson, of the Woodland Cultural Centre, Brantford, were co-curators of this exhibit in collaboration with the Royal Ontario Museum, Toronto (2001–2).

9 Canniff, *Medical Profession*, 210–11; CPSO, historical register: Dr. Oronhyatekha graduated from the University of Toronto, registered with the college on 22 May 1867, and was granted licence no. 709; "Dr. Oronhyatekha," in William Cochrane, ed., *The Canadian Album: Men of Canada; or, Success by Example*, vol. 2 (Brantford: Bradley, Garretson & Co., 1893), 67.

10 Minutes of the Senate of Queen's University, Kingston, 27 March 1866, 28, QUA; CPSO historical register, Dr. Peter Edmund Jones was granted Ontario medical licence no. 678.

11 Smith, *Sacred Feathers*, 247; Elizabeth Field Jones Carey to John Dunlop, 22 November 1856, box 4, PJC, VUL.

12 Amalie M. Kass and Edward H. Kass, *Perfecting the World: The Life and Times of Dr. Thomas Hodgkin 1798–1866* (Boston: Brace Jovanovich Publishers, 1988), 446, 600, n. 20. Hodgkin neglected his practice and busied himself with charitable causes. He had urged the Quakers to protect the Canadian Aboriginals living in the Hudson's Bay Territories.

13 Margaret Sharpe Angus, *Kingston General Hospital: A Social and Institutional History* (Montreal: McGill-Queen's University Press, 1973), 21–41, 43, 205; H. Pearson Gundy, "Growing Pains: The Early History of the Queen's Medical Faculty," *Historic Kingston*, 4 (1955); James Low, "Kingston General Hospital, a National Treasure," *Historic Kingston*, 46 (1998), 31–42.

14 Queen's University, *Student Register*, autumn 1864, QUA.

15 Queen's University, *Register of Students*, list of their religious affiliations: 1864–66, QUA.
16 Peter Oliver, "Lavell, Michael," in *DCB*, vol. 13, 1900–1910 (Toronto: University of Toronto Press, 1994), 589–82.
17 Margaret Sharpe Angus, "Dickson, John Robinson," in *DCB*, vol. 11, 1881–1890 (Toronto: University of Toronto Press, 1982), 263–64; David A. Nock, "Yates, Horatio," in *DCB*, vol. 11, 1881–1890 (Toronto: University of Toronto Press, 1982), 940–41; Canniff, *The Medical Profession,* 674–76.
18 Anthony A. Travill, *Medicine at Queen's, 1854–1920: A Peculiarly Happy Relationship* (Kingston: Faculty of Medicine, Queen's University, 1988), 14–19; J.K. Johnson and P.B. Waite, "Macdonald, Sir John Alexander," in *DCB*, vol. 12, 1891–1900 (Toronto: University of Toronto Press, 1990), 591–612.
19 Nock, "Yates, Horatio," 940–41.
20 Angus, *Kingston General Hospital,* 27–41.
21 Travill, *Medicine at Queen's*, 39–41.
22 Queen's University, *Student Register*, autumn 1864, QUA; Peter Jones, *History of the Ojebway Indians: With Especial Reference to Their Conversion to Christianity* (London: A.W. Bennett, 1861), reprint (Freeport: Books for Libraries, 1970), 141–55.
23 Eliza Jones Carey's Diary contains numerous descriptions of illness, including a heartrending account of her progressive blindness.
24 Jones, *History*, 152–53; Queen's University, *Student Register*, autumn 1864. Students had to provide the topic of their graduating thesis at the time of registration.
25 Suzanne Zeller, "Lawson, George," in *DCB*, vol. 12, 1891–1900 (Toronto: University of Toronto Press, 1990), 539–42; Travill, *Medicine at Queen's*, 45–50, 66–69.
26 Ibid.
27 Travill, *Medicine at Queen's,* 69–71; Queen's University, Robert Bell fonds, Acc. 79-44, QUA; McGill University, Robert Bell fonds, MG 2042, Acc. 2640, MUA.
28 Queen's University, minutes of the Senate, 1865–66, 19–28, QUA.
29 Ibid.
30 W.A. Waiser, "Bell, Robert," in *DCB*, vol. 14, 1911–1920 (Toronto: University of Toronto Press, 1998), 55–56.
31 Robert Bell, "The Medicine-Man; or Indian and Esquimo Notions of Medicine," *Canadian Medical & Surgical Journal* (March and April 1886) (Montreal: Gazette Printing Company, 1886), 1–13.
32 Travill, *Medicine at Queen's*, 102.
33 Walter E. Finkbeiner, Philip C. Ursell, and Richard L. Davis, *Autopsy Pathology: A Manual and Atlas* (Philadelphia: Churchill Livingston, 2004), 24.
34 Ibid., 74–75; Charles Darwin, *On the Origin of Species by Means of Natural Selection, or the Preservation of Favoured Races in the Struggle for Life* (London: Murray, 1860).
35 René Vallery-Radot, *The Life of Pasteur*, trans. R.L. Devonshire (New York: McClure Phillips & Co., 1906); Abraham Groves, *All in a Day's Work: Leaves from a Doctor's Case Book (*Toronto: Macmillan, 1934), 3–8. Allegedly, Dr. Groves performed Canada's first appendectomy in 1885 on a kitchen table in Fergus, a mere 100 kilometres from Dr. Jones's Hagersville clinic.
36 Queen's University, minutes of the Faculty of Medicine, 1864–66, QUA.
37 Angus, *Kingston General Hospital,* 10–11.

38 R. Douglas Francis, Richard Jones, and Donald B. Smith, *Journeys: A History of Canada* (Toronto: Nelson Division of Thomson Canada, 2006), 143–44; Réal Bertrand, *Célébrités Canadiennes: Louis-Hippolyte LaFontaine* (Montreal: Lidec Inc., 1993), 1–2.
39 Interview with Dr. James A. Low, curator, Kingston General Hospital, National Historic Site, 8 December 2007.
40 B.M. Duncum, *The Development of Inhalation Anaesthesia with Special Reference to the Years 1846–1900* (London: Oxford University Press, 1944).
41 Michael Bliss, *William Osler: A Life in Medicine* (Toronto: University of Toronto Press, 1999), 61.
42 Jane Errington, *Greater Kingston: Historic Past Progressive Future* (Burlington: Windsor Publications, 1998), 53–57.
43 *Kingston Daily News,* 11 June 1862, KGHA; Angus, *Kingston General Hospital,* 38–39.
44 Queen's University, *Calendar of the Faculty of Medicine for 1865–1866*, 43, QUA.
45 Travill, *Medicine at Queen's*, 40.
46 In the nineteenth century medical education was entirely theoretical; students used a cadaver when learning simple operative procedures, such as how to treat a dislocation of the shoulder.
47 Ibid.
48 "Dr. P.E. Jones, Coroner," in Don Brown, ed., *Down Memory Lane: A Glimpse of Hagersville's Past* (Hagersville: Haldimand Press, 1992), 266.
49 Queen's University, *Calendar of the Faculty of Medicine for 1865–1866,* QUA.
50 George B. Wood and Franklin Bache, *The Dispensatory of the United States of America* (Philadelphia: J.B. Lippincott, 1858), 1084–95.
51 Thomas Watson, *Lectures on the Principles and Practice of Physic Delivered at King's College London* (Philadelphia: Blanchard and Lea, 1858), 167.
52 Kingston General Hospital, admission records for 1865–66, KGHA; James A. Low, *The Faculty 1854–1956, Queen's University at Kingston: Obstetrics and Gynecology* (Kingston: Queen's University, 1985), 5–8.
53 Travill, *Medicine at Queen's*, 74, 77–78; Joseph J. Lister, "On the Antiseptic Principle in the Practice of Surgery," *British Medical Journal*, 2 (1867):246–48.
54 Kingston General Hospital, Annual Report 1865, KGHA.
55 Travill, *Medicine at Queen's*, 77–78.
56 D.O. Lynch, "A Century of Psychiatric Teaching at Rockwood Hospital, Kingston," *Canadian Medical Association Journal*, 70, no. 3 (1954):283–87.
57 Ibid.; Wendy Mitchinson, "R.M. Bulka: A Victorian Asylum Superintendent," *Ontario History*, 63 (1981):239–54.
58 Watson, *Lectures*, 408–17.
59 William Osler, *The Principles and Practice of Medicine* (New York: D. Appleton & Company, 1892), 1079. Dedicated to Osler's teachers, including Professor James Bovell, of the Toronto School of Medicine. Peter Edmund Jones was also a former student of Bovell.
60 Jacalyn Duffin, "A Rural Practice in Nineteenth-Century Ontario: The Continuing Medical Education of James Miles Langstaff," *Canadian Bulletin of Medical History*, 5 (1988):3–25.
61 Fielding H. Garrison, *An Introduction to the History of Medicine,* 4th ed. (Philadelphia: W.B. Saunders Co., 1929), 411–13.

62 Douglas J. Lanska, "The History of Reflex Hammers," *Neurology*, 39 (1989):1542–49.
63 Angus, *Kingston General Hospital*, 46.
64 Jaclyn Duffin, *Langstaff: A Nineteenth-Century Medical Life* (Toronto: University of Toronto Press, 1993).
65 William B. Spaulding, "Abraham Groves (1847–1935): A Pioneer Ontario Surgeon, Sufficient unto Himself," *Canadian Bulletin of Medical History,* 5 (1991):249–62; Abraham Groves, *All in a Day's Work: Leaves from a Doctor's Case Book* (Toronto: Macmillan, 1934); Charles G. Roland, "The Medical Life of Dr. Abraham Groves," *Wellington County History*, 16 (2003):31–48.
66 Fielding H. Garrison, "Lister in Relation to the Victorian Background," in *Contributions to the History of Medicine* (New York: Hafner Publishing, 1966), 907–12.
67 E.H. Ackernecht, *A Short History of Medicine* (Baltimore: Johns Hopkins University Press, 1982), 187–88.
68 Garrison, *History of Medicine,* 575–80; Godfrey, *Medicine for Ontario,* 161. Peter Edmund received instruction in hygiene in his course entitled "The Institutes of Medicine."
69 Queen's University, *Calendar of the Faculty of Medicine for 1863-64,* 66, QUA.
70 Travill, *Medicine at Queen's,* 39.
71 The 1856 revised edition of the *Pharmacopoeia of the United States of America [USP]*, first published in 1820, would be available in the library of Queen's University, as would its companion volume, *The National Formulary of the United States*.
72 No author, *The Pharmacopoeia of the United States of America* (Boston: Charles Ewer, 1820), mfm 413, Osler Library, McGill University.
73 Ibid.
74 Virgil J. Vogel, "American Indian Influence on the American Pharmacopoeia," in *Folk Medicine and Herbal Healing*, ed. George G. Meyer, Kenneth Blum, and John G. Cull (Springfield: Chas. C. Thomas, 1981), 111–12.
75 Virgil J. Vogel, "American Indian Influence on Medicine and Pharmacology," *Indian Historian*, 1, December (1967):12–15; Carl A. Weslager, *Magic Medicines of the Indians* (Wallingford: Middle Atlantic Press, 1973), 138–44.
76 Francis Densmore, *Indian Use of Wild Plants for Crafts, Food, Medicine, and Charms* (Originally published as: *Uses of Plants by the Chippewa Indians*), Annual Report of the Bureau of American Ethnology, 1926–1927 (Washington, DC: 1928), reprint (Ohsweken: Irocrafts, 1993), 329; Gladys Tantaquidgeon, *A Study of Delaware Indian Medicine Practice and Folk Beliefs* (Philadelphia: Pennsylvania Historical Commission, 1942), 82–83; Weslager, *Magic Medicines,* 131–37. Herbs cited are effective medicinal substances when administered alone, though many Aboriginal herbalists preferred to prescribe mixtures, sometimes with secret ingredients.
77 Jones, *History*, 152–55.
78 Queen's University, minutes of the Senate, 27 March 1866, 28, QUA; Kass and Kass, *Dr. Thomas Hodgkin*, 511–14. Hodgkin died in his sixty-eighth year in Jaffa, Palestine, of an intestinal disorder likely aggravated by cholera.
79 Peter S. Schmalz, *The Ojibwa of Southern Ontario* (Toronto: University of Toronto Press, 1991), 174; *The Civilization Act 1857,* Statutes of the Province of Canada, 20 Vict., third session, fifth Parliament, 84.

80 Peter Edmund Jones, "Red Man v. White Man," communication to the editor, *The Toronto Mail*, 14 December 1875.
81 Canniff, *Medical Profession*, 341.
82 D. Gidney and W.P.J. Millar, "The Origins of Organized Medicine in Ontario: 1850," in *Health, Disease, and Medicine: Essays in Canadian History*, ed. Charles G. Roland (Toronto: Hannah Institute for the History of Medicine, 1982), 65–95; CPSO, historical register; Dr. Peter Edmund Jones, 14 November 1866, licence no. 678; Dr. Oronhyatekha (Peter Martin), 22 May 1867, licence no. 709.

Chapter 3 Country Doctor

1 A.A. Travill, *Medicine at Queen's, 1854–1920: A Peculiarly Happy Relationship* (Kingston: Faculty of Medicine, Queen's University, 1988), 34–39; Queen's University, *Calendar of the Faculty of Medicine for 1865–1866.*
2 F. Douglas Revelle, *The History of the County of Brant, Ontario* (Toronto: Warner Beers and Company, 1883), 508–9; Robert W. Powell, *The Doctor in Canada: His Whereabouts and the Laws Which Govern Him, A Ready Book of Reference* (Montreal: Gazette Printing Company, 1890), 302, 309; Eliza Jones Carey's Diary, 25 March 1882, mfm, PJC, VUL. Eliza Jones Carey's Diary records her visits to Dr. and Mrs. Griffin's home in Brantford.
3 Donald B. Smith, *Sacred Feathers: The Reverend Peter Jones (Kahkewaquonaby) and the Mississauga Indians* (Toronto: University of Toronto Press, 1987), 246.
4 Ibid., 247; Donald B. Smith, "Field (Jones; Carey), Elizabeth (Eliza)," in *DCB*, vol. 11, 1881–1890 (Toronto: University of Toronto Press, 1982), 316–17; Jennifer Lund, "Negotiating Race and Gender in the Diaries of Eliza Jones, British Wife of an Ojibwa Missionary in Upper Canada, 1823–1883" (Ph.D. dissertation, York University, 2010), 24.
5 Charles A. Jones to Eliza Jones Carey, box 5, files 1–3, PJC, VUL.
6 John A. Macdonald to P.E. Jones Esq. M.D., 18 June 1866, Macdonald Letterbook, vol. 512, part 2, reel C-24, 330, LAC. There were many British Canadian applicants for the job. Dr. Oronhyatekha, a Mohawk, applied for the post to no avail.
7 John Disturnell, ed., *Trip through the Lakes of North America* (Ann Arbour: University of Michigan Library, 2006), 369.
8 Charles A. Jones to Eliza Jones Carey, 19 April 1867, box 5, PJC, VUL.
9 Mary Beacock Freyer, *Emily Stowe: Doctor and Suffragist* (Toronto: Hannah Institute of the History of Medicine, Dundurn Press, 1990), 44.
10 Charles A. Jones to Eliza Jones Carey, 14 September 1868, box 5, PJC, VUL.
11 Ibid.
12 No author, "A Descriptive Sketch of the Flourishing Village of Hagersville," in *The Illustrated Trade Edition of Hagersville* (Hagersville: Hagersville Board of Trade, 1908), HCL.
13 Eliza Jones Carey's Diary, 6 March 1869, box 4, mfm, PJC, VUL.
14 Jacalyn Duffin, *Langstaff: A Nineteenth-Century Medical Life* (Toronto: University of Toronto Press, 1992), 73–91; ibid., "Therapies in Langstaff's Day Books," 273–76; ibid., Appendix D, Properties, 272; ibid., Credit Sale, 244; Steve Thorning, "Dr. Abraham Groves: Businessman and Entrepreneur," *Wellington County History*, 16 (2003):5–17.

15 Indian Affairs, Annual Report 1885, Roseau River band, 97; Peter Jones, *History of the Ojebway Indians: With Especial Reference to Their Conversion to Christianity* (London: A.W. Bennett, 1861), reprint (Freeport: Books for Libraries, 1970), 153; Vogel, *Indian Medicine*, 372, 457, n. 1011.
16 Indian Affairs, Sessional Papers 1885 (no. 14), Mississaugas of the New Credit, 516–17.
17 "A Mississauga in Japan [Frank G.H. Wilson]," in *The Indian*, 21 July 1886, 162; Indian Affairs, Annual Report 1885, Part II, 36, lists his widowed mother, Phoebe Wilson.
18 Charles A. Jones to Eliza Jones Carey, 29 April 1869, box 5, PJC, VUL.
19 Ibid., 3 April 1870.
20 Canada, *Census of 1871,* District 17, Haldimand County, Walpole district, Province of Ontario: Jones, Peter E., male 26 years old, doctor, member of the Church of England, born in Ontario. In the column listing the person's race, the word "Canadian" is crossed out and replaced by "Indian." Jones was boarding with Mrs. Dorothy Cuthbert, a widow with three children, HCMA.
21 Interview with Charlotte's grand-nephew, Macdonald Holmes, then seventy-five years old, of Edmonton, AB, on 3 October 1976, courtesy of Donald B. Smith. Mr. Holmes's father was physician to the Six Nations; British Columbia, registration of death, Charlotte Elvin-Dixon-Jones, 9 September 1921, archive no. B13120, GSU mfm no. 1927297, ABC; Jones family bible in possession of Louise Thorp, Vancouver, BC; Charlotte Elvin, daughter of William and Faith Elvin, born Burlington, Yorkshire, England, 11 April 1844. Copy of entry courtesy of Donald B. Smith.
22 Ontario, Her Majesty's Surrogate Court, *Affidavit of Value of Property*, estate of William Dixon, yeoman, sworn at Cayuga, County of Haldimand, 5 January 1871. Because he was a small landowner (a yeoman), Dixon was erroneously considered to be a member of the minor gentry; the local people called him Sir William Dixon; Charlotte was called Lady Dixon, a title that adorned her death certificate.
23 Peter E. Jones M.D. to Sir John A. Macdonald, 28 December 1888, Macdonald Papers, 232539-42, LAC; Dr. P. Jones, M.D., of Hagersville, was a lay delegate to the Anglican Church of Canada's Synod of Niagara, courtesy of Dorothy Kealy, archivist, 11 October 1984.
24 Obituary of Charlotte Jones, October 1921, entitled "Called Home" in a Vernon, BC, newspaper. Charlotte Jones's Diary in possession of Louise Thorp, Vancouver.
25 Victoria Freeman, "Attitudes towards 'Miscegenation' in Canada and the United States, New Zealand, and Australia, 1860–1914," *Native Studies Review*, 16, no. 1:205; Katherine Ellinghaus, "Margins of Acceptability: Class, Education, and Interracial Marriage in Australia and North America," *Frontiers*, 23, no. 2 (2002):63, 69.
26 Douglas Leighton, "Johnson, George Henry Martin," in *DCB*, vol. 11, 1881–1890 (Toronto: University of Toronto Press, 1982), 451–53; Smith, *Sacred Feathers*, 228–29.
27 Eliza Jones Carey's Diary, 3 July 1882, box 4, mfm, PJC, VUL.
28 Jones family bible, in the possession of Louise Thorp, Vancouver. Copy of original entry, courtesy of Donald B. Smith.

29 Smith, *Sacred Feathers*, 335, n. 45; Indian Affairs, P.E. Jones, Indian agent, to deputy superintendent general re. Frederick Jones, 18 June 1896, RG 10, vol. 1974, file 5620/2, LAC.
30 Assessment roll for Municipality of Hagersville, no. 168, P.E. Jones, physician, Main Street, 1899, mfm GS2712, AO.
31 The late Lloyd S. King, educator and New Credit historian, generously granted me an interview on 17 June 2002. Mr. King, who was born in 1915, remembered his grandmother Bessie King's comment that band members wondered why Charlotte did not have any more children after she married the doctor; Indian Affairs, minutes of the Grand General Indian Council of the Chippewas, Munsees, Six Nations, &c., &c., held on the Sarnia Reserve, 25 June to 3 July 1874, RG 10, vol. 1942, file 4103, 14–15, LAC.
32 Donald B. Smith, "Jones, Peter Edmund (Kahkewaquonaby)," in *DCB*, vol. 13, 1901–1910 (Toronto: University of Toronto Press, 1993), 530–31.
33 "Peter E. Jones to Sir John A. Macdonald," 28 December 1888, Macdonald Papers 232539-42, LAC; Smith, "Jones, Peter Edmund (Kahkewaquonaby)," 530–31.
34 No author, *Trade Edition of Hagersville*, 1908, HPL.
35 Charles A. Jones to Eliza Jones Carey, box 5, files 1–3, PJC, VUL.
36 Indian Affairs, RG 10, vol. 1971, file 5415, LAC; Augustus and Reverend Peter Jones file, *Hagersville News*, 3 June 1898, HCMA. In his application to join the civil service, Dr. Jones described his nationality as Indian, Welsh, and English.
37 H.F. Bland, "A Visit to New Credit," *Christian Guardian*, Toronto, 25 March 1868.
38 Smith, *Sacred Feathers*, 247, 336, n. 62; ibid., "Peter and Eliza Jones: Their Last Years, 23; *Orange Directory of Western Ontario*, 1871, Part 2, District of Oneida, online at http://www.members.tripod.com/~Roughian/index-410/; Obituaries, *The Toronto Globe*, 30 June 1909, "Dr. Jones Dead: An Authority on Indian Affairs...."
39 Smith, *Sacred Feathers*, 317, n. 78.
40 Lawrence Leighton, "A Victorian Civil Servant at Work: Lawrence Vankoughnet and the Canadian Indian Department," in *As Long as the Sun Shines and the Water Flows: A Reader in Canadian Native Studies*, ed. Ian A.L. Getty and Antoine Lussier (Vancouver: University of British Columbia Press, 1983), 104–19.
41 Canniff, *Medical Profession*, 565–66.
42 Ibid.; Indian Affairs, RG 10, vol. 1866, file 451, mfm C-11, 104.
43 Ibid.
44 Indian Affairs, Dr. T. Pyne to J.T. Gilkison, 17 June 1872.
45 Indian Affairs, RG 10, vol. 1866, file 451, mfm C-11,104.
46 Indian Affairs, RG 10, vol. 1878, file 996, mfm C11-105, Superintendent Gilkison to Indian Affairs, 29 October 1872.
47 Indian Affairs, RG 10, vol. 1897, file 1836, mfm C-11,107, LAC, New Credit Band Council minutes, Mission Schoolhouse, Tuscarora, 13 May 1873.
48 Indian Affairs, RG 10, vol. 1876, file 919, mfm C-11,105, 30 July 1873; Peter E. Jones, M.D., to the Honorable Alexander Campbell, minister of the interior; Donald Swanson, "Campbell, Sir Alexander," in *DCB*, vol. 12, 1891–1900 (Toronto: University of Toronto Press, 1990), 150–54.

49 Ibid., 8 October 1872; Robert H. Dee, M.D., to the Honorable Joseph Howe, secretary of state. Dr. Dee, CPSO license no. 109, had passed the 1852 examination of the Medical Board of Upper Canada.
50 Duffin, *Langstaff*, 94, Table 5.1.
51 Ibid., 27 January 1873; J.T. Gilkison to the superintendent general of Indian Affairs; Indian Affairs, Annual Report for the year ending 30 June 1873, 7, 10, 11, LAC.
52 Sally Weaver, *Medicine and Politics among the Grand River Iroquois: A Study of the Non-Conservatives* (Ottawa: National Museum of Man, Publications in Ethnology, no. 4, 1972), 41–42; ibid.; "The Iroquois: The Grand River Reserve, 1875–1945," in *Aboriginal Ontario: Historical Perspectives on the First Nations*, ed. Edward S. Rogers and Donald B. Smith (Toronto: Dundurn Press, 1994), 227–28.
53 Eliza Jones Carey's Diary, 4 June 1874, box 4, mfm, PJC, VUL.
54 Indian Affairs, RG 10, vol. 1932, file 3390/91, C-11,114, LAC; minutes of the New Credit Band Council, 30 April 1874: Dr. Jones elected, vote 18 in favour, 17 against; John Elliot elected second chief and Charles Herkimer third chief, LAC; Olive P. Dickason, *Canada's First Nations: A History of Founding Peoples from Earliest Times* (Toronto: Oxford University Press, 2002), 211; Eliza Field Jones Carey's Diary, 1874, box 4, PJC, VUL.
55 Jasper T. Gilkison, "Narative: Visit of the Governor-General and the Countess of Dufferin to the Six Nations Indians, 25 August 1874" (Brantford: Department of the Interior, Indian Branch, 1875).
56 Ibid., councillors William Elliott and Leonard Herchmer represented the Mississaugas, Dr. Dee and Dr. McCargow, physicians to the Six Nations, and Dr. Pyne, formerly the medical attendant of the Mississaugas of New Credit, were also honoured with seats on the dais.
57 Indian Affairs, minutes of the New Credit council, 30 April 1874, RG 10, vol. 1932, file 3390, mfm C-11,114.
58 Dr. P.E. Jones to J.T. Gilkison, Esq., Indian Office, Brantford, 27 September 1875, RG 10, vol. 1971, file 5415, mfm C-11124, LAC; minutes of the Special Council meeting held 3 September 1875, RG 10, vol. 1971, file 5415, LAC; Ethyl Brant Monture, "Oronhyatekha," in *Canadian Portraits, Famous Indians: Brant, Crowfoot, Oronhyatekha* (Toronto: Clarke, Irwin, 1960), 131–58.
59 Indian Affairs, RG 10, vol. 1987, file 6370, mfm C-11,128, 22 June 1876, LAC, Report of Deputy Superintendent Lawrence Vankoughnet supporting the increase of Jones's pay to $250.
60 Indian Affairs, Annual Report 1876, Census of Resident and Nomadic Indians by Provinces, Return F. 89, LAC.
61 Indian Affairs, Annual Report 1894, Mississaugas of the New Credit, 42–43.
62 Virgil J. Vogel, *American Indian Medicine* (Norman: University of Oklahoma Press, 1970), 203–5.
63 James B. Waldram, "Aboriginal Peoples and the Health Transition," in *Aboriginal Health in Canada*, 2nd ed., ed. James B. Waldram, D. Ann Herring, and T. Kue Young (Toronto: University of Toronto Press, 2006), 73–125.
64 Indian Affairs, Mississaugas of the New Credit band, Sessional Papers, vol. 35, no. 27, 1901, 19.
65 E.H. Ackernecht, *A Short History of Medicine* (Baltimore: Johns Hopkins University Press, 1982), 210–17.

66 Indian Affairs, Annual Report of the superintendent general for the year ended 31 December 1883, 12–13.
67 Indian Affairs, Annual Report of the superintendent general for the year ended 31 December 1885, 13–14, LAC.
68 Donald B. Smith, "Peter and Eliza Jones: Their Last Years," *The Beaver*, Winter (1977), 20–21.
69 Indian Affairs, RG 10, vol. 1733, file 63-16, part 1, mfm C-15021, 9, LAC. Minutes of the Mississaugas of the New Credit council, 19 October 1883.
70 Indian Affairs, RG, vol. 2238, file 45,742, mfm C-12780, 8 February 1888, 86203, 15–17, LAC. Report of A. Dingman, commissioner under the Indian Act.
71 Ibid., presentations by Dr. P.E. Jones, David Sawyer, John Henry, James Tobico, and John Laform.
72 Ibid., 15 May 1888, 1½–5½, "Analysis of vote by Agent Dr. P.E. Jones." For continued membership, males 13, females 19, total 32; for exclusion, males 18, females 18, total 36.
73 Indian Affairs, minutes of the Mississaugas of the New Credit Band Council, 10 and 11 October 1878, RG 10, vol. 2070, file 10,513, mfm C-11149.
74 Ibid., 9, 10, and 21 January 1879, RG 10, vol. 2076, file 11,156, LAC.
75 Indian Affairs, minutes of the Mississaugas of the New Credit Band Council, April 1882, RG 10, vol. 2207, file 41,812, mfm, C-11180, LAC.
76 Ibid.; Eliza's Diary, 25 December 1880, "Peter poorly with bronchitis," box 4, mfm, PJC, VUL.
77 Indian Affairs, RG 10, vol. 2207, 41,812, mfm C-11,180; minutes of the Mississaugas of the New Credit Band Council, 28 February 1883.
78 Dr. Oronhyatekha accused of non-attendance, online at http://www.woodland-centre.library.cornell.edu/synoptic/.
79 Donald B. Smith, "Maungwudaus Goes Abroad," *The Beaver*, Autumn (1976), 4–8; Smith, *Sacred Feathers*, 187–88, 218–19.
80 George Henry [Sr.], *Remarks Concerning the Indians, by One of Themselves Called Maungwudaus Who Has Been Traveling in England, France, Belgium, Ireland, and Scotland* (Leeds: C.A. Wilson & Co., 1847). Portraits of Maungwudaus by Paul Kane hang in the National Gallery of Canada, Ottawa, and in the Royal Ontario Museum, Toronto.
81 Smith, *Sacred Feathers*, 317, n. 78.
82 Advertisement in the *Oswego [NY] Daily Palladium* of Friday, 11 April 1873: "Dr. Maungwudaus from the Chippewa Nation, will receive health seekers at Fitzburgh House, Oswego, NY, 15–18 April."
83 Ibid.
84 Forbes B. Geddes [advocate] to superintendent general of Indian Affairs, dated 18 April 1894, respecting the death of George Francis Henry, c. 4 November 1893, courtesy of Margaret Sault, MNCA.
85 Indian Affairs, P.E. Jones, Indian agent, to Hayter Reed, deputy superintendent of Indian Affairs, dated 5 June 1894, MNCA; Indian Affairs, Annual Report, Mississaugas of the New Credit (no. 18), 1894, part 2, 36.

Chapter 4 Pride in His Heritage

1 Indian Affairs, RG10, vol. 2139, file 28,650, LAC.
2 Indian Affairs, Sessional Papers (no. 4), 1884, Return B, Mississaugas of the New Credit band (no. 18), 38–39, LAC.
3 Indian Affairs, minutes of the Grand General Indian Council, held upon the New Credit Reserve near Hagersville, Ontario, from 13 September to 18 September 1882 (Hagersville: Hagersville Book and Job Rooms, 1883), 8.
4 Ibid., 21.
5 Ibid., 23.
6 Ibid., 24.
7 Ibid.
8 Ibid., 9.
9 Ibid., 24–25.
10 Ibid., 25.
11 Ibid., 22–25.
12 R.W. Phipps, "Reasons against Prohibition," communication to the editor, 30 November 1875, mfm, no. 9. *The Toronto Mail* was founded in 1872 by Sir John A. Macdonald, leader of the Conservative party; *The Toronto Globe* was founded in 1844 by George Brown, leader of the Reform party. In 1895 *The Mail* merged with *The Empire*, and in 1936 *The Globe* merged with *The Mail and Empire* to form *The Toronto Globe and Mail.*
13 Oronhyatekha, M.D., communication to the editor, *The Toronto Mail*, 4 December 1875. B.A., communication to the editor, "Red Men v. White Men," *The Toronto Mail*, 8 December 1875.
14 Peter Edmund Jones, M.D., communication to the editor, "Red Man v. White Man," *The Toronto Mail*, 14 December 1875.
15 Oronhyatekha, M.D., "Red Man v. White Man," communication to the editor, *The Toronto Mail*, 14 December, 1875.
16 Oronhyatekha, M.D., "The Mohawk Language," *The Canadian Journal*, new series vol. 10 (1865), 182–94 and vol. 15 (1876–78), 1–12.
17 Eliza's Diary, box 4, mfm, p. 5, PJC, VUL; Charles, age ten years, sent to preparatory school, box 11, file 11, PJC, VUL.
18 Smith, *Sacred Feathers*, 245.
19 Ibid.
20 Eliza Jones, Correspondence, box 5, PJC, VUL.
21 R. Douglas Francis, Richard Jones, and Donald B. Smith, *Journeys: A History of Canada* (Toronto; Nelson/Thomson Canada, 2006), 236–59.
22 Charles Augustus Jones to Eliza Jones, 19 November 1867, box 5, PJC, VUL; Eliza Jones Carey to the captain of C.A. Jones Company, n.d., PJC, VUL; Charles A. Jones to Eliza, 24 September 1867, box 5, PJC, VUL.
23 Smith, *Sacred Feathers,* 245.
24 Indian Affairs, P.E. Jones, Indian agent to deputy superintendent general, 18 June 1896, RG 10, vol. 1974, file 5620/2, LAC.
25 Charles A. Jones to Eliza Jones Carey, 17 February 1870, box 5, PJC, VUL.
26 Copy of a letter in Charles Jones's handwriting of the testimonial supplied by Henry George, editor, *The Reporter*, Sacramento, 1 May 1870, box 5, PJC, VUL.
27 Indian Affairs, RG 10, vol. 1986, file 6306, 3 June 1876.
28 Personal communication from Don G. Jones, Dundas, ON, a United Empire Loyalist descendant of Augustus Jones's elder brother Robert, Dr. P.E. Jones's great uncle.

29 Obituary, "The Late C.A. Jones," *The Brantford Weekly Expositor*, 23 June 1882, 3.
30 Photograph of Frederick Jones from Eliza Jones Carey's Album, courtesy of Donald B. Smith; Smith, "Peter and Eliza Jones: Their Last Years," 23; Indian Affairs, RG 10, vol. 1974, file 5620/2, LAC.
31 Frederick Jones to Eliza, 13 February 1876, box 5, file 4, PJC, VUL.
32 Ibid.; Ontario, registration of deaths, schedule G, County of Brant, division of Town of Brantford, 20 March 1876, no. 001321, AO.
33 "In Memory of Brother Fred," by Charles A. Jones. A handwritten copy of the complete poem in Eliza Jones Carey's Album, which is in possession of Louise Thorp, Vancouver, courtesy of Donald B. Smith.
34 Brant Memorial Committee, *The Joseph Brant Memorial*, Brantford, ON, online at http://www.grandriveruel.ca/Grand_River_Brant_Monument.jtm, p. 3 of 6; Ke-che-ah-gah-me-qua [Eliza Jones Carey], *The Life of Captain Joseph Brant (Thayendanegea): An Account of His Re-interment at Mohawk, 1850 and of the Corner Stone Ceremony in the Erection of the Brant Memorial* (Brantford: B.H. Rothwell, 1886).
35 Obituary, "The Late C.A. Jones," *Christian Guardian*, 19 June 1882; ibid., *Brantford Weekly Expositor*, 23 June 1882, 3.
36 Indian Affairs, the Brant Memorial Committee, C.A. Jones, secretary, July 1876, RG 10, vol. 434, mfm C-9632, 432.
37 E. Bocquet, painter in Smith, *Sacred Feathers*, 132, 298, n. 8; J. Russell Harper, *Early Painters and Engravers in Canada* (Toronto: University of Toronto Press, 1970), 176; Elisabeth Fields, "On the Life of Benjamin West," in no author, *Essays and Letters on Various Subjects* (London: Johnson's Court, Fleet Street, 1819), 148–49; Jennifer Lund, "Eliza Field Jones Carey's Mission to 'Civilize' the Native Women of Early Nineteenth-Century Upper Canada" (M.A. thesis, University of Toronto, 1991), 25.
38 Eliza's Diary, entry in cash accounts for November 1882, box 4, mfm, PJC, VUL.
39 Ibid., entry for 25 December 1882.
40 Canada, Charles A. Jones, son of George D. Jones, Mississaugas of the New Credit band, no. 235, enfranchised 25 March 1920 by order in council, P.C. 39/656, and his brother Peter Alfred Jones, band no. 234, enfranchised 21 April 1922 by order in council, P.C. 40/846.
41 Peter E. Paul Dembski, "Ryerson, George Ansel Sterling," in *DCB*, vol. 15, 1921–1930 (Toronto: University of Toronto Press, 2005), 900–1.
42 Eliza's Diary, 2 May 1882, PJC, VUL.
43 Jean Waldie, "Description of Eliza Jones Carey's quilt, Century pattern done in silk which was unusual," *Brantford Expositor*, 15 December 1949; Eliza Field Jones Carey, Last Will and Testament, 1 January 1889. Dr. P.E. Jones, executor, Brant Will/Estate file no. 1433, GSI-228.
44 Obituary of Mrs Eliza [Jones] Carey, *Christian Guardian*, 5 November 1890, box 4, file 2, PJC, VUL.
45 Ibid.
46 Ontario registration of deaths, RG 80-8 on MS 935, reel 56, AO.
47 Indian Affairs, Sessional Papers (no. 14) 58 Vict., 1895, 18–19; P.E. Jones, obituary of George D. Jones (13 June 1846 to 16 July 1903); name of newspaper not recorded, clipping in the scrapbook of Elvin Dixon, Vernon, BC, courtesy of Donald B. Smith; Ontario registration of deaths, RG 80-8, Ms 935, reel 67, no.

001726, 16 July 1893. Brant County, town of Brantford, 20 March 1876, no. 001321.

48 Peter E. Jones, "Salutatory," *The Indian,* 30 December 1885, 1; no author, "Prehistoric Man," *The Indian*, 15 December 1886, 24.

49 Gerald Killan, *David Boyle: From Artisan to Archaeologist* (Toronto: University of Toronto Press, 1983); Gerald Killan, "Boyle, David," in *DCB*, vol. 14, 1911–1920 (Toronto: University of Toronto Press, 2001), 130–34.

50 R.S. MacNeish, "*Iroquois Pottery Types: A Technique for the Study of Iroquois Prehistory* (Ottawa: National Museum of Man, Bulletin 124, 1952).

51 Ontario, David Boyle, "Fourth Annual Archaeological Report of the Canadian Institute (Session of 1890–91)," Sessional Papers (no. 21), 1891, 10–12 (esp. Fig. 2); no author, Board Policy, Royal Ontario Museum, Repatriation of Canadian Aboriginal Objects, ROMA.

52 Bruce Trigger, "Indians and Ontario's History," *Ontario History*, 74, no. 4 (1982):246–57; no author, *Hagersville News,* 3 June 1898, HCMA, courtesy of Donald B. Smith.

53 Ibid.

54 News clipping, *Hagersville News*, 3 June 1898, HCMA.

55 Horatio Hale, ed., *The Iroquois Book of Rites* (Philadelphia: D.G. Brinton, 1883); Horatio Hale, "An Iroquois Condoling Council: A Study of Aboriginal American Society and Government," *Transactions of the Royal Society of Canada*, second series, 1895–1896, vol. 1, section 2 (Ottawa: John Durie & Son, 1895); William N. Fenton, "Hale, Horatio Emmons," in *DCB*, vol. 12, 1891–1900 (Toronto: University of Toronto Press, 1990), 400–3.

56 Smithsonian Institution, Washington, DC, "The Meaning of Place Names Asked by Mr. H.F. Gardner and Supplied by Dr. P.E. Jones, Chief Kahkewaquonaby, 25 May 1898," *Anthropological Archives*, Smithsonian record no. 3732, 1–5; Smith, *Sacred Feathers*, 255–57.

57 James Constantine Pilling, *Bibliography of the Algonquian Languages* (Washington: Smithsonian Institution, Bureau of Ethnology, 1891), 272.

Chapter 5 Active Critic of the Indian Act

1 *Minutes of the Eighth Grand General Indian Council held upon the Cape Crocker Indian Reserve, County of Bruce, 10–15 September 1884* (Hagersville: Indian Publishing Co., 1884), 35, AO.

2 Norman Shields, "Anishinabek Political Alliance in the Post Confederation Period: The Grand General Indian Council of Ontario, 1870–1936" (M.A. thesis, Queen's University, 2001); Norman Shields, "The Grand General Indian Council of Ontario and Indian Status Legislation," in *Lines Drawn Upon the Water: First Nations and the Great Lakes Borders and Borderlands*, ed. Karl S. Hele (Waterloo: Wilfrid Laurier University Press, 2008), 205–18.

3 John C. Mohawk, "Iroquois Confederacy," in *Encyclopaedia of North American Indians*, ed. Frederick E. Hoxie (Boston: Houghton Mifflin, 1996), 298–302.

4 Canada, S.C. 20 Vict., c. 26, 10 June 1857; John Leslie and Ron Maguire, *The Historical Development of the Indian Act,* 2nd ed. (Ottawa: Treaties and Research Centre, Research Branch, Indian and Northern Affairs Canada, 1978); Donald B. Smith, "John A. Macdonald and Aboriginal Canada," in *Historic Kingston, Annual Publication of the Kingston Historical Society*, 50 (2002):24, n. 22; Julia Jarvis, "Robinson, William Benjamin," in *DCB*, vol. 10, 1871–1880 (Toronto: University of Toronto Press, 1972), 622–24.

5 Sidney L. Harring, *White Man's Law: Native People in Nineteenth-Century Canadian Jurisprudence* (Toronto: University of Toronto Press, 1998), 32–34, 99–100.
6 Edward S. Rogers and Donald B. Smith, eds., *Aboriginal Ontario: Historical Perspectives on the First Nations* (Toronto: Dundurn Press, 1994), 199–201.
7 Comments of Reverend H.P. Chase, who had attended the 1858 Grand Council meeting. See *Minutes of the General Council of the Six Nations, and Delegates from Different Bands in Western and Eastern Canada, 10 June 1870* (Hamilton: Office of the Spectator Newspaper, 1870), 16.
8 John Ralston Saul, *A Fair Country: Telling Truths about Canada* (Toronto: Penguin Group Canada), 2008.
9 Canada, S.C. 31 Vict. Cc 26, 22 June 1869, online at http://www.ainc-inac.gc.ca/pr/lib/phi/histlws/hln/a69c6_e/.
10 Grand Council, *Minutes of the General Council of the Six Nations, and Delegates from Different Bands in Western and Eastern Canada, 10 June 1870* (Hamilton: Office of the Spectator Newspaper, 1870).
11 Grand Council, minutes of 1870 meeting, list of bands in attendance, 3–4.
12 Shields, "Ashinabek Political Alliance," 137–38.
13 Grand Council, minutes of 1870 meeting, 14–15, 25.
14 Norman Shields, "Ashinabek Political Alliance in the Post Confederation Period: The Grand General Indian Council of Ontario, 1870–1936" (M.A. thesis, Queen's University, 2001), 36–37.
15 *Minutes of the Grand General Council of the Chippewas, Munsees, Six Nations, etc. held on the Sarnia Reserve, 25 June to 3 July, 1874* (Sarnia: Canadian Steam Publishing, 1874).
16 Oronhyatekha appears to have left the meeting following the election. He had recently moved to London, ON, where he served as physician to the Oneidas of the Thames. Indian Affairs, Annual Report 1884, 5, noted: "A hall was built on the reserve chiefly through the exertions and supervision of Dr. Oronhyatekha."
17 Shields, "Anishinabek Political Alliance," 58–63; minutes of the Grand General Council, 1874, 4–8.
18 Andrew Robb, "Laird, David," in *DCB,* vol. 13, 1900–1910 (Toronto: University of Toronto Press, 1994), 578–81.
19 Canada, Indian Act, S.C. 1876, 39 Vict., c. 18, 43–73; Donald B. Smith, "John A. Macdonald and Aboriginal Canada," in *Historic Kingston, Annual Publication of the Kingston Historical Society* (Kingston: Kingston Historical Society, 2002), 10–29.
20 Peter S. Schmalz, *The Ojibwa of Southern Ontario* (Toronto: University of Toronto Press, 1991), 296, n. 25; Reverend Allan Salt Papers, 1865–1906, MG 29 H 11, LAC.
21 Ibid.; Schmalz, *The Ojibwa*, 195–96; Robb, "Laird, David," 578–81.
22 Indian Affairs, RG 10, vol. 1994, file 6829, report of the proceedings of the Chippewa Grand Council approving the new Indian Act [1876] and Reverend H.P. Chase's supporting letter.
23 Schmaltz, *The Ojibwa*, 295–96; ibid.
24 No author, report of the "First Session of The Grand Indian Council of the Province of Ontario held at Sarnia, 27 June 1878," in *The Wiarton Echo,* 15 August 1879; ibid., serialized account of remaining sessions of the 1878 council, 29 August, 5, 12, 19, and 26 September, 5, 10, 17, 24, and 31 October; Schmalz, *The Ojibwa*, 196.

25 David Sawyer in minutes of 1878 Grand Indian Council, *The Wiarton Echo*, 10 October 1878.

26 Conrad Van Dusen (alias, Enemikeese), *The Indian Chief: An Account of the Labours. Losses, Sufferings, and Oppression of Ke-zig-ko-e-ne-ne (David Sawyer), a Chief of the Ojibbeway Indians in Canada West* (London: William Nichols, 1867), facsimile edition (Toronto: Coles Publishing, 1974).

27 Donald B. Smith, *Sacred Feathers: The Reverend Peter Jones (Kahkewaquonaby) and the Mississauga Indians* (Toronto: University of Toronto Press, 1987), 241.

28 Minutes of 1878 Grand Indian Council, *The Wiarton Echo*, 24 October 1878.

29 Ibid., 10 October 1878; Rogers and Smith, *Aboriginal Ontario*, 68–77.

30 Shields, "Anishinabek Political Alliance," 61; Canada, An Act to Amend and Consolidate the Laws Respecting Indians. Statutes of Canada 1880, 43 Vict., c. 18.

31 *Minutes of the Seventh Grand General Indian Council Held upon the New Credit Reserve, Near Hagersville, Ontario from 13 September to 18 September 1882*, Hagersville, ON (Hagersville: Book & Job Rooms, 1883), 32, LAC.

32 Peter E. Jones, M.D., head chief, Mississaugas of the New Credit, to Sir John A. Macdonald, 28 August, 1882, Macdonald Papers, 182861-62, LAC.

33 Minutes of the Grand Council 1882, 14.

34 Schmalz, *The Ojibwa*, 207.

35 Ibid., 208, 297, n. 41.

36 Dr. Peter E. Jones to Sir John A. Macdonald, 19 September 1885, Macdonald Papers, 203490-203495, LAC.

37 Indian Affairs, *Minutes and Correspondence Relating to Grand General Indian Council Held at Cape Croker, June 1896*, RG 10, vol. 2639, file 129,690-1, mfm C-11255, LAC; Shields, "Anishinabek," 94–95.

38 J.A. Macrae's travel expenses, in Indian Affairs, Annual Report 1900, 946, LAC.

39 Minutes of the Grand General Indian Council, September 1892, Indian Affairs, RG 10, vol. 2639, file 129,690-1, mfm 11255, LAC; *Minutes of 13th Grand General Indian Council-Ontario and Quebec, Held upon the Moraviantown Indian Reserve from 16th to 20th October 1894* (Wiarton: Printed at the Wiarton Canadian Office, n.d.); RG 10, vol. 2639, file 129,690-1, mfm C-11255, LAC.

40 Delgamuukw and Nisga'a Treaty, Indian and Northern Affairs Canada, online at http://www.bctreaty.net.

41 Canada, Statutes of Canada, Constitution Act 1982, online at http://www.laws.justice.gc.ca/en/const/annex_e/.

42 Minutes of the Grand Council, 1882, 30.

43 Shields, "Anishinabek Political Alliance," 69–72.

44 General Council, *Minutes of the Eighth Grand General Indian Council, Held upon the Cape Croker Reserve ... Sept 10th to Sept. 15th, 1884* (Hagersville: Indian Publishing Co., 1885), 10–12.

45 Ibid., 17.

46 Ibid., 18–19.

47 Ibid., 22.

48 Sidney L. Harring, *White Man's Law: Native People in Nineteenth-Century Canadian Jurisprudence* (Toronto: University of Toronto Press, 1998), 150–52.

49 Ontario, *The Algoma District* (Toronto: Commissioner of Crown Lands, Grip Printing and Publishing Co., 1884); no author, "Ontario's Mineral Wealth," *The Indian*, 22 December 1886, 223.

50 Janet Chute, *The Legacy of Shingwaukonse: A Century of Native Leadership* (Toronto: University of Toronto Press, 1998).
51 Human Rights Committee of the United Nations, 30 July 1981 meeting, *Sandra Lovelace v. Canada*, University of Minnesota Human Rights Library, online at http://www.1.umn.edu/humanrts/undocs/session36/6-24/.
52 Minutes of the Grand Council, 1884, 15.
53 Canada, Indian Advancement Act, 1884, S.C. 1884, c. 28, s. 5.
54 Dean Neu and Richard Therrien, *Accounting for Genocide: Canada's Bureaucratic Assault on Aboriginal People* (Black Point: Fernwood Publishing, 2003), 84.
55 Ibid.
56 Dr. Peter E. Jones to Sir John A. Macdonald, 19 September 1885, Macdonald Papers, 203490–203495, LAC.
57 P.E. Jones to John A. Macdonald, 28 December 1888, Macdonald Papers, 232539-42, Macdonald's marginal note on 232542.
58 Smith, "Macdonald and Aboriginal Canada," 13; Richard Gywn, *John A.: The Man That Made Us* (Toronto: Vintage Canada, 2008), 155.
59 Ibid.
60 Rogers and Smith, *Aboriginal Ontario*, 146–47.
61 Dr. P.E. Jones to Sir John A. Macdonald, Macdonald Papers, MG 26A, vol. 152, part 2, 62344–69 (esp. 6259–60). This attachment contains Dr. Jones's suggested amendments to the Indian Act.
62 Ibid.
63 Toby Elaine Morantz, *The White Man's Gonna Getcha: The Colonial Challenge to the Crees in Quebec* (Montreal: McGill-Queen's University Press, 2002), 241.
64 Dr. P.E. Jones to Sir John A. Macdonald, Macdonald Papers, MG 26A, vol. 152, pt. 2, 62344–69 (esp. 6259–60).
65 Macdonald Correspondence, MG 26A, vol. 152, pt. 2, 62344–69, especially 62359–60.
66 Ibid.
67 P.E. Jones to John A. Macdonald, 31 March 1886, Macdonald Papers, 208742-45, includes a marginal note by Macdonald, LAC; Oronhyatekha to an unknown recipient, online at http://woodland-centre.library.cornell.edu/synoptic.html/; Blair Stonechild and Bill Waiser, *Loyal Till Death: Indians and the North-West Rebellion* (Calgary: Fifth House, 1997).
68 P.E. Jones to Joseph Pope, 28 July 1887, regarding Jones's wish to receive acknowledgement of receipt of his last letter, Macdonald Correspondence, 1011001, 221605–06, LAC.
69 P.E. Jones to Sir John A. Macdonald, 28 December 1888, Macdonald Correspondence 232539-42, LAC. Letter includes a marginal note by Macdonald.
70 Edwin C. Guillet, *You'll Never Die John A* (Toronto: Macmillan Canada, 1967), 144–45.
71 Richard Gwyn, *John A: The Man Who Made Us: The Life and Times of John A. Macdonald*, vol. 1: 1815–1891 (Toronto: Vintage Canada, 2008), 155; Richard Gwyn, *John A.: Nation Maker, Sir John A. Macdonald, His Life, Our Times*, vol. 2: 1867–1891 (Toronto: Random House, 2011), 420.

Chapter 6 Aboriginal Rights Advocate

1 Order in council authorizing payment of Dr. Jones's land claim on behalf of the Mississaugas of the New Credit, P.C. 1884–1432 re: Mississauga Indians, 30 June 1884, LAC.
2 Indian Affairs, RG 10, vol. 2238, file 45,742, mfm C-12780, LAC.
3 Indian Affairs, Dr. Peter E. Jones, Hagersville, to superintendent general of Indian Affairs, Ottawa, 30 January 1909, file 213957-339795, courtesy of Margaret Sault, copy stamped 339795, six pages written and signed by Dr. Jones, MNCA.
4 Indian Affairs, RG 10, vol. 1968, file 5209, authorizing Dr. Jones's expenses for trip to Ottawa.
5 Canada, order in council: PC 1884-1432, re: Mississauga Indians, 30 June 1884, RG 2, A-1-a, vol. 452, mfm C-3351.
6 Canada, order in council (OC): PC 1884-1931, 8 September 1884, amending OC 1884–1432, 30 June 1884, confirmed 7 October 1884, RG 2, A-1-a, vol. 456, mfm C-3352, LAC.
7 Canada, "David Mills, MP," Commons Debates, 27 May 1885, 2144–46.
8 Peter Edmund Jones to Sir John A. Macdonald, 27 February 1885, Macdonald Papers, LAC.
9 *The Indian*, 17 February 1886, 30.
10 John Kendle, "Daly, Thomas Mayne," in *DCB*, vol. 14, 1911–1920 (Toronto: University of Toronto Press, 1998), 265–66.
11 Indian Affairs, Annual Report 1884, pt. 2, 36; Indian Affairs, Annual Report 1893, 431; Indian Affairs, Annual Report, 1894, 435, LAC.
12 Indian Affairs, "Mississaugas of the New Credit," Sessional Papers (no. 14), 1892, pt. 2, 143–44; ibid., 1896, 488, LAC.
13 Indian Affairs, Annual Report, "Mississaugas of the New Credit," 1896, 12–13, LAC.
14 Indian Affairs, "Report of the Superintendent General," 56 Vict., Sessional Papers (no. 14), 1896, 17, LAC.
15 P.E. Jones to superintendent general of Indian Affairs, 30 January 1909, copy of letter stamped Indian Affairs, Accountants Branch, courtesy of MNCA.
16 Indian Affairs, P.E. Jones to the department, 30 Jan. 1909, file 213957-339795, LAC.
17 Dr. Peter E. Jones to Miss Merritt, MG29, Original four pages, 1899, 7-1521, LAC; no author, *Indian Treaties and Surrenders: From 1688–1890,* vol. 1–2 (Ottawa: Queen's Printer, 1891).
18 Richard C. Daniel, "The Board of Arbitrators and the Mississaugas of the Credit," in *A History of Native Claims Processes in Canada* (Ottawa: Research Branch, Department of Indian and Northern Affairs, 1980), 56–62.
19 Ibid., 56.
20 Malcolm Montgomery, "The Six Nations and the Macdonald Franchise," *Ontario History*, 57 (1965):13–25.
21 Canada, Constitution Act, 1867, 30 and 31 Vict., c. 3. (UK).
22 Cynthia M. Smith and Jack McLeod, eds., *Sir John A.: Anecdotal Life of John A. Macdonald* (Toronto: Oxford University Press, 1989), 132. In 1898, the newly elected Liberal government's Franchise Act, 1898 (S.C. 1898, c. 14), restored control of voting lists to the provinces; In 1920, the Dominion Elections Act (S.C. 1920, c. 46, s. 38) re established federal control of voting lists in federal elections. Aboriginals were denied the vote until Bill C-2, which repealed the offending parts of Section 86 of the Indian Act, was passed in 1960.

23 Canada, "Sir John A. Macdonald," Commons Debates, 30 April 1885, 1487–88.
24 Ibid., 1489–90.
25 Ibid., 1487–88.
26 Ibid., 27 May 1885, 2144–45; 8 June 1885, 2374–75.
27 Ibid., 8 June 1885, 2374–76.
28 Robert C. Vipond, "Mills, David," in *DCB*, vol. 13, 1901–1910 (Toronto: University of Toronto Press, 1884), 707–12.
29 Dr. P.E. Jones, "An Indian's View of the Indian Question," *The Toronto Daily Mail*, 16 May 1885.
30 Indian Affairs, Report on the Affairs of the Indian's of Canada (Bagot Commission), Laid before the Legislative Assembly, 20 March 1845, Montreal, 1847; Peter (Kahkewaquonaby) Jones, *History of the Ojebway Indians: With Especial Reference to Their Conversion to Christianity* (London: A.W. Bennett, 1861), reprint (Freeport: Books for Libraries, 1970), 242–45.
31 Peter E. Jones, "The Indian Franchise, Views of a Head Chief," *The Toronto Mail*, 22 May 1885, TRL.
32 Ibid.
33 The Electoral Franchise Act, S.C. 1885, c. 40 ss. 2, 11, LAC.
34 Smith and McLeod, *Sir John A.*, 48.
35 Donald Creighton, *John A. Macdonald, The Old Chieftain* (Toronto: Macmillan, 1955), 410; Sir Joseph Pope, "The Day of Sir John A. Macdonald," in *Chronicles of Canada*, vol. 29, ed. George M. Wrong and H.H. Langdon (Ottawa: J. Durie & Son, 1894), reprint (Toronto: University of Toronto Press, 1964, 133–38.
36 P.E. Jones to John A. Macdonald, 28 August 1886, Macdonald Papers, 209783, LAC.
37 No author, "An Indian Picnic, a Day among the Six Nations on Their Reserve: The Franchise Act Discussed," *The Toronto Mail*, 15 August 1885; Montgomery, "The Macdonald Franchise," 16–17, TRL.
38 Ibid.
39 Ibid.
40 Sir John A. Macdonald to Dr. Peter E. Jones, 31 August 1886, Macdonald Papers, Letterbook 24, 8, LAC.
41 Ibid.
42 Dr. P.E. Jones to Sir John A. Macdonald, 30 August 1886, Macdonald Papers, 209818, LAC.
43 Donald B. Smith, "Sir John A. Macdonald and Aboriginal Canada," in *Historic Kingston, Annual Publication of the Kingston Historical Society* 50 (2002):19.
44 Indian Affairs, RG 10, vol. 2357, file 72, 563, 2–18, LAC. Memorandum by the deputy superintendent general of Indian Affairs upon the controversy between the Six Nations of the Grand River and the Mississaugas of the Credit, LAC.
45 Ibid.
46 Indian Affairs, RG 10, vol. 2358, file 72,566, part 2, LAC.
47 Ibid.
48 Sally M. Weaver, "The Iroquois: The Consolidation of the Grand River Reserve in the Mid-Nineteenth Century, 1847–1875," in *Aboriginal Ontario: Historical Perspectives on the First Nations,* ed. Edward S. Rogers and Donald B. Smith (Toronto: Dundurn Press, 1994), 184.
49 Indian Affairs, Annual Report 1888, Return A (2), officers of the outside service.
50 Indian Affairs, RG 10, vol. 2358, file 72,566, part 2.

51 Genesis, 23:3–16.
52 Indian Affairs, RG 10, vol. 2358, file 72,566, part 1, LAC.
53 Ibid.
54 Indian Affairs, RG 10, vol. 2357, file 72, 563, 2, LAC.
55 No author, "Long-standing disagreement resolved, the Six Nations have accepted the Mississaugas offer of $10,000 for the Mississaugas right to undisturbed occupancy of New Credit," transcript of letter dated June 1903, MNCA.

Chapter 7: Canada's First Aboriginal Publisher

1 *The Indian* (Hagersville: The Indian Publishing Company), 30 December 1885 and 29 December 1886. Frequency varied. Subtitle: "A paper devoted to the Aborigines of North America, and especially to the Indians of Canada." On one mfm reel (Maclaren Micropublishing, 1974), TRL.
2 Donald B. Smith, *Sacred Feathers: The Reverend Peter Jones (Kahkewaquonaby) and the Mississauga Indians* (Toronto: University of Toronto Press, 1987), 21–22.
3 Ibid.
4 Sam G. Riley, "The Cherokee Phoenix: The Short, Unhappy Life of the First American Indian Newspaper," *Journalism Quarterly*, 53, no. 4 (1976):666–71; *Cherokee Phoenix*, online at http://www.wcu.edu/library/Cherokee Phoenix; Shannon Avison, "Aboriginal Newspapers: Their Contribution to the Emergence of an Alternative Public Sphere in Canada" (M.A. thesis, Concordia University, 1996). The Cherokees' writing system or syllabary employs eighty-six signs that enabled thousands to read and write. James Evans later developed a Cree syllabary that was used in a book printed in western Canada in 1841 using type cast from lead salvaged from tea boxes.
5 "Cherokee Phoenix," in *The New Georgia Encyclopedia*, online at http://georgiaencyclopedia.org/nge/ArticlePrintable.jsp?id=h-611.
6 Frederick E. Hoxie, ed., *North American Indians* (Boston: Houghton Mifflin, 1996), 639–40.
7 Indian Affairs, Annual Report 1883, 13, LAC. Report of Sir John A. Macdonald, superintendent general of Indian Affairs.
8 P.E. Jones to Sir John A. Macdonald, 19 September 1885, Macdonald Correspondence, 203490-94 (esp. 203492), LAC.
9 P.E. Jones, "Prospectus of *The Indian:* A paper devoted to Aborigines of North America," Dept. of the Interior, RG 15, series D-11-1, vol. 403, file 104,198, mfm T-13109, LAC.
10 No author, *The Toronto Globe*, 10 November 1885, TRL.
11 P.E. Jones to Prime Minister Sir John A. Macdonald, 31 March 1886, Macdonald Papers, 208742-45, LAC.
12 Peter Edmund Jones, "Salutatory," *The Indian*, 30 December 1885, 1.
13 No author, "Editorial in Ojibway," *The Indian*, 30 December 1885, 3, TRL.
14 Edward Furlong, "Notes on the Franchise Act," *The Indian*, 30 December 1885, 6; 3 February 1886, 2; 17 February, 1886, 31, TRL.
15 Reverend Peter Jones, "Jesus Lord We Look to Thee, in the Tongue" in *The Indian*, 3 February 1886, 4.
16 "Editorial in Ojibway," *The Indian*, 30 December 1885, 3, TRL. 17 February 1886, 31, and 3 March 1886, 44, columns in the Mohawk language, TRL.
17 David Boyle, "Names and Names," *The Indian*, 17 February, 1886, 25, TRL.

18 Edith G. Firth, "Bain, James," in *DCB*, vol. 13, 1990–1910 (Toronto: University of Toronto Press, 1994), 34–35; Gerald Kilan, "Boyle, David," in *DCB*, vol. 14, 1911–1920 (Toronto: University of Toronto Press, 1998), 130–4; Edith G. Firth and Curtis Fahey, "Scadding, Henry," in *DCB*, vol. 13, 1900–1910 (Toronto: University of Toronto Press, 1994), 927–29. The Pioneer Association of Ontario was the forerunner of the Ontario Historical Association.

19 *The Indian*, vol. 1, no. 1, "Prospectus," objective number eight; articles on archaeology appeared on 30 December 1885, 1 and 17 March 1886, 49, TRL.

20 Horatio Hale, "Chief George H.M. Johnson (Onwanonsyshon), His Life and Work among the Six Nations," *The Indian*, 24 November 1886, 219–20, TRL; The Hirschfelder collection of prehistoric Aboriginal artifacts now graces the Canadian Museum of Civilization in Ottawa, online at http://www.civilization.ca/cmc/exhibitions/tresors/ethno/etb0360e/.

21 Charles A. Hirschfelder, "Gi-Ye-Wa-No-Us-Qua-Go-Wa," or the sacrifice of the white dog," *The Indian,* 14 April 1886, 7; 28 April 1886, 86–87; 12 May 1886, 96, 99, TRL; Bruce E. Johansen and Barbara A. Mann, eds., *Encyclopedia of the Haudenosaunee* (Westport: Greenwood Press, 2000), 52–53.

22 *The Indian*, 9 June 1886; 15 December 1886, 247, TRL.

23 *The Indian*, 3 February 1886, 11, TRL.

24 *The Indian,* 23 June 1886, 136, TRL.

25 *The Toronto Mail*, 15 August 1885, TRL.

26 *The Indian,* 3 March 1886, 42, TRL.

27 Ibid.

28 *The Indian*, 26 May 1886, 111

29 *The Indian,* 3 February 1886, 11.

30 *The Indian,* 17 and 25 February.

31 Dr. P.E. Jones, "Prospectus of *The Indian*," 30 December 1885, TRL.

32 R. Douglas Francis, Richard Jones, and Donald B. Smith, *Journeys: A History of Canada* (Toronto: Nelson/Thomson Canada, 2006), 266.

33 Calvin Helm, *Dances with Dependency, Indigenous Success through Self-Reliance* (Vancouver: Orca Spirit Publishing, 2006), 97–99.

34 Indian Affairs, Sessional Papers (no. 14), 1893, 18–19.

35 Indian Affairs, Annual Report 1894, Dr. Jones's annual report, 18; ibid., part 2, 36, LAC.

36 Indian Affairs, Annual Report 1883, 13.

37 *The Indian*, "Prospectus," objective number 11, 30 December 1885, TRL.

38 *The Indian*, 3 February 1886, 11, TRL.

39 *The Indian,* 30 December 1885 to 29 December 1886, TRL.

40 Smith, *Sacred Feathers*, 138.

41 *The Indian,* 30 December 1885, 4; 3 February 1886, 1–2; 27 February 1886, 28; 3 March 1886, 40–41; 17 March 1886, 52; 31 March 1886, 63; 14 April 1886, 75–76, TRL.

42 *The Indian,* 3 February 1886, 8, TRL.

43 No author, "How Do Indians Know? Indian Medicine Men and Women," *The Indian*, 9 June 1886, 125, TRL.

44 No author, editorial, "The Indian Advancement Act," *The Indian,* 3 February 1886, 5 and 3 March 1886, 3, TRL.

45 Eliza Field Jones's Diary, box 11, file 11, PJC, VUL.

46 *The Indian*, 28 June 1886, 137, TRL.

47 Geo. S. Conover (Hy-We-Saus), "Indian Delicacies—Nut Oil &c," *The Indian*, 1 December 1886, 225, TRL.
48 Ibid.
49 Ibid.
50 *The Indian*, 1 December 1886, 225.
51 *The Indian*, 21 July 1886, 162.
52 *The Indian*, 4 August 1886, 174.
53 *The Indian*, 9 June 1886, 126.
54 Indian Affairs, RG 10, vol. 2615, file 124,391, LAC.
55 Masthead of *The Indian*, 8 September 1886, 198, TRL.
56 Peter Edmund Jones, "The Indians of Haldimand," in *The Illustrated Historical Atlas of the County of Haldimand, Ontario* (Toronto: H.R. Page Co., 1879), 9–10.
57 *The Indian*, 17 March 1886, 54, TRL.
58 Indian Affairs, report of A. McDonald, RG 10, vol. 8618, file 1/1-15-2-2; Annual Report 1887, report of the superintendent general, 117, LAC.
59 Ibid.
60 No author, editorial notes, "Indian Chiefs" (letter to *The Globe*), *The Indian*, 17 February 1886, 30, TRL.
61 Ibid.
62 Carl A. Weslager, *Magic Medicines of the Indians* (Wallingford: Middle Atlantic Press, 1973), 138–44; Kickapoo Indian Medicine Company, online at http://www.bottlebooks.com/kickapoo/.
63 No author, *The Pharmacopoeia of the United States of America*, 4th rev. ed. (Philadelphia: J.B. Lippincott & Co., 1864).
64 No author, *The British Pharmacopoeia* (London: Spottiswood & Co., 1867).
65 *The Indian*, 15 December 1886, 243, TRL.
66 Vic. Duy, *A Brief History of the Canadian Patent System prepared for the Canadian Biotechnology Advisory Committee,* online at http://www.cbac-cccb.ca.
67 *The Indian*, 12 May 1886, 108, TRL. The chief would collect the money when the band received their next interest payment and pay the merchant.
68 *The Indian*, 26 May 1886, 120, TRL.
69 Peter Edmund Jones to Sir John A. Macdonald, 31 March 1886, Macdonald Papers, 208742-45, LAC.
70 P.E. Jones to John A. Macdonald, 28 December 1888, Macdonald Papers, 2325-42, LAC.
71 Indian Affairs, Annual Report 1894, Dr. Jones's annual report, 18; ibid., part 2, 36, LAC.
72 Dr. P.E. Jones's departure for Washington, DC, *Hagersville News*, May 1896, HPL.
73 Indian Affairs, Peter E. Jones to T. Mayne Daly, Jr., RG 10, vol. 2755, file 149259, 3 May 1894, LAC.
74 *Tekawennake: Two Voices: Six Nations & New Credit News,* Oshweken, ON.
75 Peter E. Jones, "Salutatory," *The Indian,* 30 December 1885, 1, TRL.

Chapter 8: Federal Indian Agent

1 Donald B. Smith, *Sacred Feathers: The Reverend Peter Jones (Kahkewaquonaby) and the Mississauga Indians* (Toronto: University of Toronto Press, 1987), 225–26.
2 Indian Affairs, RG 10, vol. 1971, file 5416, mfm C-11124, LAC.
3 Indian Affairs, RG 10, vol. 2356, file 71911.
4 Wm. Hamilton Merritt to Sir John A. Macdonald, 2 December 1886, Macdonald Papers, vol. 432, 212382-83, mfm C 1780, LAC.
5 William H. Montague to Sir John A. Macdonald, Macdonald Papers, 28 September 1887, vol. 449, 222642-45, LAC.
6 Indian Affairs, "Lawrence Vankoughtnet to Sir John A. Macdonald," RG 10, vol. 2356, file 71,911, LAC.
7 P.E. Jones to Sir John A. Macdonald, 16 November 1886, Macdonald Papers, MG 26A, vol. 431, 21192-95, mfm C 1779, LAC.
8 Dorothy D. Aiello and Julie K. Silver, "Aging with Polio," in *Postpolio Syndrome,* ed. Julie K. Silver and Anne C. Gawne (Philadelphia: Hanley and Belfus, 2004), 275–85.
9 P.E. Jones to Sir John A Macdonald, Macdonald Papers, 16 November 1886, 211893, LAC.
10 Donald B. Smith, "John A. Macdonald and Aboriginal Canada," in *Historic Kingston, Annual Publication of the Kingston Historical Society*, 50 (2002):15.
11 Olive P. Dickason, *Canada's First Nations: A History of Founding Peoples from Earliest Times* (Toronto: Oxford University Press, 2002), 292–318.
12 Douglas Leighton, "A Victorian Civil Servant at Work: Lawrence Vankoughnet and the Canadian Indian Department," in *As Long as the Sun Shines and the Water Flows: A Reader in Canadian Native Studies*, ed. Ian A.L. Getty and Antoine Lussier (Vancouver: University of British Columbia Press, 1983), 104–19.
13 P.B. Waite, "White, Thomas," in *DCB,* vol. 11, 1881–1890 (Toronto: University of Toronto Press, 1982), 919–21.
14 Ibid.
15 Leighton, "Lawrence Vankoughnet," 104–19; Indian Affairs, Sessional Papers (no. 18), 1891 (part II), Return A, 3. Officers and employees at headquarters, Return A, LAC.
16 Photocopy courtesy of Donald B. Smith.
17 P.E. Jones to John A. Macdonald, 25 April 1888, Macdonald Papers 227894-96, LAC.
18 Indian Affairs, Annual Report, Index, reports of superintendents and agents, Nova Scotia, Part 1, 4.
19 Indian Affairs, Annual Report 1888, Return A (2), officers of the outside service, LAC.
20 Waite, "Thomas White," 919–21.
21 P.E. Jones to John A. Macdonald, 25 April 1888, Macdonald Papers, 227894-96, LAC; E. Brian Titley, "Dewdney, Edgar," in *DCB*, vol. 14, 1911–1920 (Toronto: University of Toronto Press, 1998), 295–98.
22 Leighton, "Lawrence Vankoughnet," 104–19; Edward Marion Chadwick, *Ontario Families Genealogies of United Empire Loyalists and Other Families of Upper Canada*, vol. 1 (Black Point: Fernwood Publishing, 2003), 60–62; "Lawrence Vankoughnet: Fiscal Responsibility and the Criminalization of Potlach," in Dean Neu and Richard Therrien, *Accounting for Genocide: Canada's*

Bureaucratic Assault on Aboriginal People (Black Point: Fernwood Publishing, 2003), 84–87.

23 Indian Affairs, Sessional Papers (no. 18), 1891, part 2, 3, LAC.

24 Indian Affairs, RG 10, vol. 2638, file 129,467, mfm, reel C-11255, LAC.

25 Indian Affairs, RG 10, vol. 2238, file 45,742; Christopher Vecsey, *Traditional Ojibwe Religion and Its Historical Changes* (Philadelphia: American Philosophical Society, 1983), 39, LAC.

26 "The Iroquois: The Grand River Reserve, 1875–1945," in *Aboriginal Ontario: Historical Perspectives on the First Nations*, ed. Edward S. Rogers and Donald B. Smith (Toronto: Dundurn Press, 1994), 227–30.

27 Indian Affairs, Annual Report 1896, Mississaugas of the New Credit, 12–13.

28 Ibid., report of the deputy superintendent general, 93.

29 Leighton, "Lawrence Vankoughnet," 108–11.

30 Indian Affairs, Annual Report 1891, New Credit Agency, Hagersville, Dr. Jones, Indian agent, 58, LAC.

31 Indian Affairs, Annual Report 1889, Sessional Papers (no. 16), vol. 22, part 1, 17–19, LAC.

32 Indian Affairs, Annual Report, Sessional Papers (no. 14), 1895, Mississaugas of the New Credit, 18–19, LAC.

33 Indian Affairs, Annual Report 1888, 16.

34 Indian Affairs, Annual Report 1895, report of the deputy superintendent general of Indian Affairs, 21; Indian Affairs, Annual Report 1914, Prevention and Spread of Tuberculosis, $4,685, Part H, 67, LAC.

35 Ronald F. Williamson and Susan Pfieffer, "Studying the Bones of the Ancestors," in *Bones of the Ancestors: The Archaeology and Osteobiography of the Moatfield Ossuary,* ed. Ronald F. Williamson and Susan Pfieffer (Ottawa: Archaeological Survey of Canada Mercury Series, vol. 163, Canadian Museum of Civilization, 2003), 5–16.

36 James B. Waldram, D. Ann Herring, and T. Kue Young, *Aboriginal Health in Canada: Historical, Cultural, and Epidemiological Perspectives*, 2nd ed. (Toronto: University of Toronto Press, 2006), 46.

37 M. Clark, P. Riben, and E. Nowegesic, "The Association of Housing Density, Isolation, and Tuberculosis in Canadian First Nations Communities," *International Journal of Epidemiology*, 31 (2002):940–45; Waldram et al., *Aboriginal Health*, 68–70, 86–88, 115.

38 Deborah C. Merrett and Susan Pfeiffer, "Maxillary Sinusitis as an Indicator of Respiratory Health in Past Populations," *American Journal of Physical Anthropology*, 11 (2000):301–18; Karen Morris, Marcia Morganlander, John L. Coulehan, Sheila Gahagen, and Vincent C. Arena, "Wood-Burning Stoves and Lower Respiratory Tract Infection in American Indian Children," *American Journal of Diseases of Children*, 144 (1990):105–8.

39 Merrett and Pfeiffer, "Maxillary Sinusitis," 301–18; Morris et al., "Wood-Burning Stoves," 105–8; Nancy Benac, "Dirty Cookstoves Pose Enormous Health Risk," *Canadian Medical Association Journal*, 182 (2010):1718–19.

40 Susan Pfieffer, "Commentary," in A.K. Wilber, A.W. Farnbach, K.J. Knudson, and J.E. Buikstra, "Diet, Tuberculosis, and the Paleopathological Record," *Current Anthropology*, 49 (2008):963–91, esp. 981.

41 Carl Benn, "Colonial Transformations," in *A Short Illustrated History of Its First 12,000 Years*, ed. Ronald F. Williamson (Toronto: James Lorimer & Co., 2008), 53; Smith, *Sacred Feathers*, 17–33.

42 Indian Affairs, Sessional Papers (no. 18), 1891 (part 1), Annual Report of the Mississaugas of the New Credit, 101, LAC.
43 Thomas M. Daniel, *Captain of Death: The Story of Tuberculosis* (Rochester: University of Rochester Press, 1997).
44 Indian Affairs, Annual Report, Sessional Papers (no. 14), 56 Vict., 1893, part I, 18. Mississaugas of the New Credit reported six deaths, four due to consumption, LAC.
45 Indian Affairs, Annual Report, Sessional Papers (no. 14), 56 Vict., 1893, part I, 36.
46 Sally M. Weaver, *Medicine and Politics among the Grand River Iroquois: A Study of the Non-Conservatives* (Ottawa: National Museum of Man, Publications in Ethnology, no. 4, 1972), 42; Dr. L. Secord cited in David Boyle, "The Pagan Iroquois," in *Archaeological Report: Appendix to the Report of the Minister of Education of Ontario* (Toronto: Government of Ontario, 1898), 190–94.
47 No author, *Report of the Proceedings of the New England Company, for the Civilization and Conversion of Indians, Blacks, and Pagans in the Dominion of Canada, South Africa, and the West Indies, during the years 1871–1872* (London: Taylor & Co., 1874), 190–1, 340.
48 Michael Bliss, *William Osler: A Life in Medicine* (Toronto: University of Toronto Press, 1999), 65–66.
49 Joseph Hanaway and Richard Cruess, *McGill Medicine, vol. 1, 1829–1885: The First Half Century, List of graduates: George E. Bomberry, M.D., 1875* (Montreal: McGill-Queen's University Press, 1996), 126–27.
50 No author, *Canadian Journal of Medical Science*, 10 (1 July 1878):346.
51 No author, CPSO, historical register, Dr. George Bomberry, granted licence no. 01955, 15 June 1878; no author, *A Sketch of the Origin and the Recent History of the New England Company by the Senior Member of the Company* (London: Spottiswoode & Co., 1844), 41.
52 The attending physician's medical diagnoses were carefully transcribed by the officiating clergyman in the burial records of the New Credit reserve cemeteries, MNCA, courtesy of Margaret Sault.
53 Gloria Pare, "Old Band Cemetery, Tuscarora Township, Brant County, Ontario," *The Cemetery Transcription Library*, online at http://www.internment.net/data/canada/ontario/brant/tuscarora/oldband/oldband.html.
54 Charles M. Godfrey, *Medicine for Ontario: A History* (Belleville: Mika Publishing, 1979), 157, Table C, 254.
55 Jacalyn Duffin, *Langstaff: A Nineteenth-Century Medical Life* (Toronto: University of Toronto Press, 1993), 99.
56 Burial records of the New Credit reserve cemeteries, MNCA.
57 Ibid., Chief David Sawyerm, MNCA; Tuhbenahneequay, Ontario Methodist Indian Mission, reel 1, 77.202, UCA.
58 Donald Brown, *Down Memory Lane: A Glimpse of Hagersville's Past* (Hagersville: Haldimand Press, 1992), 266, HPL; Ontario, http://www.yellowpages.ca/bus/Ontario/Hagersville/LCBO-Hagersville/5986175/.
59 Ibid.
60 Indian Affairs, Sessional Papers (no. 12), 1890, report of the superintendent general; Dewdney's visit to Jones's home is mentioned in Charlotte Dixon Jones's obituary, in possession of Louise Thorp, Vancouver.
61 Indian Affairs, Annual Report 1889, 36, LAC.

62 S. Dixon, moving schoolhouse, $173, in Indian Affairs, Sessional Papers (no. 14), 1895, Part 2, 18–19, LAC.
63 Indian Affairs, Annual Report 1889, in Sessional Papers (no. 12), 1890, part 1, 147–49, LAC. S. Dixon, moving schoolhouse, $173.
64 Indian Affairs, 55 Vict., Sessional Papers (no. 14), 1893, 15–16, LAC.
65 Indian Affairs, 55 Vict., Sessional Papers (no. 14), 1993, 18–19, LAC.
66 Indian Affairs, Annual Report, the Mississaugas of the New Credit, 1894, 42–43, LAC.
67 Indian Affairs, Annual Report, the Mississaugas of the New Credit, 1895, 53–54, LAC.
68 Lauro S. Halstead, "Diagnosing Postpolio Syndrome: Inclusion and Exclusion Criteria," in *Postpolio Syndrome*, ed. Julie K. Silver and Anne C. Gawne (Philadelphia: Hanley and Belfus, 2004), 1–20.
69 CPSO, historical register.
70 Peter E. Jones to Sir John A. Macdonald, 28 December 1888, Macdonald Papers, 232539-42, LAC.
71 Ibid.
72 Ibid.
73 Ibid.
74 Ibid.
75 J.K. Johnson and P.B. Waits, "Macdonald, Sir John Alexander," in *DCB*, vol. 12, 1891–1900 (Toronto: University of Toronto Press, 1985), 591–612.
76 Leighton, "Lawrence Vankoughnet," 106–7; Blair Stonechild and Bill Waiser, *Loyal Till Death: Indians and the North West Rebellion* (Calgary: Fifth House, 1997), 52–54. The authors note that the majority of Northwest Indians were loyal to the Queen, but emphasize that this fact has never been sufficiently recognized.
77 Indian Affairs, Annual Report, 55 Vict., Sessional Papers (no. 14), 1993, LAC; Leighton, "Lawrence Vankoughnet," 114–17.
78 David Wistow, "Bruce, William Blair," in *DCB*, vol. 13, 1900–1910 (Toronto: University of Toronto Press, 1994), 117–18; Phillip Buckner, "Tupper, Sir Charles," in *DCB*, vol. 14, 1911–1920 (Toronto: University of Toronto Press, 1998), 1014–23; obituary of Charlotte Jones, October 1921, entitled "Called Home," in a Vernon, BC, newspaper, in possession of Louise Thorp, Vancouver.
79 Peter E. Jones to Sir John A. Macdonald, 28 December 1888, Macdonald Papers, 232539–42, LAC.
80 Indian Affairs, RG 10, vol. 1116, deputy superintendent general's Letterbook, 17 November 1894 to 21 May 1895, 219–20, 621–23, LAC. Transcribed copy obtained 16 June 2006, courtesy of Margaret Sault, MNCA.
81 Duffin, *Langstaff*, 82–83.
82 Ibid., 75, Table 4.2.
83 Indian Affairs, minutes of the Mississaugas of the Credit council, 11 June 1878.
84 Indian Affairs, L. Vankoughnet to A. Dingman, Indian Office, Brantford, 24 April 1889, MNCA.
85 Canada, fourth census, 1901, Ontario, District no. 67, Haldimand & Monck, p. 11, 107 Main St., Robert McDonald, head of family, Charlotte Jones reported to be a sister-in-law; Indian Affairs, Annual Report, 60 Vict. 1896, Return A (2), officers and employees, outside service, Ontario, 456, LAC.
86 Indian Affairs, Annual Report, 59 Vict., 1895, 488, LAC. Dr. Jones's last payment as band physician was 31 July 1895.

87 Indian Affairs, Hayter Reed to Hon. T. Mayne Daly, superintendent general, 8 November 1895, file no. 81740, 621-23, copy held by MNCA; Hayter Reed to superintendent general, 22 December 1896, 612, re. withholding Dr. Jones's salary as $250 for an Indian's estate unaccounted for; photocopy June 16, 2006, courtesy of MNCA.
88 Ibid.
89 Indian Affairs, Hayter Reed to T. Mayne Daly in deputy superintendent general's Letterbook, 17 November 1894 to 21 May 1895, RG 10, vol. 1116, 219–20, LAC.
90 Indian Affairs, Memorandum, 30 March 1898, deputy superintendent general's Letterbook, 10 August 1897 to 9 June 1898, RG 10, vol. 1121, 571 re. order in council relieving Dr. Peter E. Jones of his post in the Outside Service of the Department of Indian Affairs approved on 25 January 1897, LAC and MNCA.
91 Peter S. Schmalz, *The Ojibwa of Southern Ontario* (Toronto: University of Toronto Press, 1991), 211.
92 Ibid., 212.
93 Dr. P.E. Jones to David Boyle, 11 March 1998, David Boyle Correspondence, 1893–1900, SCI, box 1, ROMA.
94 Indian Affairs, Annual Report, Mississaugas of the New Credit, 1896, 12–13.
95 Ibid.

Chapter 9: The Later Years

1 Donald Brown, *Down Memory Lane: A Glimpse of Hagersville's Past* (Hagersville: Haldimand Press, 1992), 11, HCL; M.L.A. Willard, A. Graham, and J. Carr, eds., *Roots and Branches: A History of Hagersville* (Hagersville: Haldimand Press, 1992), 11, HPL.
2 Indian Affairs, Annual Report 1898, Sessional Papers, 1898, 516, LAC.
3 CPSO, historical register, Robert George McDonald, registered 28 June 1869, M.D.; Eclectic Medical College, 1868; licensed by Ontario's Eclectic Medical Board in 1868.
4 Rose Hoover was born on 30 April 1884. I thank Donald B. Smith for sending me these details, which were obtained during his interview with Mr. Senn, of Victoria, BC.
5 No author, "Dr. Jones Leaves for Washington, DC," *Hagersville News*, 3 June 1898, retrieved from the Augustus and Peter Jones file, HCMA.
6 Donald B. Smith, *Sacred Feathers: The Reverend Peter Jones (Kahkewaquonaby) and the Mississauga Indians* (Toronto: University of Toronto Press, 1987), 255–57.
7 Smithsonian Institution, Washington, DC, photo no. 498, 25 August 1898.
8 W.J. McGee, " Feather Symbolism," *American Anthropologist*, 11 (1898):177–80; list and descriptions of twenty-four items purchased by Mr. W.J. McGee of the Bureau of Ethnology, accession no. 3732. Dr. Jones received US $198 for the collection.
9 Donald B. Smith, "Historic Peace-Pipe," *The Beaver*, Summer (1984):4–7; Edward S. Rogers, "The Algonquian Farmers of South Ontario, 1830–1945," in *Aboriginal Ontario: Historical Perspectives on the First Nations*, ed. Edward S. Rogers and Donald B. Smith (Toronto: Dundurn Press, 1994), 94.
10 P.E. Jones to W.L. Stone, 31 October 1882, PJC, VUL.

11 Dr. Peter Edmund Jones to William L. Stone, Esq., Jersey City, NJ, 31 October 1882. Draper/Brant Papers, 13 F13, Wisconsin State Historical Society; Dr. P.E. Jones to Dr. Lyman C. Draper, 12 November 1882, Draper/Brant Papers, 13F14, Wisconsin State Historical Society, Madison, WI.

12 P.E. Jones, *Hagersville News*, 3 June 1898.

13 Peter E. Jones Collection of the Bureau of Ethnology, Smithsonian Institution, Washington, DC, accession 33939, 25 August 1898.

14 Brown, *Hagersville's Past,* 266.

15 David T. McNab, ed., *Earth, Water, Air, and Fire: Studies in Canadian Ethnohistory* (Waterloo: Wilfrid Laurier University Press, 1998), 176, n. 117.

16 Stephen Laurent, "The Abenakis: Aborigines of Vermont," part 2, *Vermont History*, 24 (1956), 5; Paul Radin, *Primitive Religion* (New York: Dover, 1957), 206.

17 Charles Darwin, *On the Origin of Species by Means of Natural Selection, or the Preservation of Favoured Races in the Struggle for Life* (London: Murray, 1860), 502. Bird specimens prepared by Dr. Jones were still on display in the high schools and museum in Vernon, BC, a century after his death.

18 Dr. P.E. Jones to Dr. Lyman C. Draper, 12 November 1882, Draper/Brant Papers, 13F14, Wisconsin State Historical Society, Madison, WI.

19 Ibid.; Henry R. Schoolcraft, *The American Indians Their History, Condition, and Prospects, from Original Notes and Manuscripts* (Buffalo: G.H. Derby, 1851), online at http://www.canadiana.org/ECO/mtq?doc=41884.

20 Scrapbook containing press clippings and photographs from the *First Canadian Historical Exhibition*, held at Victoria College, Queen's Park, Toronto, June 1899, plus catalogue, AO.

21 Brown, *Hagersville's Past*, 266.

22 Obituary of Hannah E., relict of the late Chas. A. Jones, 2 May 1902, copy of unnamed newspaper clipping, courtesy of Donald B. Smith.

23 *Hagersville News*, 3 June 1898, HCMA. Postcards showing Dr. Jones's chess moves, two games per card, in possession of Louise Thorp, Vancouver; photocopies courtesy of Donald B. Smith.

24 Eliza Field's Diary, 2 April 1833, PJC, VUL.

25 Indian Affairs, Deputy Superintendent General Hayter Reed to A.E. Forget, assistant Indian commissioner, Regina, 14 February 1895, deputy superintendent's Letterbook, 345; copy obtained 16 June 2006, MNCA.

26 Indian Affairs, superintendent general of Indian Affairs to His Excellency, the governor general in council, 4 April 1898, re. refund of Dr. Jones's past payments to the civil service's superannuation fund, RG 10, vol. 1121, DSG Letterbook, 10 August 1897 to 9 June 1898, LAC.

27 Indian Affairs, RG 10, vol. 1733, file 63-16, LAC. Dr. Jones granted a $1,500 loan to repair his barn in January 1896.

28 *Six Nations of the Grand River, Land Rights, Financial Justice, Creative Solutions* (2006), 9, online at http://www.myhamilton.ca/NR/rdonlyres/0FCA0BC2-A78F-47AC-9577-016BB397F1D7/0/sixnationsclaimsbooklet.pdf.

29 Canada's passenger rail system, Via Rail, continued this tradition by offering all qualified Aboriginals a thirty-three percent discount off the full adult regular fare; online at http://www.viarail.ca/en/help/faq/discounts/.

30 *Jones v. Grand Trunk Railway Company* (1904), 3 O.W.R. 705, Ontario High Court, Britton, J., 3 June 1904 (appealed to Ontario Court of Appeal, *infra* p. 139), AO.

31 Ibid.
32 Ibid.
33 Ibid.
34 Ibid.
35 *Jones v. Grand Trunk Railway Company* (1905), 9 O.L.R. 723 (also reported: 5 O.W.R. 611), Ontario Court of Appeal, Moss C.J.O., Osler, MacLennan, Garrow, and MacLaren, J.A., 12 April 1905. (On appeal from judgment of Ontario High Court, supra p. 134.) I thank David Smith for discovering this legal case while a student at Ryerson University.
36 Grand Trunk Railway Company of Canada, online at http://www.collectionscanada.gc.ca/confederation/023001-2997-e/.
37 D.T. Max, "A Man of Taste: A Chef with Cancer of the Tongue Fights to Save His Taste," *The New Yorker* (12 May 2008):82–93; Ken Flegel, Noni MacDonald, and Paul C. Herbert, "Binge Drinking: All Too Prevalent and Hazardous," *Canadian Medical Association Journal*, 183 (2011):411.
38 Michael Bliss, *William Osler: A Life in Medicine* (Toronto: University of Toronto Press, 1999), 365.
39 Macdonald Holmes, then seventy-five years of age, was interviewed by Donald B. Smith at his home in Edmonton in 1976.
40 Richard C. Daniel, "The Board of Arbitrators and the Mississaugas of the Credit," in *Native Claims Processes in Canada* (Ottawa: Research Branch, Department of Indian and Northern Affairs, 1980), 61.
41 Indian Affairs, file 213957-339795, 30 January 1909, LAC.
42 Indian Affairs, RG 10, vol. 1731, file 63-16, mfm C-15022, 282, LAC.
43 Holmes interview, 1976.
44 P.E. Jones to Sir John A. Macdonald, 19 September 1885, Macdonald Papers, 2003490-95, LAC.
45 Ontario, registrations of death, RG 80-8, vol. 8, 1909, no. 12092, mfm Ms 935, reel 144, AO; obituary, *The Toronto Globe*, 30 June 1909, TRL; *Hagersville News*, obituary of 29 June 1909, reprinted in Brown, *Hagersville's Past*, 157; Indian Affairs, RG 10, vol. 1734, file 63-16, part 4, mfm C-15022, 262; voucher passed 21 July 1909 to pay burial expenses of Dr. Jones, LAC. The same bill was paid twice in error. Jones, who long suffered from departmental parsimony, would have had a good laugh.
46 Registrar of burials, Greenwood Cemetery, Parks and Cemetery Commission Office, 1 Sherwood Drive, Brantford, location: E½ & W½ 37. Time has erased the names.
47 Assessment roll, Hagersville, 1899, no. 168, P.E. Jones, physician, value of property $750, five occupants [parents, three sons], mfm GS2712, AO.
48 Indian Affairs, RG 10, vol. 3156, file 358,000-25, mfm C-11332, minutes of the New Credit Band Council, 15 January 1913; minutes of 24 Jan 1913, LAC. The band offered Charlotte Jones $1,200 for her farm, which boasted considerable improvements. Offer confirmed by vote of twenty-one to six.
49 Ontario register of deaths, RG 80-8, Ms 935, reel 175, AO.
50 The late Lloyd S. King, Mississaugas of the New Credit First Nation educator and band historian, kindly granted the author an interview on 17 June 2002.
51 British Columbia death certificate, no. B13120, reg. no. 1921-09-290186, GSU mfm 1927297, ABC.
52 Obituary of Charlotte Dixon Jones in the Vernon newspaper by her daughter-in-law, Jessie Blanche Ritchie Dixon, courtesy of Louise Thorp and Donald B.

Smith. Following the demise of *The Indian,* Dr. Jones's stepson, Alpheus Dixon, became assistant commercial editor of *The Toronto Empire*. Later he owned and edited the *Orchard and Farm* magazine in California and in 1902 he was on the board of the Frisco Press Club.

53 PJC, VUL, Dr. Peter E. Jones's collection of Indian books, relics, and taxidermy was stored by his stepson, Elvin Dixon, of Vernon. British Columbia, probate file, reg. no. 1943-09-618/888, no. B13178, GSU mfm no. 1953635, ABC, the Woodland Cultural Centre and Museum in Brantford, among others.

54 Linda Wills, archivist, Greater Vernon Museum and Archives, Vernon, to Donald B. Smith, Department of History, University of Calgary, Calgary, AB, 10 and 24 August and 15 December 1989. My thanks to Judy Hill, acting director of the Woodland Cultural Centre for allowing the author to examine these artifacts. Preliminary estimate of their age by Gary Warrick and Paul Racher, archaeologists, Wilfrid Laurier University.

55 Donald B. Smith, "Historic Peace-Pipe," *The Beaver*, Summer (1984):4–7.

56 Canada, the Franchise Act, 1898, S.C. 1898, 61 Vict., c. 14.

Appendix: Effective Herbal Therapies of Aboriginal Women

1 Cited in William Osler, *The Evolution of Modern Medicine* (New Haven: Yale University Press, 1921), 7.

2 According to Gillian Barlow, Queen's University archivist, Jones's M.D. graduation thesis was read by the faculty's examiners but not archived.

3 Lewis Paul Hill, "Understanding Indigenous Canadian Traditional Health and Healing" (Ph.D. dissertation, Wilfrid Laurier University, 2008).

4 The Jones sailed to New York; only their excess luggage was on this ship, and these items were later donated to the McCord Museum of Canadian History, Montreal, Quebec.

5 Peter Jones, *History of the Ojebway Indians: With Especial Reference to Their Conversion to Christianity* (London: A.W. Bennett, 1861), reprint (Freeport: Books for Libraries, 1970), 152–55.

6 Peter Jones (Kahkewaquonaby), "The Indian Nations: A Short Account of the Customs and Manners of the North American Indians, Particularly of the Chippeway Nation," *The Monthly Review: Devoted to the Government of Canada, Toronto*, 1, May (1841):313–26.

7 Judith Sumner, *The Natural History of Medicinal* Plants (Portland: Timber Press, 2000), 49.

8 Christina M. Clavelle, "Ethnobotany of Two Cree Communities in the Southern Boreal Forest of Saskatchewan" (M.A. thesis, University of Saskatchewan, 1997), 45–46.

9 Jacques Rousseau and Marcel Raymond, Études Ethnobotaniques Québécoises (Montreal: Institut Botanique de l'Université de Montréal, 1945), 8.

10 Cary Miller, *Ogimaag: Anishinaabeg Leadership, 1760–1845* (Lincoln: University of Nebraska Press, 2010).

11 Miller, *Ogimaag*, 66–70.

12 Sarah Carter, "First Nations Women of Prairie Canada in the Early Reserve Years, the 1870s to the 1920s: A Preliminary Inquiry," in *Women of the First Nations: Power, Wisdom, and Strength*, ed. Christine Miller and Patricia Marie Chuchryk (Winnipeg: University of Manitoba Press, 1996), 63–64.

13 Anthony J. Cichoke, *Secrets of Native American Herbal Remedies* (New York: Penguin Putnam, 2001), 33–34; Joan Heather Brown and Pamela Taylor, "Muscarinic Receptor Agonists and Antagonists," in *Goodman & Gilman's: The Pharmacological Basis of Therapeutics*, 11th ed., ed. Lawrence L. Brunton (New York: McGraw Hill, 2006), 183–200; Virgil J. Vogel, *American Indian Medicine* (Norman: University of Oklahoma Press, 1970), 330; Frank Chandler, ed., *Herbs: Everyday Reference for Health Professionals* (Ottawa: Canadian Pharmacists Association, 2000), 211–12; Cichoke, *Herbal Remedies*, 54. These plants are also called American valerian because of their sedative effect.
14 Carter, "First Nations Women of Prairie Canada," 63–64.
15 Thor Arnason, Richard J. Hebda, and Timothy Johns, "Use of Plants for Food and Medicine by Native Peoples of Eastern Canada," *Canadian Journal of Botany*, 59 (1981):2189–2325.
16 Gladys Tantaquidgeon, "Mohegan Medicinal Practices, Weather-Lore, and Superstition," *Forty-third Annual Report of the Bureau of American Ethnology, 1925–26* (Washington, DC: Government Printing Office, 1928), 264–79.
17 Carl A. Weslager, *Magic Medicines of the Indians* (Wallingford: Middle Atlantic Press, 1973), 76.
18 Ibid.
19 Vogel, *Indian Medicine*, 311–12; Chandler, ed., *Herbs*, 139–41, 395; Walter H. Lewis and Memory P.F. Elvin-Lewis, *Medical Botany: Plants Affecting Man's Health* (New York: John Wiley, 1944), 224.
20 Vogel, *Indian Medicine*, 225.
21 Ibid., 395–96.
22 Fielding H. Garrison, *An Introduction to the History of Medicine, with Medical Chronology, Suggestions for Study and Bibliographic Data*, 4th ed. (Philadelphia: W.B. Saunders Company, 1929), 606; Chandler, ed., *Herbs*, 54–56; Cichoke, *Herbal Remedies*, 25–26.
23 Garrison, *History of Medicine*, 346–48.
24 Weslager, *Magic Medicines,* 71.
25 Frances Densmore, *Indian Use of Wild Plants for Crafts, Food, Medicine, and Charms, originally published as: Uses of Plants by the Chippewa Indians* (Washington, DC: Annual Report of the Bureau of American Ethnology, 1926–27), reprint (Ohsweken: Iroqrafts Limited, 1993), 301; Vogel, *Indian Medicine*, 230.
26 Vogel, *Indian Medicine*, 225.
27 Ibid., 400.
28 Lewis and Elvin-Lewis, *Medical Botany,* 225.
29 Vogel, *Indian Medicine*, 402–3.
30 Weslager, *Magic Medicines*, 84.
31 Jacques Mathieu, *L'Annedda, l'Arbre de vie* (Quebec: Les éditions du Septentrion, 2009), 73–109.
32 N. Shakuntala Manay and M. Shadaksharaswamy, *Foods: Facts and Principles* (New Delhi: New Age International Ltd., 2001), 77–79; Weston A. Price, *Nutrition and Physical Degeneration: A Comparison of Primitive and Modern Diets and Their Effects* (Los Angeles: American Academy of Applied Nutrition, 1939); Mathieu, *L'Annedda, l'Arbre de vie*, 73–109; Hans Selye, "Studies on Adaptation," *Endocrinology*, 21 (1937):169–88.
33 Vogel, *Indian Medicine*, 253–60, 403; Weslager, *Magic Medicines*, 102–4.
34 Weslager, *Magic Medicines*, 93–104.

35 Cichoke, *Herbal Remedies*, 55; Chandler, ed., *Herbs*, 149–52. Students working under the direction of Malcolm King, Ph.D., a professor at the University of Alberta, demonstrated by means of *in vitro* studies that constituents of this herb can liquefy mucus.
36 Vogel, *Indian Medicine*, 388–90; Densmore, *Indian Use of Wild Plants*, 302.
37 T. Arnason, R. Hebda, and T. Johns, "Uses of Plants for Food and Medicine by Native Peoples of Eastern Canada," *Canadian Journal of Botany*, 58 (1981):2202.
38 Vogel, *Indian Medicine*, 302–4.
39 Densmore, *Wild Plants*, 300; Weslager, *Magic Medicines*, 76.
40 Lewis, *Medical Botany*, 82; Vogel, *Indian Medicine*, 277–79.
41 Vogel, *Indian Medicine*, 1026
42 Ibid.; Densmore, *Wild Plants*, 331.
43 Vogel, *Indian Medicine*, 374.
44 Weslager, *Magic Medicines*, 116.
45 Vogel, *Indian Medicine*, 303, 315–16.
46 Ibid., 289, 366; David Hoffmann, *The Complete Illustrated Holistic Herbal* (Rockport: Element Books, 1996), 143; Vogel, *Indian Medicine*, 334–36.
47 Vogel, *Indian Medicine*, 296; Weslager, *Magic Medicines*, 69; Vogel, *Indian Medicine*, 282.
48 Densmore, *Wild Plants*, 331–32; Vogel, *Indian Medicine*, 184–86.
49 L.P.E. Choquette, "Significance of Parasites in Wildlife," *Canadian Journal of Comparative Medicine*, 20 (1956):418–26; Thomas J. Riley, "Ascarids, American Indians, and the Modern World: Parasites and the Prehistoric Record of a Pharmacological Tradition," *Perspectives in Biology and Medicine*, 36 (1993):369–75.
50 Eric O. Callen, T.W.M. Cameron, "A Prehistoric Diet Revealed in Coprolites," *New Scientist*, 8 (1960):35–40; Vaughn M. Bryant and Glenna W. Dean, "Archaeological Coprolyte Science: The Legacy of Eric O. Callen (1912–1970), *Palaeogeography, Palaeoclimatology, Palaeoecology*, 237 (2006):51–66.
51 Alfred Stillé, *Therapeutics and Materia Medica: A Systematic Treatise on the Action and Uses of Medicinal Agents Including Their Description and History*, 3rd ed., vol. 2 (Philadelphia: Henry C. Lee, 1868), 611–12.
52 Vogel, *Indian Medicine*, 317.
53 Ibid., 304–5.
54 Robert W. Wolfgang, "Indian and Eskimo Diphyllobothriasis," *Canadian Medical Association Journal*, 70, May (1954):536–39; James B. Waldram, D. Ann Herring, and T. Kue Young, *Aboriginal Health in Canada: Historical, Cultural, and Epidemiological Perspectives*, 2nd ed. (Toronto: University of Toronto Press, 2006), 45; Vogel, *Indian Medicine*, 304.
55 Robert Bell, "The Medicine-Man; or Indian and Esquimo Notions of Medicine," *Canadian Medical and Surgical Journal for March/April 1886* (Montreal: Gazette Printing Company, 1886), 9; Percy W. Mathews, *Notes on the Diseases among the Indians Frequenting York Factory, Hudson's Bay* (Montreal: Gazette Printing Co., 1885), online at http://www.Canadiana.org/record/30381/.
56 Carter, "First Nations Women," 63–64.
57 Ibid.
58 Weslager, *Magic Medicines*, 70–71; Vogel, *Indian Medicine*, 290, 347, 393.
59 Dominion Forest Service, bulletin 61, *Native Trees of Canada* (Ottawa: Department of Mines and Resources, 1939), 71.

60 John C. Krantz, Jr., *Historical Medical Classics Involving New Drugs* (Baltimore: Williams & Wilkins, 1974), 37–41.
61 Mark Blumenthal, ed., *Herbal Medicine: Expanded Commission E Monographs* (Newton: Integrative Medicine Communications, 2000).
62 Vogel, *Indian Medicine*, 393–95.
63 R.B. Lipton, H. Göbel, K.M. Einhäupl, K. Wilks, and A. Mauskop, "Petasites hybridus Root (Butterbar) Is an Effective Preventative Treatment for Migraine," *Neurology*, 63 (2004):2240–4; Tamara Pringsheim, W. Jeptha Davenport, and Werner J. Becker, "Prophylaxis of Migraine Headache," *Canadian Medical Association Journal*, 182 (2010):679–85.
64 Robin J. Marles, Christina Clavelle, Leslie Monteleone, Natalie Tays, and Donna Burns, *Aboriginal Plant Use in Canada's Northwest Boreal Forest* (Edmonton: Natural Resources Canada, Canadian Forest Service, 2008), 149.
65 Lewis, *Medical Botany*, 255; Densmore, *Wild Plants*, 335.
66 Mrs. Rosanna Hoover to Wilma Jamieson, dated Thessalon, ON, 16 September 1959. Catherine Russell was a member of the Six Nations.
67 Daniel E. Moerman, *Native American Ethnobotany* (Portland: Timber Press, 1998), 123; Densmore, *Wild Plants*, 334–35.
68 Vogel, *Indian Medicine*, 299–301.
69 E.H. Ackernecht, *A Short History of Medicine* (Baltimore: Johns Hopkins University Press, 1982), 123–24.
70 Densmore, *Wild Plants*, photo plate no. 46.
71 Interview on 10 September 2007 with Elisabeth Patterson, an intellectual properties lawyer representing the interests of Cree First Nations.
72 Sally M. Weaver, "The Iroquois: The Grand River Reserve in the Late Nineteenth and Early Twentieth Centuries, 1875–1945," in *Aboriginal Ontario: Historical Perspectives on the First Nations*, ed. Edward S. Rogers and Donald B. Smith (Toronto: Dundurn Press, 1994), 227–28.
73 Waldram, *Aboriginal Health*, 173–81; P. Barkwell, "The Medicine Chest Clause in Treaty no. 6," *Canadian Native Law Reporter*, 4 (1981):1–23; no author, *An Overview of Traditional Knowledge and Medicine and Public Health in Canada* (Ottawa: National Aboriginal Health Organization, 2008).

Glossary

[Modified from Aboriginal Affairs and Northern Development Canada, "Words First: An Evolving Terminology Relating to Aboriginal Peoples in Canada," online at http://www.ainc-inac.gc.ca.]

Aboriginal peoples The descendants of the original inhabitants of North America. The Canadian Constitution recognizes three separate peoples—Indians, Métis, and Inuit.

Band A community of Indians for whom lands have been set apart or money is held by the federal government. Each band has its own chief and governing Band Council chosen through election or sometimes through custom. Today many bands prefer to be known as First Nations.

First Nation A term selected to replace the word "Indian," which some people consider offensive. "First Nations peoples," however, refers to all the Indian peoples of Canada, both Status and non-Status.

Indian The term "Indian" collectively describes all the indigenous peoples in Canada who are not Inuit or Métis. There are legal reasons for the continued use of this term, which is recognized in the Canadian Constitution and the Indian Act.

Indian Act Canadian federal legislation that defines an individual's legal status as an Indian and regulates the management of their reserve lands, money, and resources.

Indigenous peoples The word "indigenous" means "native to the area." Its meaning is similar to "Native peoples," "Aboriginal peoples," or "First peoples."

Métis People with mixed Aboriginal and non-Aboriginal ancestry who identify themselves as Métis. Métis communities have their own unique culture, which draws on their ancestral origins such as Cree, Ojibwe, French, or British. Métis peoples are entitled to certain rights both under Canada's Constitution and in the law of the land.

Non-Status Indian A person who considers himself or herself to be Indian, but is not recognized as such by the government and is not entitled to the rights and benefits of a Status Indian.

Reserve Lands set apart for the use and benefit of an Aboriginal band, but the federal government retains ownership of the tract of land. Band members, all Status Indians, receive location certificates for their properties, which usually remain in the family. Many bands now prefer the term "First Nation community."

Status Indian A person who is recognized as an Indian under the Indian Act and is entitled to various rights and benefits, but is also subject to restrictions.

Bibliography

I. Archival Collections

Archives of Ontario, Toronto
BC Archives, Victoria
Brant County Museum and Archives, Brantford
Brantford Public Library, Brantford
College of Physicians and Surgeons of Ontario, historical register, Toronto
Government Information Service, McGill University Library, Montreal
Haldimand County Archives, Cayuga
Haldimand County Library, Hagersville
Kingston General Hospital Archives, Kingston
Library and Archives Canada, Ottawa
    Indian Affairs, RG 10
    Macdonald Papers; correspondence with Dr. P.E. Jones
McGill University Rare Book Room, Montreal
    Pilling, James Constantine. *Bibliography of the Algonquian Languages*
Mississaugas of the New Credit First Nation Archives, Hagersville
National Library of Scotland, Edinburgh
Orange Directory of Western Ontario
Queen's University Archives, Kingston
    A.A Travill fonds
    Faculty of Medicine calendars
    Minutes of Queen's University Faculty of Medicine
    Minutes of Queen's University Senate
    Robert Bell fonds
Queen's University Library, Kingston
    Rare book collection
Royal Ontario Museum, Toronto
    David Boyle correspondence
Smithsonian Institution, Washington, DC.
    Dr. Peter E. Jones, photographs, Aboriginal relics, and translations of Ojibwe words

Toronto Reference Library, Toronto
Toronto Star Newspaper Centre
United Church Archives, Toronto
Dr. Peter E. Jones collection
University of Toronto Archives
Toronto School of Medicine fonds
Victoria University Library and Archives, Toronto
Peter Jones Collection
Welcome Trust History of Medicine Library, London, UK
Wisconsin State Historical Society, Madison
Draper/Brant Papers
Woodland Educational and Cultural Centre, Brantford

II. Government and University Documents

Canada (Province of). An Act for the Better Protection of the Indians of Upper Canada from the Imposition, and the Property Occupied or Enjoyed by Them from Trespass or Injury. Statutes of the Province of Canada, 1850, 13 Vict., c. 74.

———. An Act to Encourage the Gradual Civilization of the Indian Tribes in the Province, and to Amend the Laws Respecting Indians. Statutes of the Province of Canada 1857, 20 Vict., c.26.

Canada. An Act for the Gradual Enfranchisement of Indians, the Better Management of Indian Affairs, and to Extend the Provisions of the Act, 31st Victoria, Chapter 42. Statutes of Canada 1869, 32–33 Vict., c. 6.

———. An Act Providing for the Organization of the Department of the Secretary of State of Canada, and for the Management of Indian and Ordinance Lands. Statutes of Canada, 31 Vict., c. 42: 91–100.

———. An Act to Amend and Consolidate the Laws Respecting Indians. Statutes of Canada 1880, 43 Vict., c. 18.

———. "David Mills, MP," Commons Debates, 27 May 1885, 2144–46.

———. Exchequer Court, *Henry et al. [Mississaugas of the New Credit] v. The King*, (1905), 9 Ex. C.R. 417, Burbidge J., 8 May 1905.

———. "Frank Oliver, M.P.," Commons Debates, Session 1906–7, vol. 4, 7292–93.

———. Indian Act, Statutes of Canada 1876, 39 Vict., c. 18: 43–73, 43–44.

———. Indian Advancement Act. Statutes of Canada 1884, 47 Vict., c. 28.

———. Indian Affairs. *Annual Reports*. Online at http:// www.collectionscanada .gc.ca/indianaffairs/.

———. The Dominion Electoral Franchise Act, Statutes of Canada 1898, c.14, s. 5(a).

———. The Electoral Franchise Act, Statutes of Canada, 48 Vict., c. 40, ss. 2, 11.

———. "Sir John A. Macdonald," Commons Debates, 30 April 1885, 1487–88.

———. "Sir John A. Macdonald," Commons Debates, 48 Victoria, 8 June 1885, 19:2371.

Ontario. Assessment Roll for the Municipality of Hagersville, no. 168, P.E. Jones, physician, Main Street, 1899, mfm GS2712, AO.

———. College of Physicians and Surgeons, Toronto, historical register, list of licensed physicians and surgeons.

———. Court of Appeal, *Jones v. Grand Trunk Railway Company* (1905) 9. O.L.R. 723 (also reported: 5 O.W.R. 611), Ontario Court of Appeal, Moss C.J.O., Osler, MacLennan, Garrow, and MacLaren, J.A., 12 April 1905. Charlotte Jones was awarded $10 and her legal costs.

———. *High Court, Jones v. Grand Trunk Railway Company* (1904), 3 O.W.R. 705, Britton, J., 3 June 1904 (Appealed to Ontario Court of Appeal, infra p. 139).

———. Legislative Assembly. *Annual Archaeological Report; Being Part of an Appendix to the Report of the Minister of Education, Ontario, 1899.* Toronto: Government of Ontario, 1900.

Queen's University, Kingston. Minutes of the Faculty of Medicine, 1864–66, QUA.

———. Calendar of the Faculty of Medicine for 1865–66, 43, QUA.

———. Calendar for 1875–76, Cumulative list of Students, QUA.

———. Minutes of Senate from 11 February 1963 to 25 April 1887. Minutes of meeting held 27 March 1866, 28, QUA.

Toronto School of Medicine. Calendar 1871, Cumulative List of Students, UTA.

III (A) Newspapers

Anishinabek News, North Bay
Brantford Expositor, Brantford
Cherokee Phoenix and Indian Advocate, New Echota
Christian Guardian, Toronto
Eagle Press Newsletter, Mississaugas of the New Credit, Hagersville
Empire, Toronto
Globe and Mail, Toronto
Hagersville News, Hagersville
Hamilton Daily Spectator, Hamilton
Kingston Daily News, Kingston
Montreal Gazette, Montreal
Ottawa Citizen, Ottawa
Tekawennake: Two Voices: Six Nations & New Credit News, Oshweken
The Indian, Hagersville
Toronto Mail, Toronto
Wadrihwa, Woodland Cultural Centre Newsletter, Brantford

III (B) Selected Articles

B.A. "Red Men vs White Men." Communication to the editor. *The Toronto Mail*, 8 December 1875.

Jones, P.E. "An Indian's View of the Indian Question." *The Toronto Mail*, 16 May 1885.

———. "Red Man v. White Man." Communication to the editor. *The Toronto Mail*, 14 December 1875.

———. "The Indian Franchise: Views of a Head Chief." *The Toronto Mail*, 22 May 1885.

No author. "An Indian Picnic, a Day among the Six Nations on Their Reserve: The Franchise Act Discussed." *The Toronto Mail*, 15 August 1885.

———. "Obituary: Dr. Jones Dead: An Authority on Indian Affairs—Son of Famous Missionary." *The Toronto Globe*, 30 June 1909.

———. "The Mississauga Indians, an Important Meeting of the Tribe Yesterday. A Claim to Be Made to the Government for a Large Tract of Land on the North Shore, Including the Site of Oakville." *The Hamilton Spectator*, 21 November 1894.

———. "The Red-Skinned Wards of the Dominion Will Present an Address of Welcome to His Excellency [the Governor General]." *The Hamilton Daily Spectator*, 8 November 1888 [Head Chief P.E. Jones, secretary-treasurer of the Grand General Indian Council of Ontario, travelled to Ottawa and read the address accompanied by the president and executive of the council, dressed in their traditional costumes].

Oronhyatekha, M.D. Communications to the Editor, *The Toronto Mail*, 4 December 1875.

———. "Red Man v. White Man." Communication to the editor. *The Toronto Mail*, 14 December 1875.

Phipps, R.W. "Reasons against Prohibition." Communication to the editor. *The Toronto Mail*, 30 November 1875, mfm no. 9.

IV. Published Works and Theses, and Dissertations

Ackernecht, E.H. *A Short History of Medicine*. Baltimore: Johns Hopkins University Press, 1982.

Aiello, Dorothy D., and Julie K. Silver. "Aging with Polio." In *Postpolio Syndrome*, ed. Julie K. Silver and Anne C. Gawne, 275–85. Philadelphia: Hanley and Belfus, 2004.

Angus, Margaret. "Dickson, John Robertson." In *DCB*, vol. 11, 1881–1890, 263–64. Toronto: University of Toronto Press, 1982.

———. *Kingston General Hospital: A Social and Institutional History*. Montreal: McGill-Queen's University Press, 1973.

Arnason, T., R. Hebda, and T. Johns. "Use of Plants for Food and Medicine by Native Peoples of Eastern Canada." *Canadian Journal of Botany*, 58 (1981):2189–325.

Avison, Shannon. "Aboriginal Newspapers: Their Contribution to the Emergence of an Alternative Public Sphere in Canada." M.A. thesis, Concordia University, 1996.

Badham, J. "Paralysis in Childhood: Four Remarkable Cases of Suddenly Induced Paralysis in the Extremities, Occurring in Children, without Any Apparent Cerebral or Cerebro-Spinal Lesion." *London Medical Gazette*, n.s. 17 (1834–35):17.

Barbeau, Marius. "Our Indians—Their Disappearance." *Queen's Quarterly*, 38 (1931):691–707.

Barkwell, P. "The Medicine Chest Clause in Treaty no. 6." *Canadian Native Law Reporter*, 4 (1981):1–23.

Bates, J. "Tuberculosis: Susceptibility and Resistance." *American Review of Respiratory Disease*, 125, no. 3 (1982):20–24.

Bell, Charles. "Case 183: Case of Wasting of a Child's Leg in Consequence of an Epidemic of Fever in St. Helena." In *The Nervous System of the Human Body as Explained in a Series of Papers Read before the Royal Society of London*, 434–35. London: Henry Renshaw, 1844.

Bell, Robert. "The Medicine-Man; or Indian and Esquimo Notions of Medicine. *Canadian Medical and Surgical Journal for March/April 1886* (1886):1–13. Montreal: Gazette Printing Company.

Benac, Nancy. "Dirty Cookstoves Pose Enormous Health Risk." *Canadian Medical Association Journal*, 182 (2010):1718–19.

Benn, Carl. "Colonial Transformations." In *Toronto: A Short Illustrated History of Its First 12,000 Years*, ed. Ronald F. Williamson, p. 53. Toronto: James Lorimer & Co., 2008.

Bertrand, Réal. *Célébrités Canadiennes: Louis-Hippolyte Lafontaine.* Montreal: Lidec Inc., 1993.

Bigelow, Jacob. *American Medical Botany, Being a Collection of the Native Medicinal Plants of the United States.* Boston: Cummings & Hilliard, 1817–20.

Bliss, Michael. *William Osler: A Life in Medicine.* Toronto: University of Toronto Press, 1999.

Blumenthal, Mark, ed. *The Complete German Commission E Monographs: Therapeutic Guide to Herbal Medicines*, trans. S. Klein. Austin: American Botanical Council Boston, 1998.

Boyle, David. *Ontario Provincial Museum: Fourth Annual Archaeological Report, 1890–1891.* 54 Victoria, Sessional Papers no. 21, 1891, 10–12.

Brant, Clare Clifton. "Native Ethics and Rules of Behaviour." *Canadian Journal of Psychiatry*, 35 (1990):534–39.

Brant, Clare, and Bruce Sealy. "The Ethics of Non-interference." In *Indian Thinking and Indian Ways.* Kenora: Office of the Crown Attorney, 1988.

Briante, John G. *The Old Root and Herb Doctor or the Indian Method of Healing.* Claremont: Granite Book Co., 1870.

Brock, Daniel J. "Clench, Joseph Brant," In *DCB*, vol. 8, 1851–1860, 161–63. Toronto: University of Toronto Press, 1985.

Brown, Donald. *Down Memory Lane: A Glimpse of Hagersville's Past.* Hagersville: Haldimand Press, 1992.

Brown, Joan Heather, and Pamela Taylor. "Muscarinic Receptor Agonists and Antagonists." In *Goodman & Gilman's: The Pharmacological Basis of Therapeutics*, 11th ed., ed. Lawrence L. Brunton, 183–200. New York: McGraw-Hill, 2006.

Bryant, Vaughn M., and Glenna W. Dean. "Archaeological Coprolite Science: The Legacy of Eric O. Callen (1912–1970)." *Palaeogeography, Palaeoclimatology, Palaeoecology*, 237 (2006):51–66.

Buddle, Kathleen. "Media, Markets, and Powwows: Matrices of Aboriginal Cultural Mediation in Canada." *Cultural Dynamics*, 16 (2004):29–63.

Burkholder, Mabel. "Doctors of the Horse and Buggy Days: Dr. Peter E. Jones." In *The Hagersville Story, Haldimand County Centennial*, 266. Hagersville: n.p., 1950.

Burley, David G. *A Particular Condition in Life: Self Employment and Social Mobility in Mid-Victorian Brantford, Ontario.* Montreal: McGill-Queen's University Press, 1994.

Byers, Mary, and Margaret McBurney. "Missionaries' Home Has Classical Look." *Toronto Globe and Mail*, May 12, 1983.

Callen, Eric O., and T.W.M. Cameron. "A Prehistoric Diet Revealed in Coprolites." *New Scientist*, 8 (1960):35–40.

Cameron, J. Stewart. "Milk or Albumin? The History of Proteinuria before Richard Bright." *Nephrology, Dialysis, Transplantation*, 18 (2003):1281–85.

Canadian Department of Indian Affairs and Northern Development. *Indians of Ontario: An Historical Review.* Ottawa: Indian Affairs Branch, 1966. Reprint, Ottawa: Information Canada, 1971.

Canniff, William. *The Medical Profession in Upper Canada 1738–1850.* Toronto: William Briggs, 1894. Reprint, Toronto: Clarke, Irwin & Co. for the Hannah Institute for the History of Medicine, 1980.

Careless, J.M.S., and R. Craig Brown, eds. *The Canadians: 1867–1967.* Toronto: Macmillan Canada, 1967.

Chandler, Frank, ed. *Herbs: Everyday Reference for Health Professionals.* Ottawa: Canadian Pharmacists Association and Canadian Medical Association, 2000.

Choquette, L.P.E. "Significance of Parasites in Wildlife." *Canadian Journal of Comparative Medicine*, 20 (1956):418–26.

Chute, Janet E. "Shinwauk, George (Menissino, Messinowini, also Known as George Pine)." In *DCB*, vol. 15, 1921–1930, 1095–97. Toronto: University of Toronto Press, 2005.

———. *The Legacy of Shingwaukonse: A Century of Native Leadership*. Toronto: University of Toronto Press, 1998.

Cichoke, Anthony J. *Secrets of Native American Herbal Remedies*. New York: Penguin Putnam, 2001.

Clark, Bruce. *Native Liberty, Crown Sovereignty: The Existing Aboriginal Right of Self-Government in Canada*. Montreal: McGill-Queen's University Press, 1990.

Clark, M., P. Riben, and E. Nowegesic. "The Association of Housing Density, Isolation, and Tuberculosis in Canadian First Nations Communities." *International Journal of Epidemiology*, 31 (2002):940–45.

Clavelle, Christina M. "Ethnobotany of Two Cree Communities in the Southern Boreal Forest of Saskatchewan." M.A. thesis, University of Saskatchewan, 1997.

Cochrane, William, ed. "Peter Edmund Jones, M.D." In *The Canadian Album: Men of Canada; or, Success by Example*, vol. 2, 330. Brantford: Bradley Garretson and Company, 1893.

Comeau-Vasilopoulos, Gayle M. "Oronhyatekha (Peter Martin)." In *DCB*, vol. 13, 1901–1910, 791–95. Toronto: University of Toronto Press, 1994.

Creighton, Donald. *John A. Macdonald: The Old Chieftain*. Toronto: Macmillan Canada, 1955.

Cumming, Peter A., and Neil H. Mickenberg, eds. *Native Rights in Canada*. Toronto: General Publishing Co., 1972.

Daniel, Thomas M. *Captain of Death: The Story of Tuberculosis*. Rochester: University of Rochester Press, 1997.

Darwin, Charles. *On the Origin of Species by Means of Natural Selection, or the Preservation of Favoured Races in the Struggle for Life*. London: Murray, 1860.

Dee, R.H., and L. Secord. "Disease among the Six Nations." in *Thirteenth Annual Archaeological Report Ontario,* part of Appendix to the Report of the Minister of Education of Ontario, 189–94. Toronto: Warwick Bros. & Rutter, 1898.

Dembski, Peter E. Paul. "Ryerson, George Ansel Sterling." In *DCB*, vol. 15, 1921–1930, 900–1. Toronto: University of Toronto Press, 2005.

Densmore, Frances. *Indian Use of Wild Plants for Crafts, Food, Medicine, and Charms, originally published as: Uses of Plants by the Chippewa Indians*. Annual Report of the Bureau of American Ethnology, 1926–27. Washington, DC: n.p., 1928. Reprint, Ohsweken: Iroqrafts Limited, 1993.

Dickason, Olive P. *Canada's First Nations: A History of Founding Peoples from Earliest Times*. Toronto: Oxford University Press, 2002.

Dickson, George, and G. Mercer Adam, eds. *A History of Upper Canada College, 1829–1892*, 297. Toronto: Rowsell & Hutchison, 1893.

Disturnell, J.A., ed. *Trip through the Lakes of North America; Embracing a Full Description of the St. Lawrence River Together with All the Principal*

Places on Its Banks, from Its Sources to Its Mouth, etc. New York: n.p. 1857. Digitalized version, Ann Arbour: University of Michigan Library, 2006.

Doleman, Claude E. "Bovell, James." In *DCB*, vol. 10, 1871–1880, 83–85. Toronto: University of Toronto Press, 1972.

Duffin, Jacalyn. "A Rural Practice in Nineteenth-Century Ontario: The Continuing Medical Education of James Miles Langstaff." *Canadian Bulletin of Medical History*, 5 (1988):3–28.

———. *Langstaff: A Nineteenth-Century Medical Life.* Toronto: University of Toronto Press, 1993.

Dailey, Robert C. "The Midewiwin, Ontario's First Medical Society." *Ontario History*, 50 (1958):133–38.

Daniel, Richard C. "The Board of Arbitrators and the Mississaugas of the Credit." In *A History of Native Claims Processes in Canada*, 56–62. Ottawa: Research Branch, Department of Indian and Northern Affairs, 1980.

Duncum, B.M. *The Development of Inhalation Anaesthesia with Special Reference to the Years 1846–1900.* London: Oxford University Press, 1994.

Dupuis, Renée. *Justice for Canada's Aboriginal Peoples.* Trans. Robert Chodos and Susan Joanis. Toronto: James Lormer and Company, 2002.

Ellinghaus, Katherine. "Margins of Acceptability: Class, Education, and Interracial Marriage in Australia and North America." *Frontiers: A Journal of Women's Studies*, 23 (2002):55–75.

Erichsen-Brown, Charlotte. *Medicinal and Other Uses of North American Plants: A Historical Survey with Special Reference to the Eastern Indian Tribes*, 43. New York: Dover Publications, 1989.

Errington, Jane. *Greater Kingston: Historic Past, Progressive Future.* Burlington: Windsor Publications, 1998.

Finkbeiner, Walter E., Phillip C. Ursell, and Richard Davis. *Autopsy Pathology: A Manual and Atlas*, 24. Philadelphia: Churchill Livingston, 2004.

Fisher, Robin, and Kenneth Coates, eds. *Out of the Background: Readings on Canadian Native History.* Mississauga: Copp Clark Pitman, 1988.

Flegel, Ken, Noni MacDonald, and Pault C. Herbert. "Binge Drinking: All Too Prevalent and Hazardous." *Canadian Medical Association Journal*, 183 (2011):411.

Ford, R. "Ethnobotany in North America: An Historical Phytogeographic Perspective." *Canadian Journal of Botany*, 59 (1981):2178–88.

Francis, R. Douglas, Richard Jones, and Donald B. Smith. *Journeys: A History of Canada.* Toronto: Nelson/Thomson Canada, 2006.

Freeman, Victoria. "Attitudes towards 'Miscegenation' in Canada and the United States, New Zealand, and Australia, 1860–1914." *Native Studies Review*, 16 (2005):41–69.

Freyer, Mary Beacock. *Emily Stowe: Doctor and Suffragist.* Toronto: Hannah Institute of the History of Medicine, Dundurn Press, 1990.

Friedland, Martin L. *The University of Toronto: A History.* Toronto: University of Toronto Press, 2002.

Friesen, Joe. "Ethnic Constituencies: Natives Can 'Turn the Tide' in 10 Key Ontario Ridings, Chief Tells Aboriginals." *The Globe and Mail*, 9 October 2008, A9.

Froman, Tara. "History Is Everyone's Business." *Wadrihwa*, 16 Summer/Fall (2001):1. Woodland Indian Cultural and Educational Centre. Brantford.

Garrison, Fielding H. *An Introduction to the History of Medicine, with Medical Chronology, Suggestions for Study and Bibliographic Data.* 4th ed. Philadelphia: W.B. Saunders Company, 1929.

———. "Lister in Relation to the Victorian Background." In *Contributions to the History of Medicine*, 907–12. New York: Hafner Publishing, 1966.

George, P., and B. Nahwegahbow. "Anishinaabe Health." In *Royal Commission on Aboriginal Peoples: The Path to Healing*, 241–43. Ottawa: Royal Commission on Aboriginal Peoples, 1993.

Gibson, Marian M. *In the Footsteps of the Mississaugas.* Mississauga: Mississauga Heritage Foundation, 2006.

Gidney, D., and W.P.J. Miller. "The Origins of Organized Medicine in Ontario: 1850–1869." In *Health, Disease, and Medicine: Essays in Canadian History*, ed. Charles G. Roland, 65–95. Toronto: Hannah Institute for the History of Medicine, 1982.

Godfrey, Charles M. *Medicine for Ontario: A History.* Belleville: Mika Publishing Co., 1979.

Graham, Elizabeth. *Medicine Man to Missionary: Missionaries as Agents of Change among the Indians of Southern Ontario, 1784–1867.* Toronto: Peter Martin Associates Limited, 1975.

Graham-Cumming, George. "Health of the Original Canadians: 1867–1967." *Medical Services Journal*, 23 (1967):115–66, esp. tuberculosis, 129–42.

Grand General Council. *Grand Council of the Indians of Ontario, held on the Cape Crocker Reserve in July 1896.* Complementary report of inspector of Indian agencies, J.A. Macrea, who was in attendance. LAC, Indian Affairs, RG 10, vol. 2639, file 129,690-1. J. Macrea to deputy superintendent general of Indian Affairs, 11 July 1896, 1–9. Online at http://www.collectionscanada.gc.ca/databases/indianaffairs/001074-119.01-e,php?page_id_nbr=10443&.

———. Grand General Council Held at Sarnia. In *The Algoma Missionary News and Shingwauk Journal*, August (1878):112–14. The entire proceedings of the Grand Indian Council of the Province of Ontario were later published in instalments in *The Wiarton Echo*, 15 and 29 August; 5, 12, 19, and 26 September; 5, 10, 17, 24, and 31 October 1879.

———. Grand Ojibway Council held on the Saugeen reserve, 12 July 1976. In *Report on the Proceedings of the Chippewa Grand Council Approving of the New Indian Act*. Indian Affairs, RG 10, vol. 1994, file 6829, 1876.

———. *Minutes, Grand Council Held September 1892*. Indian Affairs, RG 10, vol. 2639, file 129,690-1, LAC.

———. *Minutes of the Eighth Grand Indian Council Held upon the Cape Crocker Indian Reserve, County of Bruce from September 10 to 15, 1884*. Hagersville: The Indian Publishing Co. Printers, n.d. Pamphlet 1884, no. 54, AO.

———. *Minutes of the Seventh Grand General Indian Council Held upon the New Credit Indian Reserve, from September 13 to September 18th*. Hagersville: Hagersville Book and Job Rooms, 1883.

———. *Minutes of the Six Nations and Delegates from Different Bands in Western and Eastern Canada, 10–18 June 1970*. Hamilton: Office of the Spectator Newspaper, 1870. The 1858 Grand Council delegates' outrage at the provisions of the 1857 Indian legislation is described by Reverend H.P. Chase, 16.

———. *Minutes of the Thirteenth Grand General Indian Council, Ontario and Quebec, Moraviantown Indian Reserve, October 16 to 20, 1894*. Wiarton: Printed at the Wiarton Canadian Office.

———. *The Grand General Council of the Chippewas, Munsees, Six Nations etc., etc., Held on the Sarnia Reserve, June 25th to July 3rd 1874*. Sarnia: Canadian Steam Publishing Co., 1874.

Grigg, E. "The Arcana of Tuberculosis." *American Review of Respiratory Disease*, 78 (1958):151–72.

Groves, Abraham. *All in a Day's Work: Leaves from a Doctor's Case-Book*. Toronto: Macmillan of Canada, 1934.

Guillet, Edwin C. *You'll Never Die John A!* Toronto: Macmillan of Canada, 1967.

Gwyn, Richard. *John A: The Man Who Made Us, the Life and Times of John A. Macdonald*, vol. 1: 1815–1891, 155. Toronto: Vintage Canada, 2008.

———. *Sir John A. Macdonald, Nation Maker, Sir John A. Macdonald: His Life, Our Times*, vol. 2: 1867–1891, 420. Toronto: Random House, 2011.

Hallowell, A. Irving. "Ojibwa World View and Disease." In *Man's Image in Medicine and Anthropology*, ed. Iago Galdston, 258–315. New York: New York Academy of Medicine; International Universities Press, 1963.

Hanaway, Joseph, and Richard Cruess. *McGill Medicine, vol. 1, 1829–1885: The First Half Century*, Graduation List, George E. Bomberry, M.D. 1875, 126–27. Montreal: McGill-Queen's University Press, 1996.

Harper, J. Russell. *Early Painters and Engravers in Canada*. Toronto: University of Toronto Press, 1970.

Harring, Sidney L. *White Man's Law: Native People in Nineteenth-Century Canadian Jurisprudence*. Toronto: University of Toronto Press, 1998.

Hatfield, Gabrielle. *Encyclopedia of Folk Medicine: Old World and New World Traditions*. Santa Barbara: ABC-CLIO, 2004.

Heagerty, John J. *Four Centuries of Medical History in Canada, and a Sketch of the Medical History of Newfoundland*, 2 vols. Toronto: Macmillan Company of Canada, 1928.

Hedican, Edward J., ed. *Applied Anthropology in Canada: Understanding Aboriginal Issues*, 2nd ed. Toronto: University of Toronto Press, 2008.

Hele, Karl S., ed. *Lines Drawn upon the Water: First Nations and the Great Lakes Borders and Borderlands*. Waterloo: Wilfrid Laurier University Press, 2008.

Helin, Calvin. *Dances with Dependency: Indigenous Success through Self-Reliance*. Vancouver: Orca Spirit Publishing and Communications, 2006.

Hewitt, David, ed. *Scott on Himself: A Selection of the Autobiographical Writings of Sir Walter Scott*, 10–16. Edinburgh: Scottish Academic Press, 1981.

Hill, Louis Paul. "Understanding Indigenous Canadian Traditional Health and Healing." Ph.D. dissertation, Wilfrid Laurier University, 2008.

Hill, Susan M. *Best Practices to Recruit Mature Aboriginal Students to Medicine. Ottawa:* Indigenous Physicians Association of Canada, 2007. Online at http://www.ipac.org.

Hodge, Frederick W., ed. "Reverend Peter Jones." Cited in *Handbook of American Indians North of Mexico*, part 1, 633–34. New York: Rowman and Littlefield, 1965.

Hoxie, Frederick E., ed. *Encyclopedia of North American Indians*. Boston: Houghton Mifflin, 1996.

Jamieson, Keith A. "Mohawk Ideals-Victorian Values, More Than a Doctor." In *Wadrihwa*, 16, no. 1 and 2 (2001):10–14. Quarterly newsletter of the Woodland Cultural Centre, Brantford.

Jenkins, D. "Tuberculosis: The Native Indian Viewpoint on Its Prevention, Diagnosis, and Treatment." *Preventive Medicine*, 6 (1977):545–55.

Johnson, Leo A. "The Mississaugas Lake Ontario Land Surrenders of 1805." *Ontario History*, 83, no. 3 (1990):233–54.

Johnston, C.M. *Brant County: A History 1784–1945*, 84–85. Toronto: Oxford University Press, 1967.

Jones, Donald G. "Augustus Jones 1758–1836." *Head-of-the-Lake Historical Society*, 15 (1988):n.p.

Jones, Eliza [Field]. *Memoir of Elizabeth Jones, a Little Indian Girl, Who Lived at River Credit Mission, Upper Canada*. London: John Mason, 1838.

[Jones-Carey, Eliza] Ke-che-ah-gah-me-qua. *Sketch of the Life of Captain Joseph Brant, Thayendanagea*. Montreal: Dougall, 1872.

———. *The Life of Captain Joseph Brant (Thayendanegea): An Account of His Re-interment at Mohawk, 1850, and of the Corner Stone Ceremony in the Erection of the Brant Memorial*, 11–15. Brantford: B.H. Rothwell, 1886.

Jones, Peter (Kahkewaquonaby). *History of the Ojebway Indians: With Especial Reference to Their Conversion to Christianity.* London: A.W. Bennett, 1861. Reprint, Freeport: Books for Libraries, 1970.

———. *Life and Journals of Kah-ke-wa-quo-na-by (Rev. Peter Jones) Wesleyan Missionary.* Toronto: Anson Green, at the Wesleyan Printing Establishment, 1860.

———. "The Indian Nations: A Short Account of the Customs and Manners of the North American Indians, Particularly of the Chippeway Nation." *The Monthly Review: Devoted to the Government of Canada*, 1, May (1841):313–26.

Jones, Peter Edmund, "The Indians of Haldimand." In *The Illustrated Historical Atlas of the County of Haldimand, Ontario*, 9–11. Toronto: H.R. Page Co., 1879.

Kalpakjian, Claire Z., Sunny Roller, and Denise G. Tate. "Psychological Well-being of Polio Survivors." In *Postpolio Syndrome,* ed. Julie K. Silver and Anne C. Gawne, 289–306. Philadelphia: Hanley and Belfus, 2004.

Kass, Amalie, M., and Edward H. Kass. *Perfecting the World: The Life and Times of Dr. Thomas Hodgkin 1798–1866.* Boston: Brace Jovanovich Publishers, 1988.

Killan, Gerald. "Boyle, David." In *DCB,* vol. 14, 1911–1920, 130–34. Toronto: University of Toronto Press, 2001.

King, Lloyd. *Early Days at New Credit*, ed. George Beaver. Hagersville: Mississaugas of the New Credit First Nation, 1997, MNCA.

———. *History of the New Credit Church & History of the Roads at New Credit.* Hagersville: Mississaugas of the New Credit First Nation, 1999, MNCA.

———. *Mississaugas of the Credit: History of Education.* Hagersville: Mississaugas of the New Credit First Nation, n.d., MNCA.

———. *Reflexions at New Credit*, ed. Margaret Sault & Lloyd King. Hagersville: Mississaugas of the New Credit First Nation, n.d., MNCA.

Kuhnlein, H.V., and N.J. Turner. *Traditional Plant Foods of Canadian Indigenous Peoples: Nutrition, Botany, and Use.* Philadelphia: Gordon and Breach, 1991.

Ladell, John L. *They Left Their Mark: Surveyors and Their Role in the Settlement of Ontario.* Toronto: Dundurn Press, 1993.

Lanska, Douglas J. "The History of Reflex Hammers." *Neurology*, 39 (1989):1542–49.

Lee, David. "The Dominion General Election of 1878 in Ontario." *Ontario History*, 51 (1959):172–90.

Leighton, Douglas. "A Victorian Civil Servant at Work: Lawrence Vankoughnet and the Canadian Indian Department." In *As Long as the Sun Shines and the Water Flows: A Reader in Canadian Native Studies*, ed. Ian A.L. Getty and Antoine Lussier, 104–19. Vancouver: University of British Columbia Press, 1983.

———. "Johnson, George Henry Martin." In *DCB*, vol. 11, 1881–1890, 451–53. Toronto: University of Toronto Press, 1982.

Lewis, Walter H., and Memory P.F. Elvin-Lewis. *Medical Botany: Plants Affecting Man's Health*, 224. New York: John Wiley, 1944.

Lind, James. *A Treatis on the Scurvey in Three Parts Containing an Inquiry into the Nature, Causes, and Cure of That Disease.* Edinburgh: Sands, Murray, and Cochran, 1753.

Lipton, R.B., H. Göbel, K.M. Einhäupl, K. Wilks, and A. Mauskop. "*Petasites hybridus* Root (Butterbar) Is an Effective Preventative Treatment for Migraine." *Neurology*, 63 (2004):2240–44.

Lischke, Ute, and David McNab, eds. *The Long Journey of a Forgotten People: Métis Identities and Family Histories.* Waterloo: Wilfrid Laurier University Press, 2007.

———. *Walking a Tightrope: Aboriginal People and Their Representations.* Waterloo: Wilfrid Laurier University Press, 2005.

Lister, Joseph Jackson. "On the Antiseptic Principle in the Practice of Surgery." *British Medical Journal*, 2 (1867):246–48.

Lloyd, John U. *History of the Vegetable Drugs of the Pharmacopoeia of the United States.* Lloyd Library, Bulletin no. 16, Pharmacy Series no. 4. Cincinnati: J.U. and C.G. Lloyd, 1911.

Longford, Elizabeth. *Victoria R I.* London: Weidenfeld and Nicolson, 1964.

Low, James A. "Kingston General Hospital: A National Treasure." *Historic Kingston*, 46 (1998):31–42.

———. *The Faculty 1854–1954, Queen's University at Kingston: Obstetrics and Gynecology.* Kingston: Queen's University, 1985.

Lund, Jennifer. "Eliza Field Jones Carey's Mission to 'Civilize' the Native Women of Early Nineteenth-Century Upper Canada." M.A. thesis, University of Toronto, 1991.

———. "Negotiating Race and Gender in the Diaries of Eliza Jones, British Wife of an Ojibwa Missionary in Upper Canada, 1823–1883." Ph.D. dissertation, York University, 2010.

Lynch, D.O. "A Century of Psychiatric Teaching at Rockwood Hospital, Kingston." *Canadian Medical Association Journal*, 70, no. 3 (1954):283–87.

MacNeish, R.S. "Iroquois Pottery Types: A Technique for the Study of Iroquois Prehistory." Ottawa: Bulletin of the National Museum of Man, 124, 1952.

Marles, Robin J., Christina Clavelle, Leslie Monteleone, Natalie Tays, and Donna Burns. *Aboriginal Plant Use in Canada's Northwest Boreal Forest.* Edmonton: Natural Resources Canada, Canadian Forest Service, 2008.

Mathews, Percy W. "Notes on the Diseases among the Indians Frequenting York Factory, Hudson's Bay." *Canadian Medical and Surgical Journal.* Montreal: Gazette Printing Co., 1885. Online at http://www.Canadiana .org/record/30381.

Mathieu, Jacques. *L'Annedda, l'arbre de vie.* Quebec: Les éditions du Septentrion, 2009.

Max, D.T. "A Man of Taste: A Chef with Cancer of the Tongue Fights to Save His Taste." *The New Yorker*, 12 May 2008, 82–93.

McNab, David T. *Circles of Time: Aboriginal Land Rights and Resistance in Ontario.* Waterloo: Wilfrid Laurier University Press, 1999.

McPhedran, N. Tait. *Canadian Medical Schools: Two Centuries of Medical History, 1822–1992*, 104. Montreal: Harvest House, 1992.

Merrett, Deborah C., and Susan Pfeiffer. "Maxillary Sinusitis as an Indicator of Respiratory Health in Past Populations." *American Journal of Physical Anthropology*, 11 (2000):301–18.

Miles, F.R. "William Adams 1820–1900." In *Oxford Dictionary of National Biography.* Oxford: Oxford University Press, 2004–8.

Miller, Cary. *Ogimaag: Anishinaabeg Leadership, 1760–1845.* Lincoln: University of Nebraska Press, 2010.

Mitchinson, Wendy. "M. Bulke: A Victorian Asylum Superintendent." *Ontario History*, 63 (1981):239–54.

Moerman, Daniel E. *Native American Ethnobotany.* Portland: Timber Press, 1998.

Montgomery, Malcolm. "The Six Nations and the Macdonald Franchise." *Ontario History*, 57 (1965):13–25.

Montour, Ethyl Brant. *Canadian Portraits: Brant, Crowfoot, Oronhyatekha.* Toronto: Clark Irwin and Co., 1960.

Morris, J.L. *Indians of Ontario.* Toronto: Ontario Department of Lands and Forests, 1943.

Morris, Karen, Marcia Morganlander, John L. Coulehan, Sheila Gahagen, and Vincent C. Arena. "Wood-Burning Stoves and Lower Respiratory Tract Infection in American Indian Children." *American Journal of Diseases of Children*, 144 (1990):105–8.

Moss, Wendy, and Elaine Gardiner-O'Tool. *Aboriginal People: History of Discriminatory Laws.* Ottawa: Law and Government Division, Government of Canada, 1991. Online at http://dsp-psd.tpsgc.gc.ca/ Collection-R/LoPBdP/BP/bp175-e.htm.

Newbold, K.B. "Aboriginal Physician Use in Canada: Location, Orientation, and Identity." *Health Economics*, 6 (1997):197–207.

No author. "A Descriptive Sketch of the Flourishing Village of Hagersville." In *Illustrated Trade Edition of Hagersville*. Hagersville: Hagersville Board of Trade, 1908. Haldimand County Library, Hagersville Branch.

———. *A Sketch of the Origin and the Recent History of the New England Company by the Senior Members of the Company*, 41. London: Spottiswoode & Co., 1884.

———. *An Overview of Traditional Knowledge and Medicine and Public Health in Canada*. Ottawa: National Aboriginal Health Organization, 2008. Online at http://www.naho.ca/publications/tkOverviewPublicHealth.pdf.

———. "Doctor Peter E. Jones Remembered." In *The Hagersville Story: Haldimand County Centennial, 1950*. HPL.

———. *Grand River Conservation Authority*. Online at http://www.grandriver.ca/About Grand.

———. "Mississaugas of the New Credit's Toronto Purchase Specific Claim Update." Hagersville: Mississaugas of the New Credit First Nation, 2004.

———. *Orange Directory of Western Ontario*, 1871, part 2, District of Oneida. Online at http://www.Members.tripod.com/~Roughian/index-410. html.

———. *Pharmacopoeia of the United States of America, by the Authority of the Medical Societies and Colleges*. Boston: Charles Ewer, 1820.

———. Registration Committee, CPSO, application of Dr. George Bomberry. *The Canadian Journal of Medical Science*, 10, 1 July (1878):346.

———. *Report of the Proceedings of the New England Company, for the Civilization and Conversion of Indians, Blacks, and Pagans in the Dominion of Canada, South Africa, and the West Indies, During the Years 1871–1872*, 190–1, 340. London: Taylor & Co., 1874.

———. *Report on the Indians of Upper Canada: By a Subcommittee of the Aborigines Protection Society (1839)*. Reprint, Toronto: Canadiana House, 1968.

———. *Toronto School of Medicine, Cumulative List of Students as of 1871*. UTA.

Nock, David A. "Yates, Horatio." In *DCB*, vol. 11, 1881–1890, 940–41. Toronto: University of Toronto Press, 1982.

Onn, David. "Egerton Ryerson's Philosophy of Education: Something Borrowed or Something New." *Ontario History*, 61, no. 2 (1969):77–86.

Ontario Historical Society. *Catalogue, Canadian Historical Exhibition Victoria College, Queen's Park, Toronto under the Patronage of His Excellency the Governor General and the Countess of Minto*. Toronto: William Briggs, 1899.

Ontario's Commissioner of Crown Lands. *The Algoma District*. Toronto: Grip Printing and Publishing Co., 1884.

Oronhyatekha. *History of the Independent Order of Foresters*. Toronto: Hunter Rose and Co., 1894.

———. "The Mohawk Language." *The Canadian Journal*, no. 90 (1876):1–2.

Osler, William. "An Address on the Haematoza of Malaria." *British Medical Journal*, 12 March (1887):556–62.

———. *The Principles and Practice of Medicine*. New York: D. Appleton and Company, 1992.

Patterson, Marian A. "The Life and Times of the Hon. John Rolph, M.D. (1793–1870)." *Medical History*, 5 (1961):15–33.

Paul, John R. *A History of Poliomyelitis*. New Haven: Yale University Press, 1971.

Petten, Cheryl. "Dr. Clare Clifton Brant, Mohawk Man and Doctor: Bridging the Divide." *Windspeaker (Six Nations)*, October (2003):34.

Pfieffer, Susan. "Commentary." In A.K. Wilber, A.W. Farnbach, K.J. Knudson, and J.E. Buikstra, "Diet, Tuberculosis, and the Paleopathological Record." *Current Anthropology*, 49 (2008):963–91, esp. p. 981.

Pilling, James Constantine. "Dr. P.E. Jones' Biography and His Translations of the Meanings of Place Names." In *Bibliography of the Algonquian Languages*, 272. Washington, DC: Smithsonian Institution, Bureau of Ethnology, 1891.

Powell, Robert W. *The Doctor in Canada: His Whereabouts and the Laws Which Govern Him, A Ready Book of Reference*. Montreal: Gazette Printing Company, 1890.

Price, Weston A. *Nutrition and Physical Degeneration: A Comparison of Primitive and Modern Diets and Their Effects*. Los Angeles: American Academy of Applied Nutrition, 1939.

Poser, Charles M., and George W. Bruyn. *An Illustrated History of Malaria*. Pearl River: Parthenon Publishing, 1999.

Pringsheim, Tamara, W. Jeptha Davenport, and Werner J. Becker. "Prophylaxis of Migraine Headache." *Canadian Medical Association Journal*, 182 (2010):679–85.

Ramenofsky, Ann F., Alicia K.Wilbur, and Anne C. Stone. "Native American Disease History: Past, Present, and Future Directions." *World Archaeology: Epidemic and Infectious Disease*, 35 (2003):241–57.

Rankin, Diana L. *Research Report: The Mississaugas of the New Credit Indian Band Land Claim to 200 Acres Adjacent to the Credit River*. Ottawa: Office of Indian Resource Policy, Ministry of Natural Resources, 1985.

Reinhard, Karl, J., J. Richard Ambler, and Magdalene McGuffie. "Diet and Parasitism at Dust Devil Cave." *American Antiquity*, 50 (1985):819–24.

Revelle, F. Douglas. *History of the County of Brant*. Brantford: Hurley Printing Co., 1920.

Riley, Thomas J. "Ascarids, American Indians, and the Modern World: Parasites and the Prehistoric Record of a Pharmacological Tradition." *Perspectives in Biology and Medicine*, 36 (1993):369–75.

Rogers, Edward S. "The Algonquian Farmers of Southern Ontario, 1830–1945." In *Aboriginal Ontario: Historical Perspectives on the First Nations*, ed. Edward S. Rogers and Donald B. Smith, 122–66. Toronto: Dundurn Press, 1994.

Rogers, Edward S., and Donald B. Smith, eds. *Aboriginal Ontario: Historical Perspectives on the First Nations*. Toronto: Dundurn Press, 1994.

Roland, Charles G. "The Medical Life of Dr. Abraham Groves." *Wellington County History*, 16 (2003):31–48.

Rousseau, Jacques, and Marcel Raymond. Études Ethnobotaniques Québécoises. Montreal: Institut Botanique de l'Université de Montréal, 1945.

Sami, Alakurtti, Makela Taru, Koskimies Salme, and Kli-Kauhaluoma Jari. "Pharmacological Properties of the Ubiquitous Natural Product Betulin." *European Journal of Pharmaceutical Sciences*, 29 (2006):1–13.

Saul, John Ralston. *A Fair Country: Telling Truths about Canada*. Toronto: Viking Press, 2008.

Schmalz, Peter S. *The Ojibwa of Southern Ontario*. Toronto: University of Toronto Press, 1991.

Sherwin, Allan L. "Dr. Peter Edmund Jones (1843–1909) Mississauga Chess Champion." An illustrated booklet prepared for the Chess Club of the Lloyd S. King Elementary School. Hagersville: Mississaugas of the New Credit First Nation Archives, 2010.

Shields, Norman. "Anishinabek Political Alliance in the Post Confederation Period: The Grand General Indian Council of Ontario, 1870–1936." M.A. thesis, Queen's University, 2001.

———. "The Grand General Indian Council of Ontario and Indian Status Legislation." In *Lines Drawn upon the Water: First Nations and the Great Lakes Borders and Borderlands*, ed. Karl S. Hele, 205–18. Waterloo: Wilfrid Laurier University Press, 2008.

Silver, Julie K., and Anne C. Gawne, eds. *Postpolio Syndrome*. Philadelphia: Hanley and Belfus, 2004.

Smith, Cynthia M., and Jack McLeod, ed. *Sir John A.: An Anecdotal Life of John A. Macdonald*. Toronto: Oxford University Press, 1989.

Smith, Donald B. "Eliza and the Reverend Peter Jones." *The Beaver*, Autumn (1977):40–46.

———. "Field, Elizabeth (Eliza) (Jones; Carey)." In *DCB*, vol. 11, 1881–1890, 316–17. Toronto: University of Toronto Press, 1982.

———. "Historic Peace-Pipe." *The Beaver*, Summer (1984): 4–7.

———. "John A. Macdonald and Aboriginal Canada." *Historic Kingston, Annual Publication of the Kingston Historical Society*, 50 (2002):10–29.

———. "Jones, Augustus." In *DCB*, vol. 7, 1836–1850, 450–52. Toronto: University of Toronto Press, 1988.

———. "Jones, Peter Edmund (Kahkewaquonaby)." In *DCB*, vol. 13, 1901–1910, 530–1. Toronto: University of Toronto Press, 1993.

———. "Jones, [Reverend] Peter." In *DCB*, vol. 8, 1851–1860, 439–43. Toronto: University of Toronto Press, 1985.

———. "Maungwudaus Goes Abroad." *The Beaver*, Autumn (1976):4–9.

———. "Peter and Eliza Jones: Their Last Years." *The Beaver*, Winter (1977):16–43.

———. *Portraits of the Mississauga: First Nations Voices from Nineteenth-Century Canada.* Toronto: University of Toronto Press, in press.

———. *Sacred Feathers: The Reverend Peter Jones (Kahkewaquonaby) and the Mississauga Indians.* Toronto: University of Toronto Press, 1987.

———. "The Mississauga, Peter Jones, and the White Man: The Algonkians' Adjustment to the Europeans on the North Shore of Lake Ontario to 1860." Ph.D. dissertation, University of Toronto, 1975.

———. "The Transatlantic Courtship of the Reverend Peter Jones." *The Beaver*, Summer (1977):4–13.

Spaulding, William B. "Abraham Groves (1847–1935): A Pioneer Ontario Surgeon, Sufficient unto Himself." *Canadian Bulletin of Medical History,* 5 (1991):249–62.

Sprague, George W. "The Trinity Medical College." *Ontario History*, 63 (1996):71.

Stillé, Alfred. *Therapeutics and Materia Medica: A Systematic Treatise on the Action and Uses of Medicinal Agents Including Their Description and History,* 3rd ed., 2 vols. Philadelphia: Henry C. Lee, 1868.

Stone, Eric. *Medicine among the American Indians*. New York: Paul B. Hoeber, 1932.

Strong-Boag, Veronica, and Carol Gerson. *Paddling Her Own Canoe: The Life and Times and Texts of E. Pauline Johnson (Tekahionwake).* Toronto: University of Toronto Press, 2000.

Surtees, Robert J. *Canadian Indian Policy a Critical Biography*. Bloomington: Indiana University Press, 1982.

———. "The Development of an Indian Reserve Policy in Canada." *Ontario History*, 61 (1969):87–98.

Swanson, Donald. "Campbell, Sir Alexander." In *DCB*, vol. 12, 1891–1900, 150–4. Toronto: University of Toronto Press, 1990.

Tantaquidgeon, Gladys. *A Study of Delaware Indian Medicine Practice and Folk Beliefs*. Philadelphia: Pennsylvania Historical Commission, 1942.

———. "Mohegan Medicinal Practices, Weather-Lore, and Superstition." *Forty-third Annual Report of the Bureau of American Ethnology, 1925–26*, 264–79. Washington: Government Printing Office, 1928.

———. "Notes on the Origin and Uses of Plants of the Lake St. John Montagnais." *Journal of American Folk-Lore*, 45 (1932):264–79.

T.E.C., Jr., M.D. "A Case of Poliomyelitis in an English Child Reported in 1835." *Pediatrics*, 80 (1987):244.

Thorning, Steve, "Dr. Abraham Groves: Businessmen and Entrepreneur." *Wellington County History*, 16 (2003):5–17.

Titley, E. Brian. *A Narrow Vision: Duncan Campbell Scott and the Administration of Indian Affairs in Canada*. Vancouver: University of British Columbia Press, 1986.

Tobias, John L. "Protection, Civilization, Assimilation: An Outline History of Canada's Indian Policy." In *As Long as the Sun Shines and Water Flows: A Reader in Canadian Native Studies*, ed. Ian L. Getty and Antoine S. Lussier, 39–55. Vancouver: University of British Columbia Press, 1983.

Tracy, Timothy S., and Richard L. Kingston, eds. *Herbal Products: Toxicology and Clinical Pharmacology*. Totowa: Humana Press, 2007.

Travill, A.A. *Medicine at Queen's, 1854–1920: A Peculiarly Happy Relationship*. Kingston: Faculty of Medicine Queen's University, 1988.

Trigger, Bruce G. *Natives and Newcomers: Canada's "Heroic Age" Reconsidered*. Montreal: McGill-Queen's University Press, 1985.

Turner, Nancy J., Lawrence C. Thompson, M. Terry Thompson, and Annie Z. York. *Thompson Ethnobotany: Knowledge and Usage of Plants by the Thompson Indians of British Columbia*. Victoria: Royal British Columbia Museum Memoir no. 3, 1990.

Underwood, Michael. *A Treatise on the Disorders of Childhood and Management of Infants from the Birth: Adapted to Domestic Use*, 3 vols. London: J. Matthews, 1801.

Vallery-Radot, René. *The Life of Pasteur*, trans. R.L. Devonshire. New York: McClure Phillips & Co., 1906.

Van Dusen, Conrad (alias Enemikeese). *The Indian Chief: An Account of the Labours, Losses, Sufferings, and Oppression of Ke-zig-ko-e-ne-ne (David Sawyer), a Chief of the Ojibbeway Indians in Canada West*. London: William Nichols, 1867. Reprint, Toronto: Coles Publishing Co., 1974.

Van Kirk, Sylvia. "From 'Marrying-in to Marrying-out,' Changing Patterns of Aboriginal/Non-Aboriginal Marriage in Colonial Canada." *Frontiers: A Journal of Women's Studies*, 23 (2002):1–11.

Vecsey, Christopher. *Traditional Ojibwa Religion and Its Historical Change*. Philadelphia: American Philosophical Society, 1983.

Vipond, Robert C. "Mills, David." In *DCB*, vol. 13, 1901–1910, 707–12. Toronto: University of Toronto Press, 1994.

Vizenor, Gerald R. "Reverend Jones." Cited in *The People Named the Chippewa: Narrative Histories*, 66–74. Minneapolis: University of Minnesota Press, 1984.

Vogel, Virgil J. "American Indian Influence on Medicine and Pharmacology." *Indian Historian*, 1, December (1967):12–15.

———. *American Indian Medicine*. Norman: University of Oklahoma Press, 1970.

Waiser, W.A. "Bell, Robert." In *DCB*, vol. 14. 1911–1920, 55–56. Toronto: University of Toronto Press, 1998.

Waite, P.B. "White, Thomas." In *DCB*, vol. 11, 1881–1890, 919–21. Toronto: University of Toronto Press, 1982.

Waldie, Jean. "Long, Colorful Story of Echo Villa." *The Brantford Expositor*, 16 November 1956.

———. "Romantic Story of "Echo Villa" Home of Peter Jones. In *Brant County: The Story of Its People,* vol. 1, 68–70. Brantford: Brant Historical Society, 1984.

Waldram, James B., D. Ann Herring, and T. Kue Young. *Aboriginal Health in Canada: Historical, Cultural, and Epidemiological Perspectives*, 2nd ed. Toronto: University of Toronto Press, 2006.

Walters, Mark D. "According to the Old Customs of Our Nation: Aboriginal Self-Government on the Credit River Mississauga Reserve, 1826–1847." *Ottawa Law Review*, 30 (1998/99):1–45.

Walton, John. *My Great Grandfather's Diary of May 1856 Voyage*. Online at http://www.personalpages.tds.net/~jonwalton/Diary.html.

Wax, Rosalie H., and Robert K. Thomas. "American Indians and White People." *Pylon*, 22 (1961):305–17.

Weaver, Sally M. "Health, Culture, and Dilemma: A Study of the Non-Conservative Iroquois, Six Nations Reserve, Ontario." Ph.D. dissertation, University of Toronto, 1967.

———. *Medicine and Politics among the Grand River Iroquois: A Study of the Non-Conservatives.* Ottawa: National Museum of Man, Publications in Ethnology, no. 4, 1972.

———. "Six Nations of the Grand River, Ontario." In *Handbook of North American Indians, Northeast.* vol. 15, ed. Bruce Trigger, 525–36. Washington, DC: Smithsonian Institution, 1978.

———. "Smallpox or Chickenpox: An Iroquoian Community's Reaction to Crisis. 1901 to 1902." Manuscript.

———. "The Iroquois: The Consolidation of the Grand River Reserve in the Mid-Nineteenth Century, 1847–1875." In *Aboriginal Ontario: Historical Perspectives on the First Nations*, ed. Edward S. Rogers and Donald B. Smith, 184. Toronto: Dundurn Press, 1994.

———. "The Iroquois: The Grand River Reserve in the Late Nineteenth and Early Twentieth Centuries, 1875–1945." In *Aboriginal Ontario: Historical Perspectives on the First Nations*, ed. Edward S. Rogers and Donald B. Smith, 213–57. Toronto: Dundurn Press, 1994.

Weslager, Carl A. *Magic Medicines of the Indians.* Wallingford: Middle Atlantic Press, 1973.

Whiteside, Don (sin a paw). *Historical Development of Aboriginal Political Associations in Canada: Documentation, Reference Aids, Indexes*, vol. 1. Ottawa: National Indian Brotherhood, 1973.

Willard, M.L., A. Graham, and J. Carr. *Roots and Branches: A History of Hagersville.* Hagersville: Funded by Opportunities for Youth, 1973. HPL.

Williamson, Ronald F., and Susan Pfeiffer. "Studying the Bones of the Ancestors." In *Bones of the Ancestors: The Archaeology and Osteobiography of the Moatfield Ossuary*, ed. Ronald F. Williamson and Susan Pfieffer, 5–16. Ottawa: Archaeological Survey of Canada Mercury Series, vol. 163, Canadian Museum of Civilization, 2000.

Wolfgang, Robert W. "Indian and Eskimo Diphyllobothriasis." *Canadian Medical Association Journal*, 70, May (1954):536–39.

Wood, George B., and Franklin Bache. *The Dispensatory of the United States of America,* 11th ed. Philadelphia: J.B. Lippincott, 1858.

Wyatt, Kyle Carsten. "Rejoicing in This Unpronounceable Name": Peter Jones's Authorial Identity." *Papers of the Bibliographical Society of Canada*, 47, no. 2, Autumn (2009):153–76.

Zaslow, Morris. *Reading the Rocks: The Story of the Geological Survey of Canada, 1842–1972.* Toronto: Macmillan Canada, 1975.

Zeller, Suzanne. "Lawson, George." In *DCB*, vol. 12, 1891–1900, 539–42. Toronto: University of Toronto Press, 1990.

Zubek, E. "Traditional Native Healing: Alternative or Adjunct to Modern Medicine?" *Canadian Family Physician*, 40 (1994):1923–31.

Index

Books in the Indigenous Studies Series
Published by Wilfrid Laurier University Press

Blockades and Resistance: Studies in Actions of Peace and the Temagami Blockades of 1988–89 / Bruce W. Hodgins, Ute Lischke, and David T. McNab, editors / 2003 / xi + 276 pp. / map, illustrations / ISBN 0-88920-381-4

Indian Country: Essays on Contemporary Native Culture / Gail Guthrie Valaskakis / 2005 / x + 293 pp. / photos / ISBN 0-88920-479-9

Walking a Tightrope: Aboriginal People and Their Representations / Ute Lischke and David T. McNab, editors / 2005 / xix + 377 pp. / photos / ISBN 978-0-88920-484-3

The Long Journey of a Forgotten People: Métis Identities and Family Histories / Ute Lischke and David T. McNab, editors / 2007 / viii + 386 pp. / maps, photos / ISBN 978-0-88920-523-9

Words of the Huron / John L. Steckley / 2007 / xvii + 259 pp. / ISBN 978-0-88920-516-1

Essential Song: Three Decades of Northern Cree Music / Lynn Whidden / 2007 / xvi + 176 pp. / photos, musical examples, audio CD / ISBN 978-0-88920-459-1

From the Iron House: Imprisonment in First Nations Writing / Deena Rymhs / 2008 / ix + 147 pp. / ISBN 978-1-55458-021-7

Lines Drawn upon the Water: First Nations and the Great Lakes Borders and Borderlands / Karl S. Hele, editor / 2008 / xxiii + 351 pp. / illustrations, maps / ISBN 978-1-55458-004-0

Troubling Tricksters: Revisioning Critical Conversations / Linda M. Morra and Deanna Reder, editors / 2009 / xii + 336 pp. / illustrations / ISBN 978-1-55458-181-8

Aboriginal Peoples in Canadian Cities: Transformations and Continuities / Heather A. Howard and Craig Proulx, editors / 2011 / viii + 256 pp. / colour and b&w photos / ISBN 978-1-055458-260-0

Bridging Two Peoples: Chief Peter E. Jones, 1843–1909 / Allan Sherwin / 2012 / xxiv + 246 pp. / 15 b&w photos / ISBN 978-1-55458-633-2